.B.M.

WITHDRAWN

809.03
QuH1a

ADVENTURES IN CRITICISM

BY

A. T. QUILLER-COUCH

NEW YORK

CHARLES SCRIBNER'S SONS

1896

Republished, 1968
Scholarly Press — 560 Cook Road — Grosse Pointe, Michigan 48236

Copyright, 1896, by
CHARLES SCRIBNER'S SONS

Library of Congress Catalog Card Number: 12-37963

Paper used in this edition is
a fine acid-free, permanent/durable paper
of the type commonly referred to as
"300-year" paper

To

A. B. WALKLEY

My dear A. B. W.

The short papers which follow have been reprinted, with a few alterations, from *The Speaker*. Possibly you knew this without my telling you. Possibly, too, you have sat in a theatre before now and seen the curtain rise on two characters exchanging information which must have been their common property for years. So this dedication is partly designed to save me the trouble of writing a formal preface.

As I remember then, Adam, it was upon this fashion bequeathed us by destiny to write side by side in *The Speaker* every week, you about Plays and I about Books. Three years ago you found time to arrange a few of your writings in a notable volume of *Playhouse Impressions*. Some months ago I searched the files of the paper with a similar design, and read my way

v

178175

through an astonishing amount of my own composition. Noble edifice of toil! It stretched away in imposing proportions and vanishing perspective—week upon week—two columns to the week! The mischief was, it did not appear to lead to anything: and for the first mile or two even the casual graces of the colonnade were hopelessly marred through that besetting fault of the young journalist, who finds no satisfaction in his business of making bricks without straw unless he can go straightway and heave them at somebody.

Still (to drop metaphor), I have chosen some papers which I hope may be worth a second reading. They are fragmentary, by force of the conditions under which they were produced: but perhaps the fragments may here and there suggest the outline of a first principle. And I dedicate the book to you because it would be strange if the time during which we have appeared in print side by side had brought no sense of comradeship. Though, in fact, we live far apart and seldom get speech together, more than one of these papers—ostensibly addressed to anybody whom they might concern—has been privately, if but sub-consciously, intended for you.   A. T. Q. C.

CONTENTS

Contents

ADVENTURES IN
CRITICISM

CHAUCER

AFTER twenty-five years of close toil, Professor Skeat has completed his great edition of Chaucer.* It is obviously easier to be dithyrambic than critical in chronicling this event ; to which indeed dithyrambs are more appropriate than criticism. For when a man writes *Opus vitæ meæ* at the conclusion of such a task as this, and so lays down his pen, he must be a churl (even if he be also a competent critic) who will allow no pause for admiration. And where, churl or no churl, is the competent critic to be found? The Professor has here compiled an entirely new text of Chaucer, founded solely on the manuscripts and the earliest printed editions that are accessible. Where Chaucer has translated, the originals have been

*The Complete Works of Geoffrey Chaucer. Edited, from numerous manuscripts, by the Rev. Walter W. Skeat, Litt.D., LL.D., M.A. In six volumes. Oxford: At the Clarendon Press. 1894.

March 17, 1894.
Professor Skeat's Chaucer.

I

carefully studied : " the requirements of metre and grammar have been carefully considered throughout " : and " the phonology and spelling of every word have received particular attention." We may add that all the materials for a Life of Chaucer have been sought out, examined, and pieced together with exemplary care.

All this has taken Professor Skeat twenty-five years, and in order to pass competent judgment on his conclusions the critic must follow him step by step through his researches—which will take the critic (even if we are charitable enough to suppose his mental equipment equal to Professor Skeat's) another ten years at least. For our time, then, and probably for many generations after, this edition of Chaucer will be accepted as final.

And the Clarendon Press. And I seem to see in this edition of Chaucer the beginning of the realization of a dream which I have cherished since first I stood within the quadrangle of the Clarendon Press—that fine combination of the factory and the palace. The aspect of the Press itself repeats, as it were, the characteristics of its government, which is con-

ducted by an elected body as an honorable
trust. Its delegates are not intent only on
money-getting. And yet the Clarendon Press
makes money, and the University can depend
upon it for handsome subsidies. It may well
depend upon it for much more. As the Bank
of England—to which in its system of government it may be likened—is the focus of all the
other banks, private or joint-stock, in the kingdom, and the treasure-house, not only of the
nation's gold, but of its commercial honor, so
the Clarendon Press—traditionally careful in its
selections and munificent in its rewards—might
become the academy or central temple of English literature. If it would but follow up Professor Skeat's Chaucer with a resolution to publish, at a pace suitable to so large an undertak-
ing, *all the great English classics*, edited with
all the scholarship its wealth can command, I
believe that before long the Clarendon Press
would be found to be exercising an influence on
English letters which is at present lacking, and
the lack of which drives many to call, from
time to time, for the institution in this country of something corresponding to the French
Academy. I need only cite the examples of
the Royal Society and the Marylebone Cricket

Club to show that to create an authority in this manner is consonant with our national practice. We should have that centre of correct information, correct judgment, correct taste—that intellectual metropolis, in short—which is the surest check upon provinciality in literature ; we should have a standard of English scholarship and an authoritative dictionary of the English language ; and at the same time we should escape all that business of the green coat and palm branches which has at times exposed the French Academy to much vulgar intrigue.

Also, I may add, we should have the books. Where now is the great edition of Bunyan, of Defoe, of Gibbon ? The Oxford Press did once publish an edition of Gibbon, worthy enough as far as type and paper could make it worthy. But this is only to be found in second-hand book-shops.   Why are two rival London houses now publishing editions of Scott, the better illustrated with silly pictures "out of the artists' heads" ?   Where is the final edition of Ben Jonson ?

These and the rest are to come, perhaps. Of late we have had from Oxford a great Boswell and a great Chaucer, and the magnificent Dictionary is under weigh. So that it may be the dream is in process of being realized, though none of us shall live to see its full realization. Meanwhile such a work as Professor Skeat's Chaucer is not only an answer to much chatter that goes up from time to time about nine-tenths of the work on English literature being done out of England. This and similar works are the best of all possible answers to those gentlemen who so often interrupt their own chrematistic pursuits to point out in the monthly magazines the short-comings of our two great Universities as nurseries of chrematistic youth. In this case it is Oxford that publishes, while Cambridge supplies the learning: and from a natural affection I had rather it were always Oxford that published, attracting to her service the learning, scholarship, intelligence of all parts of the kingdom, or, for that matter, of the world. So might she securely found new Schools of English Literature—were she so minded, a dozen every year. They would do no particular harm; and meanwhile, in Walton Street, out of earshot of the New Schools, the Clarendon Press would go on serenely performing its great work.

*March 23,
1895.
Essentials
and
Accidents
of Poetry* A work such as Professor Skeat's Chaucer puts
the critic into a frame of mind that lies about
midway between modesty and cowardice.   One
asks—" What right have I, who have given but
a very few hours of my life to the enjoying of
Chaucer ; who have never collated his MSS. ;
who have taken the events of his life on trust
from his biographers ; who am no authority on
his spelling, his rhythms, his inflections, or the
spelling, rhythms, inflections of his age ; who
have read him only as I have read other great
poets, for the pleasure of reading—what right
have I to express any opinion on a work of
this character, with its imposing commentary,
its patient research, its enormous accumulation
of special information ? "

Nevertheless, this diffidence, I am sure, may
be carried too far.   After all is said and done,
we, with our average life of three-score years
and ten, are the heirs of all the poetry of all
the ages.   We must do our best in our allotted
time, and Chaucer is but one of the poets.   He
did not write for specialists in his own age, and
his main value for succeeding ages resides, not in
his vocabulary, nor in his inflections, nor in his
indebtedness to foreign originals, nor in the

metrical uniformities or anomalies that may be discovered in his poems; but in his *poetry*. Other things are accidental; his poetry is essential. Other interests—historical, philological, antiquarian—must be recognized; but the poetical, or (let us say) the spiritual, interest stands first and far ahead of all others. By virtue of it Chaucer, now as always, makes his chief and his convincing appeal to that which is spiritual in men. He appeals by the poetical quality of such lines as these, from Emilia's prayer to Diana:

> " Chaste goddesse, wel wostow that I
> Desire to been a mayden al my lyf,
> Ne never wol I be no love ne wyf.
>
> I am, thou woost, yet of thy companye,
> A mayde, and love hunting and venerye,
> And for to walken in the wodes wilde,
> And noght to been a wyf, and be with childe. . ."

Or of these two from the Prioresses' Prologue:

> "O moder mayde !   O mayde moder free !
> O bush unbrent, brenninge in Moyses sighte.   . ."

Or of these from the general Prologue—also thoroughly poetical, though the quality differs:

> " Ther was also a Nonne, a Prioresse,
> That of hir smyling was ful simple and coy ;
> Hir gretteste ooth was but by sëynt Loy ;

7

And she was cleped madame Eglentyne.
Ful wel she song the service divyne,
Entuned in hir nose ful semely ;
And Frensh she spak ful faire and fetisly,
After the scole of Stratford atte Bowe,
For Frensh of Paris was to hir unknowe . . ."

Now the essential quality of this and of all very great poetry is also what we may call a *universal* quality; it appeals to those sympathies which, unequally distributed and often distorted or suppressed, are yet the common possessions of our species. This quality is the real antiseptic of poetry : this it is that keeps a line of Homer perennially fresh and in bloom :—

" "Ὣς φάτο τοὺς δ' ἤδη κατέχεν φυσίζοος αἶα
ἐν Λακεδαίμονι αὖθι, φίλῃ ἐν πατρίδι γαίῃ."

These lines live because they contain something which is also permanent in man : they depend confidently on us, and will as confidently depend on our great-grandchildren. I was glad to see this point very courageously put the other day by Professor Hiram Corson, of Cornell University, in an address on " The Aims of Literary Study "—an address which Messrs. Macmillan have printed and published here and in America. " All works of genius," says

8

Mr. Corson, "render the best service, in literary education, when they are first assimilated in their absolute character. It is, of course, important to know their relations to the several times and places in which they were produced; but such knowledge is not for the tyro in literary study. He must first know literature, if he is constituted so to know it, in its absolute character. He can go into the philosophy of its relationships later, if he like, when he has a true literary education, and when the 'years that bring the philosophic mind' have been reached. Every great production of genius is, in fact, in its essential character, no more related to one age than to another. It is only in its phenomenal character (its outward manifestations) that it has a *special* relationship." And Mr. Corson very appositely quotes Mr. Ruskin on Shakespeare's historical plays—

"If it be said that Shakespeare wrote perfect historical plays on subjects belonging to the preceding centuries, I answer that they *are* perfect plays just because there is no care about centuries in them, but a life which all men recognize for the human life of all time; and this it is, not because Shakespeare sought to give universal truth, but because, painting honestly and completely from the men about him, he painted that human nature which is, indeed, constant enough—a rogue in the fifteenth century being *at heart* what a rogue is in the nineteenth century and was in the twelfth ; and an honest or knightly man being, in like manner, very similar to other such at any other time. And the work of these great idealists is, therefore, always universal : not because it is *not portrait*, but because it is *complete* portrait down to the heart, which is the same in all ages ; and the work of the mean idealists is *not* universal, not because it is portrait, but because it is *half* portrait—of the outside, the manners and the dress, not of the heart. Thus Tintoret and Shakespeare paint, both of them, simply Venetian and English nature as they saw it in their time, down to the root ; and it does for *all* time ; but as for any care to cast themselves into the particular ways of thought, or custom, of past time in their historical work, you will find it in neither of them, nor in any other perfectly great man that I know of."—*Modern Painters*.

It will be observed that Mr. Corson, whose address deals primarily with literary training, speaks of these absolute qualities of the great masterpieces as the *first* object of study. But his words, and Ruskin's words, fairly support my further contention that they remain the *most important* object of study, no matter how far one's literary training may have proceeded. To the most erudite student of Chaucer in the wide world Chaucer's poetry should be the dominant object of interest in connection with Chaucer.

But when the elaborate specialist confronts us, we are apt to forget that poetry is meant for mankind, and that its appeal is, or should be, universal. We pay tribute to the unusual : and so far as this implies respect for protracted industry and indefatigable learning, we do right. But in so far as it implies even a momentary confusion of the essentials with the accidentals of poetry, we do wrong. And the specialist himself continues admirable only so long as he keeps them distinct.

I hasten to add that Professor Skeat *does* keep them distinct very successfully. In a single sentence of admirable brevity he tells us that of Chaucer's poetical excellence "it is superfluous to speak ; Lowell's essay on Chaucer in ' My Study Windows ' gives a just estimate of his powers." And with this, taking the poetical excellence for granted, he proceeds upon his really invaluable work of preparing a standard text of Chaucer and illustrating it out of the stores of his apparently inexhaustible learning. The result is a monument to Chaucer's memory such as never yet was reared to English poet. Douglas Jerrold assured Mrs. Cowden Clarke that, when her time came to

enter Heaven, Shakespeare would advance and
greet her with the first kiss of welcome, " *even*
should her husband happen to be present."
One can hardly with decorum imagine Professor
Skeat being kissed ; but Chaucer assuredly will
greet him with a transcendent smile.

The Professor's genuine admiration, however, for the poetical excellence of his poet
needs to be insisted upon, not only because
the nature of his task keeps him reticent, but
because his extraordinary learning seems now
and then to stand between him and the natural
appreciation of a passage. It was not quite at
haphazard that I chose just now the famous
description of the Prioresse as an illustration of
Chaucer's poetical quality. The Professor has
a long note upon the French of Stratford atte
Bowe. Most of us have hitherto believed the
passage to be an example, and a very pretty
one, of Chaucer's playfulness. The Professor
almost loses his temper over this : he speaks of
it as a view " commonly adopted by news-
paper-writers who know only this one line of
Chaucer, and cannot forbear to use it in jest."
" Even Tyrwhitt and Wright," he adds more
in sorrow than in anger, " have thoughtlessly

given currency to this idea." "Chaucer," the Professor explains, "merely states a *fact*" (the italics are his own), " viz., that the Prioress spoke the usual Anglo-French of the English Court, of the English law-courts, and of the English ecclesiastics of higher ranks. The poet, however, had been himself in France, and knew precisely the difference between the two dialects; but he had no special reason for thinking *more highly*" (the Professor's italics again) " of the Parisian than of the Anglo-French. . . . Warton's note on the line is quite sane. He shows that Queen Philippa wrote business letters in French (doubtless Anglo - French) with 'great propriety'" . . . and so on. You see, there was a Benedictine nunnery at Stratford-le-Bow; and as "Mr. Cutts says, very justly, 'She spoke French correctly, though with an accent which savored of the Benedictine Convent at Stratford-le-Bow, where she had been educated, rather than of Paris.'" So there you have a fact.

And, now you have it, doesn't it look rather like Bitzer's horse?

"Bitzer," said Thomas Gradgrind. "Your definition of a horse?"

"Quadruped. Graminivorous. Forty teeth, namely twenty-four grinders, four eye-teeth, and twelve incisive. Sheds coat in the spring; in marshy countries sheds hoofs too. Hoofs hard, but requiring to be shod with iron. Age known by marks in mouth." Thus (and much more) Bitzer.

March 30, 1895. The Texts of the "Canterbury Tales"

It follows, I hope, from what I said last week, that by far the most important service an editor can render to Chaucer and to us is to give us a pure text, through which the native beauty of the poetry may best shine. Such a text Professor Skeat has been able to prepare, in part by his own great industry, in part because he has entered into the fruit of other men's labors. The epoch-making event in the history of the Canterbury Tales (with which alone we are concerned here) was Dr. Furnivall's publication for the Chaucer Society of the famous "Six-Text Edition." Dr. Furnivall set to work upon this in 1868.

The Six Texts were these :—

1. The great "Ellesmere" MS. (so called after its owner, the Earl of Ellesmere). "The finest and best of all the MSS. now extant."

2. The " Hengwrt" MS., belonging to Mr. William W. E. Wynne, of Peniarth ; very closely agreeing with the " Ellesmere."

3. The " Cambridge" MS. Gg 4.27, in the University Library. The best copy in any public library. This also follows the " Ellesmere" closely.

4. The " Corpus" MS., in the library of Corpus Christi College, Oxford.

5. The " Petworth" MS., belonging to Lord Leconfield.

6. The " Lansdowne" MS. in the British Museum. " Not a good MS., being certainly the worst of the six ; but worth reprinting owing to the frequent use that has been made of it by editors."

In his Introduction, Professor Skeat enumerates no fewer than fifty-nine MSS. of the Tales : but of these the above six (and a seventh to be mentioned presently) are the most important. The most important of all is the " Ellesmere"—the great " find " of the Six-Text Edition. " The best in nearly every respect," says Professor Skeat. "It not only gives good lines and good sense, but is also (usually) grammatically accurate and thoroughly well spelt. The publication of it has been a great boon to all Chaucer students, for which Dr. Furnivall will be ever gratefully remembered. . . . This splendid MS. has also the great merit of being complete, requiring no supplement from any other source, except in a few cases when a line or two has been missed."

Professor Skeat has therefore chiefly employed the Six-Text Edition, supplemented by a seventh famous MS., the "Harleian 7334"—printed in full for the Chaucer Society in 1885—a MS. of great importance, differing considerably from the "Ellesmere." But the Professor judges it "a most dangerous MS. to trust to, unless constantly corrected by others, and not at all fitted to be taken as the basis of a text." For the basis of his text, then, he takes the Ellesmere MS., correcting it freely by the other seven MSS. mentioned.

Now, as fate would have it, in the year 1888 Dr. Furnivall invited Mr. Alfred W. Pollard to collaborate with him in an edition of Chaucer which he had for many years promised to bring out for Messrs. Macmillan. The basis of their text of the Tales was almost precisely that chosen by Professor Skeat, *i.e.* a careful collation of the Six Texts and the Harleian 7334, due preponderance being given to the Ellesmere MS., and all variations from it stated in the notes. "A beginning was made," says Mr. Pollard, " but the giant in the partnership had been used for a quarter of a century to doing, for nothing, all the hard work for other people, and could not spare from his pioneering the time necessary to enter into the fruit of his own Chaucer labors. Thus the partner who was not a giant was left to go on pretty much by himself. When I had made some progress, Professor Skeat informed us that the notes which he had been for years accumulating encouraged him to undertake an edition on a large scale, and I gladly abandoned, in favor of an editor of so much greater width of reading, the Library Edition which had been arranged for in the original agreement of Dr. Furnivall and myself with Messrs. Macmillan. I thought, however, that the work which I had done might fairly be used for an edition on a less extensive plan and intended for a less stalwart class of readers, and of this the present issue of the Canterbury Tales is an instalment." *

So it comes about that we have two texts before us, each based on a collation of the Six-Text edition and the Harleian MS. 7334—the chief difference being that Mr. Pollard adheres closely to the Ellesmere MS., while Professor Skeat allows himself more freedom. This is how they start—

" Whán that Aprílle with hise shourès soote
　The droghte of March hath percèd to the roote,
　And bathed every veyne in swich licóur
　Of which vertú engendred is the flour ;
　Whan Zephirus eek with his swetè breeth　　5
　Inspirèd hath in every holt and heeth
　The tendrè croppès, and the yongè sonne
　Hath in the Ram his halfè cours y-ronne,
　And smalè fowelès maken melodye
　That slepen al the nvght with open eye,—　　10
　So priketh hem Natúre in hir coráges,—
　Thanne longen folk to goon on pilgrimages . . ."
                                          (*Pollard.*)

" Whan that Aprille with his shoures sote
　The droghte of Marche hath perced to the rote,
　And bathed every veyne in swich licour
　Of which vertu engendred is the flour ;

* Chaucer's Canterbury Tales. Edited, with Notes and Introduction, by Alfred W. Pollard. London : Macmillan & Co.

Whan Zephirus eek with his swete breeth   5
Inspired hath in every holt and heeth
The tendre croppes, and the yong sonne
Hath in the Ram his halfe cours y ronne,
And smale fowles maken melodye,
That slepen al the night with open yë,   10
(So priketh hem nature in hir corages :)
Than longen folk to goon on pilgrimages . . ."

                                 (*Skeat.*)

On these two extracts it must be observed
(1) that the accents and the dotted e's in the
first are Mr. Pollard's own contrivances for
helping the scansion; (2) in the second, l. 10,
" yë " is a special contrivance of Professor
Skeat. "The scribes," he says (Introd. Vol.
IV. p. xix.), " usually write *eye* in the middle
of a line, but when they come to it at the end
of one, they are fairly puzzled. In l. 10, the
scribe of Hn (' Hengwrt ') writes *lye*, and that
of Ln (' Lansdowne ') writes *yhe ;* and the
variations on this theme are curious. The
spelling *ye* (= yë) is, however, common.
. . . I print it ' yë ' to distinguish it from
ye, the pl. pronoun." The other differences are
accounted for by the varying degrees in which
the two editors depend on the Ellesmere MS.
Mr. Pollard sticks to the Ellesmere. Professor
Skeat corrects it by the others. Obviously the

editor who allows himself the wider range lays himself open to more criticism, point by point. He has to justify himself in each particular case, while the other's excuse is set down once for all in his preface. But after comparing the two texts in over a dozen passages, I have had to vote in almost every case for Professor Skeat.

The differences, however, are always trifling. The reader will allow that in each case we have a clear, intelligible text: a text that allows Chaucer to be read and enjoyed without toil or vexation. For my part, I hope there is no presumption in saying that I could very well do without Mr. Pollard's accents and dotted e's. Remove them, and I contend that any Englishman with an ear for poetry can read either of the two texts without difficulty. A great deal too much fuss is made over the pronunciation and scansion of Chaucer. After all, we are Englishmen, with an instinct for understanding the language we inherit; in the evolution of our language we move on the same lines as our fathers; and Chaucer's English is at least no further removed from us than the Lowland dialect of Scott's novels. Moreover,

The Alleged Difficulty of Reading Chaucer

20

we have in reading Chaucer what we lack in reading Scott—the assistance of rhythm; and the rhythm of Chaucer is as clearly marked as that of Tennyson. Professor Skeat might very well have allowed his admirable text to stand alone. For his rules of pronunciation, with their elaborate system of signs and symbols, seem to me (to put it coarsely) phonetics gone mad. This, for instance, is how he would have us read the Tales :—

" Whán-dhat Aprílla ╱ wídh iz-shúurez sóota
  dha-drúuht' ov-Márcha ╱ hath pérsed tóo dha róota,
  and-báadhed év'ri véina ╱ in-swích likúur,
  ov-whích vertýy ╱ enjéndred iz dha flúur. . . ."

—and so on? I think it may safely be said that if a man need this sort of assistance in reading or pronouncing Chaucer, he had better let Chaucer alone altogether, or read him in a German prose translation.

Why is Chaucer so easy to read? At a first *April 6, 1895.* glance a page of the " Canterbury Tales " appears more formidable than a page of the " Faërie Queene." As a matter of fact, it is less formidable; or, if this be denied, everyone

will admit that twenty pages of the "Canterbury Tales" are less formidable than twenty
pages of the "Faërie Queene." I might bring
several recent editors and critics to testify that,
after the first shock of the archaic spelling
and the final " e," an intelligent. public will
soon come to terms with Chaucer; but the unconscious testimony of the intelligent public
itself is more convincing. Chaucer is read
year after year by a large number of men and
women. Spenser, in many respects a greater
poet, is also read; but by far fewer. Nobody,
I imagine, will deny this. But what is the
reason of it?

The first and chief reason is this—Forms of
language change, but the great art of narrative
appeals eternally to men, and its rules rest on
principles older than Homer. And whatever
else may be said of Chaucer, he is a superb
narrator. To borrow a phrase from another
venerable art, he is always " on the ball." He
pursues the story — the story, and again the
story. Mr. Ward once put this admirably—

   "The vivacity of joyousness of Chaucer's poetic
temperament . . . make him amusingly impatient of
epical lengths, abrupt in his transitions, and anxious,
with an anxiety usually manifested by readers rather than

by writers, to come to the point, 'to the great effect,'
as he is wont to call it. 'Men,' he says, 'may over-
lade a ship or barge, and therefore I will skip at once
to the effect, and let all the rest slip.' And he unconsciously suggests a striking difference between himself
and the great Elizabethan epic poet who owes so much
to him, when he declines to make as long a tale of the
chaff or of the straw as of the corn, and to describe all
the details of a marriage-feast *seriatim :*

'The fruit of every tale is for to say :
They eat and drink, and dance and sing and play.'

This may be the fruit; but epic poets, from Homer
downward, have been generally in the habit of not neg-
lecting the foliage. Spenser in particular has that im-
partial copiousness which we think it our duty to admire in the Ionic epos, but which, if truth were told,
has prevented generations of Englishmen from acquiring
an intimate personal acquaintance with the 'Fairy
Queen.' With Chaucer the danger certainly rather lay
in the opposite direction."

Now, if we are once interested in a story,
small difficulties of speech or spelling will not
readily daunt us in the time-honored pursuit
of " what happens next "—certainly not if we
know enough of our author to feel sure he
will come to the point and tell us what happens
next with the least possible palaver. We have
a definite want and a certainty of being satisfied promptly. But with Spenser this satisfac-

tion may, and almost certainly will, be delayed
over many pages: and though in the meanwhile
a thousand casual beauties may appeal to us,
the main thread of our attention is sensibly
relaxed. Chaucer is the minister and Spenser
the master: and the difference between pursuing what we want and pursuing we-know-not-
what must affect the ardor of the chase. Even
if we take the future on trust, and follow Spenser to the end, we cannot look back on a book
of the "Faërie Queene" as on part of a good
story: for it is admittedly an unsatisfying and
ill-constructed story. But my point is that an
ordinary reader resents being asked to take the
future on trust while the author luxuriates in
casual beauties of speech upon every mortal subject but the one in hand. The first principle
of good narrative is to stick to the subject; the
second, to carry the audience along in a series
of small surprises—satisfying expectation and
going just a little beyond. If it were necessary to read fifty pages before enjoying Chaucer, though the sum of eventual enjoyment were
as great as it now is, Chaucer would never
be read. We master small difficulties line
by line because our recompense comes line by
line.

Moreover, it is as certain as can be that we read Chaucer to-day more easily than our fathers read him one hundred, two hundred, three hundred years ago. And I make haste to add that the credit of this does not belong to the philologists.

The Elizabethans, from Spenser onward, found Chaucer distressingly archaic. When Sir Francis Kynaston, *temp*. Charles I., translated "Troilus and Criseyde," Cartwright congratulated him that he had at length made it possible to read Chaucer without a dictionary. And from Dryden's time to Wordsworth's he was an "uncouthe unkiste" barbarian, full of wit, but only tolerable in polite paraphrase. Chaucer himself seems to have foreboded this, towards the close of his "Troilus and Criseyde," when he addresses his "litel book"—

"And for there is so great diversitee
    In English, and in wryting of our tonge,
    So preye I God that noon miswryte thee,
    Ne thee mismetre for defaute of tonge.
    And red wher-so thou be, or elles songe,
    That thou be understoude I God beseche! . . . "

And therewith, as though on purpose to defeat his fears, he proceeded to turn three stanzas of

Boccaccio into English that tastes almost as freshly after five hundred years as on the day it was written. He is speaking of Hector's death :—

> " And whan that he was slayn in this manere,
> His lighte goost ful blisfully it went
> Up to the holownesse of the seventh spere
> In convers leting every element ;
> And ther he saugh, with ful avysement,
> The erratik starres, herkening armonye
> With sownes ful of hevenish melodye.

> " And down from thennes faste he gan avyse
> This litel spot of erthe, that with the see
> Embraced is, and fully gan despyse
> This wrecched world, and held al vanitee
> To respect of the pleyn felicitee
> That is in hevene above ; and at the laste,
> Ther he was slayn, his loking down he caste ;

> " And in himself he lough right at the wo
> Of hem that wepten for his death so faste ;
> And dampned al our werk that folweth so
> The blinde lust, the which that may not laste,
> And sholden al our harte on hevene caste.
> And forth he wente, shortly for to telle,
> Ther as Mercurie sorted him to dwelle . . ."

Who have prepared our ears to admit this passage, and many as fine? Not the editors, who point out very properly that it is a close translation from Boccaccio's "Teseide," xi. 1-3. The information is valuable, as far as it goes; but what it fails to explain is just the marvel of the passage—viz., the abiding "Englishness" of it, the native ring of it in our ears after five centuries of linguistic and metrical development. To whom, besides Chaucer himself, do we owe this? For while Chaucer has remained substantially the same, apparently we have an aptitude that our grandfathers and great-grandfathers had not. The answer surely is: We owe it to our nineteenth century poets, and particularly to Tennyson, Swinburne, and William Morris. Years ago Mr. R. H. Horne said most acutely that the principle of Chaucer's rhythm is "inseparable from a full and fair exercise of the genius of our language in versification." This "full and fair exercise" became a despised, almost a lost, tradition after Chaucer's death. The rhythms of Skelton, of Surrey, and Wyatt, were produced on alien and narrower lines. Revived by Shakespeare and the later Elizabethans, it fell into contempt again until Cowper once more began to claim freedom for English rhythm, and after him Coleridge, and the despised Leigh Hunt. But never has its full liberty been so triumphantly asserted as by the three poets I have named above. If we are at home as we read Chaucer, it is because they have instructed us in the liberty which Chaucer divined as the only true way.

"THE PASSIONATE PIL-
GRIM."

The Passionate Pilgrim (1599). *Reprinted with a Note about the Book, by Arthur L. Humphreys. London: Privately Printed by Arthur L. Humphreys, of* 187, *Piccadilly.* MDCCCXCIV. I was about to congratulate Mr. Humphreys on his printing when, upon turning to the end of this dainty little volume, I discovered the well-known colophon of the Chiswick Press—"Charles Whittingham & Co., Took's Court, Chancery Lane, London." So I congratulate Messrs. Charles Whittingham & Co. instead, and suggest that the imprint should have run "Privately Printed *for* Arthur L. Humphreys."

This famous (or, if you like it, infamous) little anthology of thirty leaves has been singularly unfortunate in its title-pages. It was first published in 1599 as *The Passionate Pilgrime. By W. Shakespeare. At London. Printed*

29

for W. Jaggard, and are to be sold by W. Leake, at the Greyhound in Paules Churchyard. This, of course, was disingenuous. Some of the numbers were by Shakespeare: but the authorship of some remains doubtful to this day, and others the enterprising Jaggard had boldly conveyed from Marlowe, Richard Barnefield, and Bartholomew Griffin. In short, to adapt a famous line upon a famous lexicon, "the best part was Shakespeare, the rest was not." For this, Jaggard has been execrated from time to time with sufficient heartiness. Mr. Swinburne, in his latest volume of Essays, calls him an "infamous pirate, liar, and thief." Mr. Humphreys remarks, less vivaciously, that "He was not careful and prudent, or he would not have attached the name of Shakespeare to a volume which was only partly by the bard— that was his crime. Had Jaggard foreseen the tantrums and contradictions he caused some commentators—Mr. Payne Collier, for instance —he would doubtless have substituted ' By William Shakespeare *and others*' for ' By William Shakespeare.' Thus he might have saved his reputation, and this hornets' nest which now and then rouses itself afresh around his aged ghost of three centuries ago."

That a ghost can suffer no inconvenience from hornets I take to be indisputable : but as a defence of Jaggard the above hardly seems convincing. One might as plausibly justify a forger on the ground that, had he foreseen the indignation of the prosecuting counsel, he would doubtless have saved his reputation by forbearing to forge. But before constructing a better defence, let us hear the whole tale of the alleged misdeeds. Of the second edition of *The Passionate Pilgrim* no copy exists. Nothing whatever is known of it, and the whole edition may have been but an ideal construction of Jaggard's sportive fancy. But in 1612 appeared *The Passionate Pilgrime, or certaine amorous Sonnets between Venus and Adonis, newly corrected and augmented. By W. Shakespeare. The third edition. Whereunto is newly added two Love Epistles, the first from Paris to Hellen, and Hellen's answere back again to Paris. Printed by W. Jaggard.* (These "two Love Epistles" were really by Thomas Heywood.) This title-page was very quickly cancelled, and Shakespeare's name omitted.

These are the bare facts. Now observe how they appear when set forth by Mr. Humphreys :

Mr. Humphrey's Hypothesis.

—" Shakespeare, who, when the first edition was issued, was aged thirty-five, acted his part as a great man very well, for he with dignity took no notice of the error on the title-page of the first edition, attributing to him poems which he had never written. But when Jaggard went on sinning, and the third edition appeared under Shakespeare's name *solely*, though it had poems by Thomas Heywood, and others as well, Jaggard was promptly pulled up by both Shakespeare and Heywood. Upon this the publisher appears very properly to have printed a new title-page, omitting the name of Shakespeare."

Upon this I beg leave to observe—(1) That although it may very likely have been at Shakespeare's own request that his name was removed from the title-page of the third edition, Mr. Humphreys has no right to state this as an ascertained fact. (2) That I fail to understand, if Shakespeare acted properly in case of the third edition, why we should talk nonsense about his " acting the part of a great man very well " and " with dignity taking no notice of the error " in the first edition. In the first edition he was wrongly credited with pieces that belonged to Marlowe, Barnefield, Griffin, and some authors unknown. In the third he was credited with these and some pieces by Heywood as well. In the name of common logic I ask why, if it were "dignified" to say nothing in the case of Marlowe and Barnefield, it suddenly became right and proper to protest in the case of Heywood? But (3) what right have we to assume that Shakespeare "took no notice of the error on the title-page of the first edition"? We know this only—that if he protested, he did not prevail as far as the first edition was concerned. That edition may have been already exhausted. It is even possible that he *did* prevail in the matter of the second edition, and that Jaggard reverted to his old courses in the third. I don't for a moment suppose this was the case. I merely suggest that where so many hypotheses will fit the scanty data known, it is best to lay down no particular hypothesis as fact.

For I imagine that anyone can, in five minutes, fit up an hypothesis quite as valu- *Another.* able as Mr. Humphreys'. Here is one which at least has the merit of not making Shakespeare look a fool: — W. Jaggard, publisher,

33

comes to William Shakespeare, poet, with the
information that he intends to bring out a
small miscellany of verse. If the poet has an
unconsidered trifle or so to spare, Jaggard will
not mind giving a few shillings for them. "You
may have, if you like," says Shakespeare, "the
rough copies of some songs in my *Love's La-
bour's Lost*, published last year"; and, being
further encouraged, searches among his rough
MSS., and tosses Jaggard a lyric or two and a
couple of sonnets. Jaggard pays his money,
and departs with the verses. When the miscellany appears, Shakespeare finds his name
alone upon the title - page, and remonstrates.
But, of the defrauded ones, Marlowe is dead;
Barnefield has retired to live the life of a country gentleman in Shropshire; Griffin dwells in
Coventry (where he died, three years later).
These are the men injured; and if they cannot,
or will not, move in the business, Shakespeare
(whose case at law would be more difficult) can
hardly be expected to. So he contents himself
with strong expressions at The Mermaid. But
in 1612 Jaggard repeats his offence, and is in-
discreet enough to add Heywood to the list of
the spoiled. Heywood lives in London, on the
spot; and Shakespeare, now retired to Strat-

ford, is of more importance than he was in 1599. Armed with Shakespeare's authority Heywood goes to Jaggard and threatens ; and the publisher gives way.

Whatever our hypothesis, we cannot maintain that Jaggard behaved well. On the other hand, it were foolish to judge his offence as if the man had committed it the day before yesterday. Conscience in matters of literary copyright has been a plant of slow growth. But a year or two ago respectable citizens of the United States were publishing our books " free of authorial expenses," and even corrected our imperfect works without consulting us. We must admit that Jaggard acted up to Luther's maxim, " *Pecca fortiter*." He went so fas as to include a piece so well known as Marlowe's *Live with me and be my love*—which proves at any rate his indifference to the chances of detection. But to speak of him as one would speak of a similar offender in this New Year of Grace is simply to forfeit one's claim to an historical sense.

What further palliation can we find? Mr. Swinburne calls the book " a worthless little volume of stolen and mutilated poetry, patched

up and padded out with dirty and dreary doggrel, under the senseless and preposterous title of *The Passionate Pilgrim.*" On the other hand, Mr. Humphreys maintains that "Jaggard, at any rate, had very good taste. This is partly seen in the choice of a title. Few books have so charming a name as *The Passionate Pilgrim.* It is a perfect title. Jaggard also set up a good precedent, for this collection was published a year before *England's Helicon*, and, of course, very many years before any authorized collection of Shakespeare's 'Poems' was issued. We see in *The Passionate Pilgrim* a forerunner of *The Golden Treasury* and other anthologies."

Now, as for the title, if the value of a title lie in its application, Mr. Swinburne is right. It has little relevance to the verses in the volume. On the other hand, as a portly and attractive mouthful of syllables *The Passionate Pilgrim* can hardly be surpassed. If not "a perfect title," it is surely "a charming name." But Mr. Humphreys' contention that Jaggard "set up a good precedent" and produced a "forerunner" of English anthologies becomes absurd when we remember that *Tottel's Miscellany* was published in June, 1557 (just forty-two years before *The Passionate Pilgrim*), and had reached an eighth edition by 1587; that *The Paradise of Dainty Devices* appeared in 1576; *A Gorgeous Gallery of Gallant Inventions* in 1578; *A Handfull of Pleasant Delights* in 1584; and *The Phœnix' Nest* in 1593.

Almost as wide of the mark is Mr. Swinburne's description of the volume as "worthless." It contains twenty-one numbers, besides that lofty dirge, so unapproachably solemn, *The Phœnix and the Turtle.* Of these, five are undoubtedly by Shakespeare. A sixth (*Crabbed age and youth*), if not by Shakespeare, is one of the loveliest lyrics in the language, and I for my part could give it to no other man. Note also that but for Jaggard's enterprise this jewel had been irrevocably lost to us, since it is known only through *The Passionate Pilgrim.* Marlowe's *Live with me and be my love*, and Barnefield's *As it fell upon a day*, make numbers seven and eight. And I imagine that even Mr. Swinburne cannot afford to scorn *Sweet rose, fair flower, untimely pluck'd, soon vaded* —which again only occurs in *The Passionate*

Pilgrim. These nine numbers, with *The Phœnix and the Turtle*, make up more than half the book. Among the rest we have the pretty and respectable lyrics, *If music and sweet poetry agree; Good night, good rest; Lord, how mine eyes throw gazes to the east. When as thine eye hath chose the dame*, and the gay little song, *It was a Lording's daughter*. There remain the *Venus and Adonis* sonnets and *My flocks feed not*. Mr. Swinburne may call these " dirty and dreary doggrel," an he list, with no more risk than of being held a somewhat over-anxious moralist. But to call the whole book worthless is mere abuse of words.

It is true, nevertheless, that one of the only two copies existing of the first edition was bought for three halfpence.

SHAKESPEARE'S LYRICS

August 25, 1894.
Shake-
speare's
Lyrics.

IN their re-issue of *The Aldine Poets*, Messrs. George Bell & Sons have made a number of concessions to public taste. The new binding is far more pleasing than the old; and in some cases, where the notes and introductory memoirs had fallen out of date, new editors have been set to work, with satisfactory results. It is therefore no small disappointment to find that the latest volume, "The Poems of Shakespeare," is but a reprint from stereotyped plates of the Rev. Alexander Dyce's text, notes and memoir.

The Rev. A. Dyce.

Now, of the Rev. Alexander Dyce it may be fearlessly asserted that his criticism is not for all time. Even had he been less prone to accept the word of John Payne Collier for gospel; even had Shakespearian criticism made no perceptible advance during the last quarter of a century, yet there is that in the Rev. Alexander Dyce's treatment of his poet which would warn us to pause before accepting his word as final.

39

As a test of his æsthetic judgment we may turn
to the " Songs from the Plays of Shakespeare "
with which this volume concludes. It had been
as well, in a work of this sort, to include all
the songs ; but he gives us a selection only, and
an uncommonly bad selection. I have tried in
vain to discover a single principle of taste under-
lying it. On what principle, for instance, can
a man include the song " Come away, come
away, death " from *Twelfth Night*, and omit
" O mistress mine, where are you roaming ? " ;
or include Amiens' two songs from *As you Like
It*, and omit the incomparable " It was a lover
and his lass " ? Or what but stark insensibility
can explain the omission of " Take, O take
those lips away," and the bridal song " Roses,
their sharp spines being gone," that opens *The
Two Noble Kinsmen ?* But stay : the Rev.
Alexander Dyce may attribute this last pair to
Fletcher. " Take, O take those lips away "
certainly occurs (with a second and inferior
stanza) in Fletcher's *The Bloody Brother*, first
published in 1639 ; but Dyce gives no hint of
his belief that Fletcher wrote it. We are,
therefore, left to conclude that Dyce thought it
unworthy of a place in his collection. On *The
Two Noble Kinsmen* (first published in 1634)

Dyce is more explicit. In a footnote to the Memoir he says: "The title-page of the first edition of Fletcher's *Two Noble Kinsmen* attributes the play partly to Shakespeare; I do not think our poet had any share in its composition : but I must add that Mr. C. Lamb (a great authority in such matters) inclines to a different opinion." When "Mr. C. Lamb" and the Rev. Alexander Dyce hold opposite opinions, it need not be difficult to choose. And surely, if internal evidence count for anything at all, the lines

> " Maiden pinks, of odour faint,
>   Daisies smell-less, yet most quaint,
>   And sweet thyme true."

or—

> " Oxlips in their cradles growing "

or—

> " Not an angel of the air,
>   Bird melodious, or bird fair,
>   Be absent hence."

—were written by Shakespeare and not by Fletcher. Nor is it any detraction from Fletcher to take this view. Shakespeare himself has left songs hardly finer than Fletcher wrote at his best—hardly finer, for instance, than that magnificent pair from *Valentinian*. Only the

41

note of Shakespeare happens to be different from the note of Fletcher: and it is Shakespeare's note—the note of

"The cowslips tall her pensioners be"

(also omitted by the inscrutable Dyce) and of

"When daisies pied, and violets blue,
And lady-smocks all silver-white,
And cuckoo buds of yellow hue
Do paint the meadows with delight . . ."

—that we hear repeated in this Bridal Song.*

* The opening lines of the second stanza of this poem have generally been printed thus:

"Primrose, firstborn child of Ver,
Merry springtime's harbinger,
With her bells dim . . . ."

And many have wondered how Shakespeare or Fletcher came to write of the "bells" of a primrose. Mr. W. J. Linton proposed "With harebell slim": although if we must read "harebell" or "harebells," "dim" would be a pretty and proper word for the color of that flower. The conjecture takes some little plausibility from Shakespeare's elsewhere linking primrose and harebell together:

"Thou shalt not lack
The flower that's like thy face, pale primrose, nor
The azured harebell, like thy veins . . . . ."
Cymbeline, iv. 2.

I have always suspected, however, that there should be a semicolon after "Ver," and that "Merry springtime's harbinger, with her bells dim," refers to a totally different

And if this be so, it is but another proof for us that Dyce was not a critic for all time.

Nor is the accent of finality conspicuous in such passages as this from the Memoir :—

"Wright had heard that Shakespeare 'was a much better poet than player'; and Rowe tells us that soon after his admission into the company, he became distinguished, 'if not as an extraordinary actor, yet as an excellent writer.' Perhaps his execution did not equal his conception of a character, but we may rest assured that he who wrote the incomparable instructions to the player in *Hamlet* would never offend his audience by an injudicious performance."

I have no more to urge against writing of this order than that it has passed out of fashion, and that something different might reasonably have been looked for in a volume that bears the date 1894 on its title-page. The public owes Messrs. Bell & Sons a heavy debt; but at the same time the public has a peculiar interest in such a series as that of *The Aldine Poets*. A purchaser who finds several of these books to

flower—the snowdrop, to wit. And I have lately learnt from Dr. Grosart, who has carefully examined the 1634 edition (the only early one), that the text actually gives a semicolon. The snowdrop may very well come after the primrose in this song, which altogether ignores the process of the seasons.

his mind, and is thereby induced to embark upon the purchase of the entire series, must feel a natural resentment if succeeding volumes drop below the implied standard. He cannot go back: and to omit the offending volumes is to spoil his set. And I contend that the action taken by Messrs. Bell & Sons in improving several of their more or less obsolete editions will only be entirely praiseworthy if we may take it as an earnest of their desire to place the whole series on a level with contemporary knowledge and criticism.

Nor can anyone who knows how much the industry and enthusiasm of Dyce did, in his day, for the study of Shakespeare, do more than urge that while, viewed historically, Dyce's criticism is entirely respectable, it happens to be a trifle belated in the year 1894. The points of difference between him and Charles Lamb are perhaps too obvious to need indication; but we may sum them up by saying that whereas Lamb, being a genius, belongs to all time, Dyce, being but an industrious person, belongs to a period. It was a period of rapid development, no doubt—how rapid we may learn for ourselves by the easy process of taking down

Volume V. of Chalmers's "English Poets," and turning to that immortal passage on Shakespeare's poems which Chalmers put forth in the year 1810:—

"The peremptory decision of Mr. Steevens on the merits of these poems must not be omitted. 'We have not reprinted the Sonnets, etc., of Shakespeare, because the strongest Act of Parliament that could be framed would fail to compel readers into their service. Had Shakespeare produced no other works than these, his name would have reached us with as little celebrity as time has conferred upon that of Thomas Watson, an older and much more elegant sonnetteer.' Severe as this may appear, it only amounts to the general conclusion which modern critics have formed. Still, it cannot be denied that there are many scattered beauties among his Sonnets, and in the Rape of Lucrece; enough, it is hoped, to justify their admission into the present collection, especially as the Songs, etc., from his plays have been added, and a few smaller pieces selected by Mr. Ellis. . . ."

No comment can add to, or take from, the stupendousness of this. And yet it was the criticism proper to its time. "I have only to hope," writes Chalmers in his preface, "that my criticisms will not be found destitute of candour, or improperly interfering with the general and acknowledged principles of taste." Indeed they are not. They were the right opinions

45

for Chalmers; as Dyce's were the right opinions for Dyce: and if, as we hope, ours is a larger appreciation of Shakespeare, we probably hold it by no merit of our own, but as the common possession of our generation, derived through the chastening experiences of our grandfathers. That, however, is no reason why we should not insist on having such editions of Shakespeare as fulfil our requirements, and refuse to study Dyce except as an historical figure.

It is an unwise generation that declines to take all its inheritance. I have heard once or twice of late that English poets in the future will set themselves to express emotions more complex and subtle than have ever yet been treated in poetry. I shall be extremely glad, of course, if this happen in my time. But at present I incline to rejoice rather in an assured inheritance, and, when I hear talk of this kind, to say over to myself one particular sonnet which for mere subtlety of thought seems to me unbeaten by anything that I can select from the poetry of this century:—

Thy bosom is endeared of all hearts
Which I by lacking have supposed dead;

46

And there reigns Love and all Love's loving parts,
And all those friends which I thought buried.
How many a holy and obsequious Tear
Hath dear religious love stol'n from mine eye,
As interest of the dead, which now appear
But things remov'd that hidden in thee lie !

Thou art the grave where buried love doth live,
Hung with the trophies of my lovers gone,
Who all their parts of me to thee did give ;
That due of many now is thine alone !
Their images I lov'd I view in thee,
And thou, all they, hast all the all of me.

SAMUEL DANIEL

February 24, 1894. Samuel Daniel. THE writings of Samuel Daniel and the circumstances of his life are of course well enough known to all serious students of English poetry. And, though I cannot speak on this point with any certainty, I imagine that our younger singers hold to the tradition of all their fathers, and that Daniel still

renidet in angulo

of their affections, as one who in his day did very much, though quietly, to train the growth of English verse; and proved himself, in everything he wrote, an artist to the bottom of his conscience. As certainly as Spenser, he was a "poet's poet" while he lived. A couple of pages might be filled almost offhand with the genuine compliments of his contemporaries, and he will probably remain a "poet's poet" as long as poets write in English. But the average reader of culture—the person who is honestly moved by good poetry and goes from time

48

to time to his bookshelves for an antidote to the common cares and trivialities of this life—seems to neglect Daniel almost utterly. I judge from the wretched insufficiency of his editions. It is very hard to obtain anything beyond the two small volumes published in 1718 (an imperfect collection), and a volume of selections edited by Mr. John Morris and published by a Bath bookseller in 1855 ; and even these are only to be picked up here and there. I find it significant, too, that in Mr. Palgrave's *Golden Treasury* Daniel is represented by one sonnet only, and that by no means his best. This neglect will appear the more singular to anyone who has observed how apt is the person whom I have called the " average reader of culture " to be drawn to the perusal of an author's works by some attractive idiosyncrasy in the author's private life or character. Lamb is a staring instance of this attraction. How we all love Lamb, to be sure ! Though he rejected it and called out upon it, " gentle " remains Lamb's constant epithet. And, curiously enough, in the gentleness and dignified melancholy of his life, Daniel stands nearer to Lamb than any other English writer, with the possible exception of Scott. His circumstances were less gloomily picturesque. But I defy any feeling man to read the scanty narrative of Daniel's life and think of him thereafter without sympathy and respect.

Life.   He was born in 1562—Fuller says in Somersetshire, not far from Taunton; others say at Beckington, near Philip's Norton, or at Wilmington in Wiltshire. Anthony Wood tells us that he came "of a wealthy family;" Fuller that "his father was a master of music." Of his earlier years next to nothing is known; but in 1579 he was entered as a commoner at Magdalen Hall, Oxford, and left the university three years afterwards without taking a degree. His first book—a translation of Paola Giovio's treatise on Emblems—appeared in 1585, when he was about twenty-two. In 1590 or 1591 he was travelling in Italy, probably with a pupil, and no doubt busy with those studies that finally made him the first Italian scholar of his time. In 1592 he published his "Sonnets to Delia," which at once made his reputation; in 1594 his "Complaint of Rosamond" and "Tragedy of Cleopatra;" and in 1595 four books of his "Civil Wars." On Spenser's death, in 1599, Daniel is said to have succeeded to the office of poet-laureate.

"That wreath which, in Eliza's golden days,
  My master dear, divinist Spenser, wore ;
That which rewarded Drayton's learned lays,
  Which thoughtful Ben and gentle Daniel wore . . ."

But history traces the Laureateship, as an
office, no further back than Jonson, and we
need not follow Southey into the mists. It is
certain, however, that Daniel was a favorite at
Elizabeth's Court, and in some way partook of
her bounty. In 1600 he was appointed tutor
to the Lady Anne Clifford, a little girl of about
eleven, daughter of Margaret, Countess of
Cumberland ; and his services were gratefully
remembered by mother and daughter during
his life and after. But Daniel seems to have
tired of living in great houses as private tutor to
the young. The next year, when presenting his
works to Sir Thomas Egerton, he writes :—
"Such hath been my misery that whilst I
should have written the actions of men, I have
been constrained to bide with children, and,
contrary to mine own spirit, put out of that
sense which nature had made my part."

Now there is but one answer to this—that
a man of really strong spirit does not suffer
himself to be "put out of that sense which

nature had made my part.'' Daniel's words
indicate the weakness that in the end made
*Self-
distrust.* futile all his powers: they indicate a certain
''donnish'' timidity (if I may use the epithet),
a certain distrust of his own genius. Such a
timidity and such a distrust often accompany
very exquisite faculties: indeed, they may be
said to imply a certain exquisiteness of feeling.
But they explain why, of the two contemporaries, the robust Ben Jonson is to-day a living
figure in most men's conception of those times,
while Samuel Daniel is rather a fleeting ghost.
And his self-distrust was even then recognized
as well as his exquisiteness. He is indeed
'' well-languaged Daniel,'' '' sweet honey-dropping Daniel,'' '' Rosamund's trumpeter, sweet
as the nightingale,'' revered and admired by
all his compeers. But the note of apprehension
was also sounded, not only by an unknown
contributor to that rare collection of epigrams,
Skialetheia, or the Shadow of Truth.

> '' Daniel (as some hold) might mount, *if he list ;*
> But others say he is a Lucanist ''

—but by no meaner a judge than Spenser, himself, who wrote in his '' Colin Clout's Come
Home Again '':

" And there is a new shepherd late upsprung
  The which doth all afore him far surpass ;
  Appearing well in that well-tunéd song
  Which late he sung unto a scornful lass.
  Yet doth his trembling Muse but lowly fly,
  As daring not too rashly mount on height ;
  And doth her tender plumes as yet but try
  In love's soft lays, and looser thoughts delight.
  Then rouse thy feathers quickly, DANIEL,
  And to what course thou please thyself advance ;
  But most, meseems, thy accent will excel
  In tragic plaints and passionate mischance."

Moreover, there is a significant passage in
the famous " Return from Parnassus," first
acted at Cambridge during the Christmas of
1601 :

" Sweet honey-dropping Daniel doth wage
  War with the proudest big Italian
  That melts his heart in sugar'd sonneting,
  Only let him more sparingly make use
  Of others' wit and use his own the more."

Now it has been often pointed out that considerable writers fall into two classes—(1) those
who begin, having something to say, and are
from the first rather occupied with their matter
than with the manner of expressing it ; and (2)
those who begin with the love of expression
and intent to be artists in words, *and come*

The 'mauvais pas' of Parnassus.

53

through expression to profound thought. It is
fashionable just now, for some reason or another, to account Class 1 as the more respectable; a judgment to which, considering that
Shakespeare and Milton belonged undeniably
to Class 2, I refuse to assent. The question,
however, is not to be argued here. I have
only to point out in this place that the early
work of all poets in Class 2 is largely imitative.
Virgil was imitative, Keats was imitative—to
name but a couple of sufficiently striking examples. And Daniel, who belongs to this class,
was also imitative. But for a poet of this class to
reach the heights of song, there must come a time
when out of imitation he forms a genuine style
of his own, *and loses no mental fertility in the
transformation.* This, if I may use the metaphor, is the *mauvais pas* in the ascent of Parnassus: and here Daniel broke down. He did
indeed acquire a style of his own; but the
effort exhausted him. He was no longer pro-
lific; his ardor had gone: and his innate self-
distrustfulness made him quick to recognize his
sterility.

Soon after the accession of James I., Daniel,

at the recommendation of his brother-in-law, John Florio, possibly furthered by the interest of the Earl of Pembroke, was given a post as gentleman extraordinary and groom of the privy chamber to Anne of Denmark; and a few months after was appointed to take the oversight of the plays and shows that were performed by the children of the Queen's revels, or children of the Chapel, as they were called under Elizabeth. He had thus a snug position at Court, and might have been happy, had it been another Court. But in nothing was the accession of James more apparent than in the almost instantaneous blasting of the taste, manners, and serious grace that had marked the Court of Elizabeth. The Court of James was a Court of bad taste, bad manners, and no grace whatever : and Daniel— " the remnant of another time," as he calls himself — looked wistfully back upon the days of Elizabeth.

" But whereas he came planted in the spring,
    And had the sun before him of respect ;
    We, set in th' autumn, in the withering
    And sullen season of a cold defect,
    Must taste those sour distastes the times do bring
    Upon the fulness of a cloy'd neglect.

Although the stronger constitutions shall
Wear out th' infection of distemper'd days .   .   ."

And so he stood dejected, while the young men of "stronger constitutions" passed him by.

In this way it happened that Daniel, whom at the outset his contemporaries had praised with wide consent, and who never wrote a loose or unscholarly line, came to pen, in the dedicatory epistle prefixed to his tragedy of "Philotas," these words—perhaps the most pathetic ever uttered by an artist upon his work :

" And therefore since I have outlived the date
    Of former grace, acceptance and delight.
    I would my lines, late born beyond the fate
    Of her* spent line, had never come to light ;
    So had I not been tax'd for wishing well,
    Nor now mistaken by the censuring Stage,
    Nor in my fame and reputation fell,
    Which I esteem more than what all the age
    Or the earth can give. *But years hath done this
        wrong,*
    To make me write too much, and live too long."

I said just now that Daniel had done much, though quietly, to train the growth of English verse. He not only stood up successfully for

* Sc. Elizabeth's.

its natural development at a time when the *Ease of his* clever but less largely informed Campion and *Verse.* others threatened it with fantastic changes. He probably did as much as Waller to introduce polish of line into our poetry. Turn to the famous " Ulysses and the Siren," and read. Can anyone tell me of English verses that run more smoothly off the tongue, or with a more temperate grace ?

> " Well, well, Ulysses, then I see
>   I shall not have thee here :
> And, therefore, I will come to thee,
>   And take my fortune there.
> I must be won that cannot win,
>   Yet lost were I not won ;
> For beauty hath created been
>   T'undo or be undone."

To speak familiarly, this is as easy as an old shoe. To speak yet more familiarly, it looks as if any fool could turn off lines like these. Let the fool try.

And yet to how many anthologies do we not turn in vain for " Ulysses and the Siren "; or for the exquisite spring song, beginning—

> " Now each creature joys the other,
>   Passing happy days and hours ;

57

> One bird reports unto another
> In the fall of silver showers . . ."

—or for that lofty thing, the " Epistle to the
Countess of Cumberland "?—which Wordsworth, who quoted it in his " Excursion,"
declares to be " an admirable picture of the
state of a wise man's mind in a time of public
commotion."   Certainly if ever a critic shall
arise to deny poetry the virtue we so commonly
claim for her, of fortifying men's souls against
calamity, this noble Epistle will be all but
the last post from which he will extrude her
defenders.

WILLIAM BROWNE

IT has been objected to the author of *Britannia's Pastorals* that their perusal sends you to sleep. It had been subtler criticism, as well as more amiable, to observe that you can wake up again and, starting anew at the precise point where you dropped off, continue the perusal with as much pleasure as ever, neither ashamed of your somnolence nor imputing it as a fault to the poet. For William Browne is perhaps the easiest figure in our literature. He lived easily, he wrote easily, and no doubt he died easily. He no more expected to be read through at a sitting than he tried to write all the story of Marina at a sitting. He took up his pen and composed : when he felt tired he went off to bed, like a sensible man : and when you are tired of reading he expects you to be sensible and do the same.

He was born at Tavistock, in Devon, about the year 1590 ; and after the manner of mild

April 21, 1894.
William Browne of Tavistock.

A placid life.

59

and sensible men cherished a particular love
for his birth-place to the end of his days.
From Tavistock Grammar School he passed to
Exeter College, Oxford—the old west-country
college—and thence to Clifford's Inn and the
Inner Temple.   His first wife died when he was
twenty - three or twenty - four.   He took his
second courtship quietly and leisurely, marrying
the lady at length in 1628, after a wooing of
thirteen years.   "He seems," says Mr. A. H.
Bullen, his latest biographer, "to have acquired in some way a modest competence,
which secured him immunity from the troubles
that weighed so heavily on men of letters."
His second wife also brought him a portion.
More than four years before this marriage he
had returned to Exeter College, as tutor to the
young Robert Dormer, who in due time became
Earl of Carnarvon and was killed in Newbury
fight.   By his fellow-collegians—as by everybody with whom he came into contact—he was
highly beloved and esteemed, and in the public
Register of the University is styled, "vir omni
humana literarum et bonarum artium cognitione
instructus."   He gained the especial favor of
William Herbert, Earl of Pembroke, whom
Aubrey calls "the greatest Mæcenas to learned

60

men of any peer of his time or since," and of whom Clarendon says, "He was a great lover of his country, and of the religion and justice, which he believed could only support it; and his friendships were only with men of those principles,"—another tribute to the poet's character. He was familiarly received at Wilton, the home of the Herberts. After his second marriage he moved to Dorking and there settled. He died in or before the year 1645. In the letters of administration granted to his widow (November, 1645) he is described as "late of Dorking, in the county of Surrey, Esquire." But there is no entry of his death in the registers at Dorking or Horsham: so perhaps he went back to lay his bones in his beloved Devon. A William Browne was buried at Tavistock on March 27th, 1643. This may or may not have been our author. "Tavistock,—Wilton,—Dorking," says Mr. Bullen, —"Surely few poets have had a more tranquil journey to the Elysian Fields."

As with his life, so with his poetry—he went about it quietly, contentedly. He learned his art, as he confesses, from Spenser and Sidney; and he took it over ready-made, with all the conventions and pastoral stock-in-trade—swains

An amiable poet.

languishing for hard - hearted nymphs, nymphs languishing for hard - hearted swains; sheep-cotes, rustic dances, junketings, anadems, and true-love knots; monsters invented for the perpetual menace of chastity; chastity undergoing the most surprising perils, but always saved in the nick of time, if not by an opportune shepherd, then by an equally opportune river-god or earthquake; episodes innumerable, branching off from the main stem of the narrative at the most critical point, and luxuriating in endless ramifications. Beauty, eluding unwelcome embraces, is never too hotly pressed to dally with an engaging simile or choose the most agreeable words for depicting her tribulation. Why indeed should she hurry? It is all a polite and pleasant make-believe; and when Marina and Doridon are tired, they stand aside and watch the side couples, Fida and Remond, and get their breath again for the next figure. As for the finish of the tale, there is no finish. The narrator will stop when he is tired; just then and no sooner. What became of Marina after Triton rolled away the stone and released her from the Cave of Famine? I am sure I don't know. I have followed her adventures up to that point (though I should be very sorry

to attempt a *précis* of them without the book)
through some 370 pages of verse. Does this
mean that I am greatly interested in her? Not
in the least. I am quite content to hear no
more about her. Let us have the lamentations
of Celadyne for a change — though " for a
change " is much too strong an expression.
The author is quite able to invent more adventures for Marina, if he chooses to, by the hour
together. If he does not choose to, well and
good.

Was the composition of *Britannia's Pastorals* then, a useless or inconsiderable feat? Not
at all : since to read them is to taste a mild but
continuous pleasure. In the first place, it is always pleasant to see a good man thoroughly
enjoying himself : and that Browne thoroughly
" relisht versing "—to use George Herbert's
pretty phrase—would be patent enough, even
had he not left us an express assurance : —

> " What now I sing is but to pass away
>   A tedious hour, as some musicians play ;
>   Or make another my own griefs bemoan—"

—rather affected, that, one suspects :

" Or to be least alone when most alone,
   In this can I, as oft as I will choose,
   Hug sweet content by my retirèd Muse,
   And in a study find as much to please
   As others in the greatest palaces.
   Each man that lives, according to his power,
   On what he loves bestows an idle hour.
   Instead of hounds that make the wooded hills
   Talk in a hundred voices to the rills,
   I like the pleasing cadence of a line
   Struck by the consort of the sacred Nine.
   In lieu of hawks . . ."

—and so on. Indeed, unless it be Wither, there is no poet of the time who practised his art with such entire cheerfulness : though Wither's satisfaction had a deeper note, as when he says of his Muse—

" Her true beauty leaves behind
   Apprehensions in the mind,
   Of more sweetness than all art
   Or inventions can impart ;
   Thoughts too deep to be express'd,
   And too strong to be suppressed."

Yet Charles Lamb's nice observation—

" Fame, and that too after death, was all which hitherto the poets had promised themselves from their art.
It seems to have been left to Wither to discover that
poetry was a present possession as well as a rich rever-

sion, and that the muse had promise of both lives—of
this, and of that which was to come."

—must be extended by us, after reading his
lines quoted above, to include William Browne.
He, at least, had no doubt of the Muse as an
earthly companion.

As for posthumous fame, Browne confides to
us his aspirations in that matter also :—

" And Time may be so kind to these weak lines
  To keep my name enroll'd past his that shines
  In gilded marble, or in brazen leaves :
  Since verse preserves, when stone and brass deceives.
  Or if (as worthless) Time not lets it live
  To those full days which others' Muses give,
  Yet I am sure I shall be heard and sung
  Of most severest eld and kinder young
  Beyond my days ; and maugre Envy's strife,
  Add to my name some hours beyond my life."

This is the amiable hope of one who lived an
entirely amiable life in

                         " homely towns,
        Sweetly environ'd with the daisied downs : "

and who is not the less to be beloved because
at times his amiability prevents him from at-
tacking even our somnolence too fiercely.   If

the casual reader but remember Browne as a poet who had the honor to supply Keats with inspiration,* there will always be others, and enough of them, to prize his ambling Muse for her own qualities.

* *Cf.* his lament for William Ferrar (brother of Nicholas Ferrar, of Little Gidding), drowned at sea—

> " Glide soft, ye silver floods,
>   And every spring :
> Within the shady woods
>   Let no bird sing . . . ."

THOMAS CAREW

July 28, 1894.
A Note on his Name.

EVEN as there is an M alike in Macedon and Monmouth, so Thomas Carew and I have a common grievance—that our names are constantly mispronounced. It is their own fault, of course ; on the face of it they ought to rhyme with " few " and " vouch." And if it be urged (impolitely but with a fair amount of plausibility) that what my name may or may not rhyme with is of no concern to anybody, I have only to reply that, until a month or so back, I cheerfully shared this opinion and acquiesced in the general error. Had I dreamed then of becoming a subject for poetry, I had pointed out—as I do now—for the benefit of all intending bards, that I do not legitimately rhyme with " vouch " (so liable is human judgment to err, even in trifles), unless they pronounce it " vooch," which is awkward. I believe, indeed (speaking as one who has never had occasion to own a Rhyming Dictionary), that the number of English words consonant

with my name is exceedingly small; but leave
the difficulty to the ingenious Dr. Alexander
H. Japp, LL.D., F.R.S.E., who has lately
been at the pains to compose and put into private circulation a sprightly lampoon upon me.
As it is not my intention to reply with a set of
verses upon Dr. Japp, it seems superfluous to
inquire if *his* name should be pronounced as it
is spelt.

But Carew's case is rather important; and it
is really odd that his latest and most learned
editor, the Rev. J. F. Ebsworth, should fall
into the old error. In a " dedicatory prelude "
to his edition of " The Poems and Masque of
Thomas Carew " (London : Reeves & Turner),
Mr. Ebsworth writes as follows :—

> " Hearken strains from one who knew
> How to praise and how to sue :
> *Celia's* lover, TOM CAREW."

Thomas Carew (born April 3d, 1590, at
Wickham, in Kent) was the son of Sir Matthew
Carew, Master in Chancery, and the grandson
of Sir Wymond Carew, of East Antony, or
Antony St. Jacob, between the Lynher and
Tamar rivers in Cornwall, where the family of

Pole-Carew lives to this day. Now, the Cornish Carews have always pronounced their name as " Carey," though, as soon as you cross the Tamar and find yourself (let us say) as far east as Haccombe in South Devon, the name becomes " Carew "—pronounced as it is written. The two forms are both of great age, as the old rhyme bears witness—

" Carew, Carey and Courtenay,
  When the Conqueror came, were here at play "—

and the name was often written " Carey " or " Cary," as in the case of the famous Lucius Carey, Lord Falkland, and his descendants. In Cornwall, however, where spelling is often an untrustworthy guide to pronunciation (I have known people to write their name " Hix " and pronounce it as " Hic "—when sober, too), it was written " Carew " and pronounced as " Carey "; and there is not the slightest doubt that this was the case with our poet's name. If anyone deny it, let him consider the verse in which Carew is mentioned by his contemporaries : and attempt, for instance, to scan the lines in Robert Baron's " Pocula Castalia," 1650—

" Sweet *Suckling* then, the glory of the Bower
  Wherein I've wanton'd many a genial hour,

69

> Fair Plant ! whom I have seen *Minerva* wear
> An ornament to her well-plaited hair,
> On highest days ; remove a little from
> Thy excellent *Carew !* and thou, dearest *Tom,*
> *Love's Oracle !* lay thee a little off
> Thy flourishing *Suckling*, that between you both
> I may find room . . . ."

Or this by Suckling—

> " *Tom Carew* was next, but he had a fault,
> That would not well stand with a Laureat ;
> His Muse was hard-bound, and th' issue of 's brain
> Was seldom brought forth but with trouble and pain."

Or this, by Lord Falkland himself (who surely may be supposed to have known how the name was pronounced), in his " Eclogue on the Death of Ben Jonson "—

> " *Let Digby, Carew, Killigrew* and *Maine,*
> *Godolphin, Waller*, that inspired train—
> Or whose rare pen beside deserves the grace
> Or of an equal, or a neighbouring place—
> Answer thy wish, for none so fit appears
> To raise his Tomb, as who are left his heirs."

In each case " Carey " scans admirably, while " Carew " gives the line an intolerable limp.

This mistake of Mr. Ebsworth's is the less easy to understand inasmuch as he has been very careful to clear up the popular confusion of our poet Thomas Carew, " gentleman of the Privy Chamber to King Charles I., and cup-bearer to His Majesty," with another Thomas Cary (also a poet), son of the Earl of Monmouth and groom of His Majesty's bed-chamber. But it is one thing to prove that this second Thomas Cary is the original of the "medallion portrait " commonly supposed to be Carew's : it is quite another thing to saddle him, merely upon guess-work, with Carew's reputed indiscretions. Indeed, Mr. Ebsworth lets his enthusiasm for his author run clean away with his sense of fairness. He heads his Introductory Memoir with the words of Pallas in Tennyson's " Œnone "—

> " Again she said—' I woo thee not with gifts :
> Sequel of guerdon could not alter me
> To fairer. Judge thou me by what I am,
> So shalt thou find me fairest.' "—

from which I take it that Mr. Ebsworth claims his attitude towards Carew to be much the same as Thackeray's towards Pendennis. But in fact he proves himself a thorough-going partisan, and anyone less enthusiastic may think himself lucky if dismissed by Mr. Ebsworth

with nothing worse than a smile of pity mingled
with contempt. Now, so long as an editor
confines this belligerent enthusiasm to the defence of his author's writings, it is at worst but
an amiable weakness ; and every word he says
in their praise tends indirectly to justify his
own labor in editing these meritorious com-
positions. But when he extends this cham-
pionship over the author's private life, he not
unfrequently becomes something of a nuisance.
We may easily forgive such talk as " There
must assuredly have been a singular frankness
and affectionate simplicity in the disposition of
Carew : " talk which is harmless, though hardly
more valuable than the reflection beloved of
local historians — " If these grey old walls
could speak, what a tale might they not un-
fold ! " It is less easy to forgive such a note
as this :—

" Sir John Suckling was incapable of understanding
Carew in his final days of sickness and depression, as he
had been (and this is conceding much) in their earlier
days of reckless gallantry. His vile address ' to T——
C——,' etc., ' Troth, *Tom*, I must confess I much admire . . . .' is nothing more than coarse badinage
without foundation ; in any case not necessarily addressed to Carew, although they were of close acquaintance ; but many other Toms were open to a similar

expression, since ' T. C.' might apply to Thomas Carey, to Thomas Crosse, and other T. C. poets."

It is not pleasant to rake up any man's faults; but when an editor begins to suggest some new man against whom nothing is known (except that he wrote indifferent verse)—who is not even known to have been on speaking terms with Suckling—as the proper target of Suckling's coarse raillery, we have a right not only to protest, but to point out that even Clarendon, who liked Carew, wrote of him that, " after fifty years of his life spent with less severity and exactness than it ought to have been, he died with great remorse for that license, and with the greatest manifestation of Christianity that his best friends could desire." If Carew thought fit to feel remorse for that license, it scarcely becomes Mr. Ebsworth to deny its existence, much less to hint that the sinfulness was another's.

As a minor criticism, I may point out that the *A correction.* song, "Come, my Celia, let us prove . . ." (included by Mr. Ebsworth, with the remark that " there is no external evidence to confirm the attribution of this song to Carew ") was

73

written by Ben Jonson, and is to be found in *Volpone*, Act III., sc. 7, 1607.

But, with some imperfections, this is a sound edition — sadly needed — of one of the most brilliant lyrical writers of his time. It contains a charming portrait; and the editor's enthusiasm, when it does not lead him too far, is also charming.

"ROBINSON CRUSOE"

MANY a book has produced a wide and beneficent effect and won a great reputation, and yet this effect and this reputation have been altogether wide of its author's aim. Swift's *Gulliver* is one example. As Mr. Birrell put it the other day, "Swift's gospel of hatred, his testament of woe — his *Gulliver*, upon which he expended the treasures of his wit, and into which he instilled the concentrated essence of his rage—has become a child's book, and has been read with wonder and delight by generations of innocents."

April 13, 1895.
Robinson Crusoe.

Generations of innocents in like manner have accepted *Robinson Crusoe* as a delightful tale about a castaway mariner, a story of adventure pure and simple, without sub-intention of any kind. But we know very well that Defoe in writing it intended a parable—a parable of his own life. In the first place, he distinctly

How far is the tale a parable?

75

affirms this in his preface to the *Serious Reflections* which form Part iii. of his great story :—

"As the design of everything is said to be first in the intention, and last in the execution, so I come now to acknowledge to my reader that the present work is not merely a product of the two first volumes, but the two first volumes may rather be called the product of this. The fable is always made for the moral, not the moral for the fable . . . ."

He goes on to say that whereas "the envious and ill-disposed part of the world" have accused the story of being feigned, and "all a romance, formed and embellished by invention to impose upon the world," he declares this objection to be an invention scandalous in design, and false in fact, and affirms that the story, "though allegorical, is also historical"; that it is

"the beautiful representation of a life of unexampled misfortunes, and of a variety not to be met with in the world, sincerely adapted to and intended for the common good of mankind, and *designed at first*, as it is now further applied, to the most serious use possible. Farther, that there is a man alive, and well known too, the actions of whose life are the just subject of these volumes, *and to whom all or most part of the story most directly alludes ;* this may be depended upon for truth, and to this I set my name."

He proceeds to assert this in detail of several important passages in the book, and obviously intends us to infer that the adventures of Robinson Crusoe of York, Mariner, were throughout and from the beginning designed as a story in parable of the life and adventures of Daniel Defoe, Gentleman. "But Defoe may have been lying?" This was never quite flatly asserted. Even his enemy Gildon admitted an analogy between the tale of Crusoe and the stormy life of Defoe with its frequent shipwrecks "more by land than by sea." Gildon admitted this implicitly in the title of his pamphlet, *The Life and Strange Surprising Adventures of Mr. D— De F—, of London, Hosier, who has lived above Fifty Years by himself in the Kingdoms of North and South Britain*. But the question has always been, To what extent are we to accept Defoe's statement that the story is an allegory? Does it agree step by step and in detail with the circumstances of Defoe's life? Or has it but a general allegorical resemblance?

Hitherto, critics have been content with the general resemblance, and have agreed that it would be a mistake to accept Defoe's statement too literally, to hunt for minute allusions in *Robinson Crusoe,* and search for exact resemblances between incidents in the tale and events in the author's life. But this at any rate may be safely affirmed, that recent discoveries have proved the resemblance to be a great deal closer than anyone suspected a few years ago.

Mr. Wright's hypothesis. Mr. Aitken supplied the key when he announced in the *Athenæum* for August 23rd, 1890, his discovery that Daniel Defoe was born, not in 1661 (as had hitherto been supposed), but earlier, and probably in the latter part of the year 1659. The story dates Crusoe's birth September 30th, 1632, or just twenty-seven years earlier. Now Mr. Wright, Defoe's latest biographer,* maintains that if we add these twenty-seven years to the date of any event in Crusoe's life we shall have the date of the corresponding event in Defoe's life. By this simple calculation he finds that Crusoe's running away to sea corresponds in time with Defoe's departure from the academy at Newington Green ; Crusoe's early period on the island

---

* "The Life of Daniel Defoe." By Thomas Wright, Principal of Cowper School, Olney. London : Cassell & Co.

(south side) with the years Defoe lived at Tooting; Crusoe's visit to the other side of the island with a journey of Defoe's into Scotland; the footprint and the arrival of the savages with the threatening letters received by Defoe, and the physical assaults made on him after the Sacheverell trial; while Friday stands for a collaborator who helped Defoe with his work.

Defoe expressly states in his *Serious Reflections* that the story of Friday is historical and true in fact—

" It is most real that I had . . . such a servant, a savage, and afterwards a Christian, and that his name was called Friday, and that he was ravished from me by force, and died in the hands that took him, which I represent by being killed; this is all literally true, and should I enter into discoveries many alive can testify them. His other conduct and assistance to me also have just references in all their parts to the helps I had from that faithful savage in my real solitudes and disasters."

It may be added that there are strong grounds for believing Defoe to have had about this time assistance in his literary work.

All this is very neatly worked out; but of course the really important event in Crusoe's life is his great shipwreck and his long solitude on the island. Now of what events in Defoe's life are these symbolical?

The 'Silence.'

Well, in the very forefront of his *Serious Reflections,* and in connection with his long confinement in the island, Defoe makes Crusoe tell the following story :—

" I have heard of a man that, upon some extraordinary disgust which he took at the unsuitable conversation of some of his nearest relations, whose society he could not avoid, suddenly resolved never to speak any more. He kept his resolution most rigorously many years ; not all the tears or entreaties of his friends—no, not of his wife and children—could prevail with him to break his silence. It seems it was their ill-behaviour to him, at first, that was the occasion of it ; for they treated him with provoking language, which frequently put him into undecent passions, and urged him to rash replies ; and he took this severe way to punish himself for being provoked, and to punish them for provoking him. But the severity was unjustifiable ; it ruined his family and broke up his house. His wife could not bear it, and after endeavouring, by all the ways possible, to alter his rigid silence, went first away from him, and afterwards from herself, turning melancholy and distracted. His children separated, some one way and some another way ; and only one daughter, who loved her father above all the rest, kept with him, tended him, talked to him by signs, and lived almost dumb like her

father *near twenty-nine years with him ; till being
very sick, and in a high fever, delirious as we call it,
or light-headed, he broke his silence*, not knowing when
he did it, and spoke, though wildly at first.   He recov-
ered of his illness afterwards, and frequently talked with
his daughter, but not much, and very seldom to anybody else."

I italicise some very important words in the
above story.   Crusoe was wrecked on his island
on September 30th, 1659, his twenty-seventh
birthday.   We are told that he remained on
the island twenty-eight years, two months and
nineteen days.   (Compare with duration of the
man's silence in the story.)   This puts the date
of his departure at December 19th, 1687.

Now add twenty-seven years.   We find that
Defoe left *his* solitude—whatever that may have
been—on December 19th, 1714.   Just at that
date, as all his biographers record, Defoe was
struck down by a fit of apoplexy and lay ill for
six weeks.   Compare this again with the story.

You divine what is coming.   Astounding as
it may be, Mr. Wright contends that Defoe
himself was the original of the story : that Defoe, provoked by his wife's irritating tongue,

81

made a kind of vow to live a life of silence—
and kept it for more than twenty-eight years !

So far back as 1859 the egregious Chadwick
nibbled at this theory in his *Life and Times of
Daniel Defoe, with Remarks Digressive and
Discursive.* The story, he says, " would be
very applicable " to Defoe himself, and again,
" is very likely to have been taken from his
own life " ; but at this point Chadwick maun-
ders off with the remark that " perhaps the
domestic fireside of the poet or book-writer is
not the place we should go to in search of domestic happiness." Perhaps not ; but Chadwick, tallyhoing after domestic happiness, misses
the scent. Mr. Wright sticks to the scent and
rides boldly ; but is he after the real fox ?

April 20,
1895.

Can we believe it ? Can we believe that on
the 30th of September, 1686, Defoe, provoked
by his wife's nagging tongue, made a vow to
live a life of complete silence ; that for twenty-
eight years and a month or two he never addressed a word to his wife or children ; and
that his resolution was only broken down by a
severe illness in the winter of 1714 ?

Mr. Aitken,* who has handled this hypothesis of Mr. Wright's, brings several arguments against it, which, taken together, seem to
me quite conclusive.   To begin with, several
children were born to Defoe during this period.
He paid much attention to their education, and
in 1713, the penultimate year of this supposed
silence, we find his sons helping him in his
work.   Again, in 1703 Mrs. Defoe was inter-
ceding for her husband's release from Newgate.
Let me add that it was an age in which person-
alities were freely used in public controversy;
that Defoe was continuously occupied with
public controversy during these twenty-eight
years, and managed to make as many enemies
as any man within the four seas; and I think
the silence of his adversaries upon a matter
which, if proved, would be discreditable in the
extreme, is the best of all evidence that Mr.
Wright's hypothesis cannot be sustained.   Nor
do I see how Mr. Wright makes it square with
his own conception of Defoe's character.   " Of
a forgiving temper himself," says Mr. Wright

* *Romances and Narratives by Daniel Defoe.*   Edited by
George A. Aitken.   Vols. i., ii., and iii.   Containing the
Life and Adventures, Farther Adventures, and Serious
Reflections of Robinson Crusoe.   With a General Intro-
duction by the Editor.   London: J. M. Dent & Co.

*Mr. Aitken
on Mr.
Wright's
hypothesis.*

on p. 86, "he (Defoe) was quite incapable of understanding how another person could nourish resentment." This of a man whom the writer asserts to have sulked in absolute silence with his wife and family for twenty-eight years, two months, and nineteen days !

An inherent improbability.

At all events it will not square with *our* conception of Defoe's character. Those of us who have an almost unlimited admiration for Defoe as a master of narrative, and next to no affection for him as a man, might pass the heartlessness of such conduct. "At first sight," Mr. Wright admits, "it may appear monstrous that a man should for so long a time abstain from speech with his own family." Monstrous, indeed— but I am afraid we could have passed that. Mr. Wright, who has what I may call a purfled style, tells us that—

"To narrate the career of Daniel Defoe is to tell a tale of wonder and daring, of high endeavour and marvellous success. To dwell upon it is to take courage and to praise God for the splendid possibilities of life. . . . Defoe is always the hero; his career is as thick with events as a cornfield with corn; his fortunes change as quickly and as completely as the shapes in a kaleidoscope—he is up, he is down, he is courted, he is spurned; it is shine, it is shower, it is *couleur de rose*, it is Stygian night. Thirteen times he was rich and poor. Achilles was not more audacious, Ulysses more subtle, Æneas more pious."

That is one way of putting it. Here is another way (as the cookery books say):—" To narrate the career of Daniel Defoe is to tell a tale of a hosier and pantile maker, who had a hooked nose and wrote tracts indefatigably—he was up, he was down, he was in the Pillory, he was at Tooting ; it was *poule de soie*, it was leather and prunella ; and it was always tracts. Æneas was not so pious a member of the Butchers' Company ; and there are a few milestones on the Dover Road ; but Defoe's life was as thick with tracts as a cornfield with corn." These two estimates may differ here and there ; but on one point they agree—that Defoe was an extremely restless, pushing, voluble person, who could as soon have stood on his head for twenty-eight years, two months, and nineteen days as have kept silence for that period with any man or woman in whose company he found himself frequently alone. Unless we have entirely misjudged his character—and, I may add, unless Mr. Wright has completely misrepresented the rest of his life—it simply was not *in* the man to keep this foolish vow for twenty-four hours.

85

No, I am afraid Mr. Wright's hypothesis will
not do.   And yet his plan of adding twenty-
seven years to each important date in Crusoe's
history has revealed so many coincident events
in the life of Defoe that we cannot help feeling he is "hot," as they say in the children's
game; that the wreck upon the island and
Crusoe's twenty-eight years odd of solitude do
really correspond with some great event and
important period of Defoe's life.   The wreck
is dated 30th September, 1659.   Add the
twenty-seven years, and we come to September
30th, 1686.   Where was Defoe at that date,
and what was he doing?   Mr. Wright has to
confess that of his movements in 1686 and the
two following years "we know little that is
definite."   Certainly we know of nothing that
can correspond with Crusoe's shipwreck.

*A sugges-
tion.*

But wait a moment—The *original* editions
of *Robinson Crusoe* (and most, if not all, later
editions) give the date of Crusoe's departure
from the island as December 19th, 1686,
instead of 1687.   Mr. Wright suggests that
this is a misprint; and, to be sure, it does
not agree with the statement respecting the
length of Crusoe's stay on the island, *if we*

86

assume the date of the wreck to be correct.
But (as Mr. Aitken points out) the mistake
must be the author's, not the printer's, because
in the next paragraph we are told that Crusoe
reached England in June, 1687, not 1688.   I
agree with Mr. Aitken ; and I suggest *that the
date of Crusoe's arrival at the island, not the
date of his departure, is the date misprinted.*
Assume for a moment that the date of departure
(December 19th, 1686) is correct.   Subtract
the twenty-eight years, two months, and nineteen days of Crusoe's stay on the island, and we
get September 30th, 1658, as the date of the
wreck and his arrival at the island.   Now add
the twenty-seven years which separate Crusoe's
experiences from Defoe's, and we come to September 30th, 1685.   What was happening in
England at the close of September, 1685 ? Why,
Jeffreys was carrying through his Bloody Assize.

" Like many other Dissenters," says Mr.
Wright on p. 21, " Defoe sympathised with
Monmouth ; and, to his misfortune, took part
in the rising."   His comrades perished in it,
and he himself, in Mr. Wright's words,
" probably had to lie low."   There is no
doubt that the Monmouth affair was the be-

ginning of Defoe's troubles : and I suggest that certain passages in the story of Crusoe's voyage (*e.g.* the " secret proposal " of the three merchants who came to Crusoe) have a peculiar significance if read in this connection. I also think it possible there may be a particular meaning in the several waves, so carefully described, through which Crusoe made his way to dry land ; and in the simile of the reprieved malefactor (p. 50 in Mr. Aitken's delightful edition); and in the several visits to the wreck.

I am no specialist in Defoe, but put this suggestion forward with the utmost diffidence. And yet, right or wrong, I feel it has more plausibility than Mr. Wright's. Defoe undoubtedly took part in the Monmouth rising, and was a survivor of that wreck " on the south side of the island " : and undoubtedly it formed the turning-point of his career. If we could discover how he escaped Kirke and Jeffreys, I am inclined to believe we should have a key to the whole story of the shipwreck. I should not be sorry to find this hypothesis upset ; for the story of Robinson Crusoe is quite good enough for me as it stands, and without any sub-intention. But whatever be the

true explanation of the parable, if time shall discover it, I confess I expect it will be a trifle less
recondite than Mr. Wright's, and a trifle more
creditable to the father of the English novel.*

* Upon this suggestion Mr. Aitken, in a postscript to
his seventh volume of the *Romances and Narratives*, has
since remarked as follows :—

"In a discussion in *The Speaker* upon Defoe's supposed period
of 'silence,' published since the appearance of the first volume of
this edition, Mr. Quiller Couch, while agreeing, for the reasons I
have given (vol. i. p. lvii.), that there is no mistake in the date of
Robinson Crusoe's departure from his island (December, 1686),
has suggested that perhaps the error in the chronology lies, not in
the length of time Crusoe is said to have lived on the island, but
in the date given for his landing (September, 1659). That this
suggestion is right appears from a passage which has hitherto
escaped notice. Crusoe was born in 1692, and Defoe makes him
say (vol. i. p. 147), 'The same day of the year I was born on,
viz. the 30th of September, that same day I had my life so
miraculously saved twenty-six years after, when I was cast ashore
on this island.' Crusoe must, therefore, have reached his island
on September 30, 1658, not 1659, as twice stated by Defoe ; and
by adding twenty-eight years to 1658 we get 1686, the date given
for Crusoe's departure.

"It is, however, questionable whether this rectification helps us
to interpret the allegory in *Robinson Crusoe*. It is true that if, in
accordance with the 'key' suggested by Mr. Wright, we add
twenty-seven years to the date of the shipwreck (1658) in order to
find the corresponding event in Defoe's life, we arrive at
September, 1685, when Jeffreys was sentencing many of those
who—like Defoe—took part in Monmouth's rising. But we have
no evidence that Defoe suffered seriously in consequence of the
part he took in this rebellion ; and the addition of twenty-
seven years to the date of Crusoe's departure from the island
(December, 1686) does not bring us to any corresponding event in
Defoe's own story. Those who are curious will find the question
discussed at greater length in *The Speaker* for April 13 and 20,
and May 4, 1895."

LAWRENCE STERNE

Dec. 19, 1891. Sterne and Thackeray.

IT is told by those who write scraps of Thackeray's biography that a youth once ventured to speak disrespectfully of Scott in his presence. "You and I, sir," said the great man, cutting him short, "should lift our hats at the mention of that great name."

An admirable rebuke !—if only Thackeray had remembered it when he sat down to write those famous Lectures on the English Humorists, or at least before he stood up in Willis's Rooms to inform a polite audience concerning his great predecessors. Concerning their work? No. Concerning their genius? No. Concerning the debt owed to them by mankind? Not a bit of it. Concerning their *lives*, ladies and gentlemen ; and whether their lives were pure and respectable and free from scandal and such as men ought to have led whose works you would like your sons and daughters to handle. Mr. Frank T. Marzials, Thackeray's latest biographer, finds the matter of these Lectures "excellent" :—

"One feels in the reading that Thackeray is a peer among his peers—a sort of elder brother,* kindly, appreciative and tolerant—as he discourses of Addison, Steele, Swift, Pope, Sterne, Fielding, Goldsmith. I know of no greater contrast in criticism—a contrast, be it said, not to the advantage of the French critic—than Thackeray's treatment of Pope and that of M. Taine. What allowance the Englishman makes for the physical ills that beset the 'gallant little cripple'; with what a gentle hand he touches the painful places in that poor twisted body !   M. Taine, irritated apparently that Pope will not fit into his conception of English literature, exhibits the same deformities almost savagely."

I am sorry that I cannot read this kindliness, this appreciation, this tolerance, into the Lectures—into those, for instance, of Sterne and Fielding: that the simile of the " elder brother" carries different suggestions for Mr. Marzials and for me: and that the lecturer's attitude is to me less suggestive of a peer among his peers than of a tall " bobby "—a volunteer constable—determined to warn his polite hearers what sort of men these were whose books they had hitherto read unsuspectingly.

* But why " elder " ?

And even so—even though the lives and
actions of men who lived too early to know
Victorian decency must be held up to shock a
crowd in Willis's Rooms, yet it had been but
common generosity to tell the whole truth.
Then the story of Fielding's *Voyage to Lisbon*
might have touched the heart to sympathy even
for the purely fictitious low comedian whom
Thackeray presented : and Sterne's latest letters
might have infused so much pity into the polite
audience that they, like his own Recording
Angel, might have blotted out his faults with
a tear. But that was not Thackeray's way.
Charlotte Brontë found "a finished taste and
ease" in the Lectures, a "something high
bred." Motley describes their style as "hovering," and their method as "the perfection of
lecturing to high-bred audiences." Mr. Marzials
quotes this expression "hovering" as admirably
descriptive. It is. By judicious selection, by
innuendo, here a pitying aposiopesis, there an
indignant outburst, the charges are heaped up.
Swift was a toady at heart, and used Stella
vilely for the sake of that hussy Vanessa. Con-
greve had captivating manners—of course he
had, the dog ! And we all know what that
meant in those days. Dick Steele drank and

failed to pay his creditors. Sterne—now really I know what Club life is, ladies and gentlemen, and I might tell you a thing or two if I would: but really, speaking as a gentleman before a polite audience, I warn you against Sterne.

I do not suppose for a moment that Thackeray consciously defamed these men. The weaknesses, the pettinesses of humanity interested him, and he treated them with gusto, even as he spares us nothing of that horrible scene between Mrs. Mackenzie and Colonel Newcome. And of course poor Sterne was the easiest victim. The fellow was so full of his confounded sentiments. You ring a choice few of these on the counter and prove them base metal. You assume that the rest of the bag is of equal value. You "go one better" than Sir Peter Teazle and damn all sentiment, and lo! the fellow is no better than a smirking jester, whose antics you can expose till men and women, who had foolishly laughed and wept as he moved them, turn from him, loathing him as a swindler. So it is that although *Tristram Shandy* continues one of the most popular classics in the language, nobody dares to confess his debt to Sterne except in discreet terms of apology.

But the fellow wrote the book. You can't deny *that*, though Thackeray may tempt you to forget it. (What proportion does my Uncle Toby hold in that amiable Lecture?) The truth is that the elemental simplicity of Captain Shandy and Corporal Trim did not appeal to the author of *The Book of Snobs* in the same degree as the pettiness of the man Sterne appealed to him: and his business in Willis's Rooms was to talk, not of Captain Shandy, but of the man Sterne, to whom his hearers were to feel themselves superior as members of society. I submit that this was not a worthy task for a man of letters who was also a man of genius. I submit that it was an inversion of the true critical method to wreck Sterne's *Sentimental Journey* at the outset by picking Sterne's life to pieces, holding up the shreds and warning the reader that any nobility apparent in his book will be nothing better than a sham. Sterne is scarcely arrived at Calais and in conversation with the Monk before you are cautioned how you listen to the impostor. "Watch now," says the critic; "he'll be at his tricks in a moment. Hey, *paillasse!* There! —didn't I tell you?" And yet I am as sure that the opening pages of the *Sentimental*

Journey are full of genuine feeling as I am that if Jonathan Swift had entered the room while the Lecture upon him was going forward, he would have eaten William Makepeace Goliath, white waistcoat and all.

Frenchmen, who either are less awed than we by lecturers in white waistcoats, or understand the methods of criticism somewhat better, cherish the *Sentimental Journey* (in spite of its indifferent French) and believe in the genius that created it. But the Briton reads it with shyness, and the British critic speaks of Sterne with bated breath, since Thackeray told it in Gath that Sterne was a bad man, and the daughters of Philistia triumphed.

We are a strenuous generation, with a New Humor and a number of interesting by-products; but a new *Tristram Shandy* stands not yet among our achievements. So Messrs. Henley and Whibley have made the best of it and given us a new edition of the old *Tristram* —two handsome volumes, with shapely pages, fair type, and an Introduction. Mr. Whibley supplies the Introduction, and that he writes

October 6, 1894.
Mr. Whibley's Edition of " Tristram Shandy."

95

lucidly and forcibly needs not to be said.   His
position is neither that so unfairly taken up by
Thackeray ; nor that of Allibone, who, writing
for Heaven knows how many of Allibone's
maiden aunts, summed up Sterne thus :—

> "A standing reproach to the profession which he
> disgraced, grovelling in his tastes, indiscreet, if not
> licentious, in his habits, he lived unhonoured and died
> unlamented, save by those who found amusement in his
> wit or countenance in his immorality." *

But though he avoids these particular excesses ;
though he goes straight for the book, as a critic
should ; Mr. Whibley cannot get quit of the
bad tradition of patronizing Sterne :—

> "He failed, as only a sentimentalist can fail, in the
> province of pathos. . . .   There is no trifle, ani-
> mate or inanimate, he will not bewail, if he be but in
> the mood ; nor does it shame him to dangle before the
> public gaze those poor shreds of sensibility he calls his
> feelings.   Though he seldom deceives the reader into
> sympathy, none will turn from his choicest agony with-
> out a thrill of disgust.   The *Sentimental Journey*, de-
> spite its interludes of tacit humour and excellent narra-
> tive, is the last extravagance of irrelevant grief. . . .
> Genuine sentiment was as strange to Sterne the writer
> as to Sterne the man ; and he conjures up no tragic
> figure that is not stuffed with sawdust and tricked out

* " Pan might *indeed* be proud if ever he begot
      Such an Allibone . . ." *Spenser (revised)*.

in the rags of the green-room. Fortunately, there is
scant opportunity for idle tears in *Tristram Shandy*.
. . . Yet no occasion is lost. . . . Yorick's
death is false alike to nature and art. The vapid emotion
is properly matched with commonness of expression,
and the bad taste is none the more readily excused by
the suggestion of self-defence. Even the humour of My
Uncle Toby is something degraded by the oft-quoted
platitude : 'Go, poor devil,' says he, to an overgrown
fly which had buzzed about his nose ; 'get thee gone.
Why should I hurt thee? This world surely is big
enough to hold both thee and me.' "

But here Mr. Whibley's notorious hatred of
sentiment leads him into confusion. That the
passage has been over - quoted is no fault of
Sterne's. Of My Uncle Toby, if of any man,
it might have been predicted that he would not
hurt a fly. To me this trivial action of his is
more than merely sentimental. But, be this
as it may, I am sure it is honestly characteristic.

Still, on the whole Mr. Whibley has justice.
Sterne *is* a sentimentalist. Sterne *is* indecent
by reason of his reticence—more indecent than
Rabelais, because he uses a hint where Rabelais
would have said what he meant, and prints a
dash where Rabelais would have plumped out
with a coarse word and a laugh. Sterne *is* a

convicted thief. On a famous occasion Charles Reade drew a line between plagiary and justifiable borrowing. To draw material from a heterogeneous work—to found, for instance, the play of *Coriolanus* upon Plutarch's *Life*—is justifiable : to take from a homogeneous work —to enrich your drama from another man's drama—is plagiary. But even on this interpretation of the law Sterne must be condemned ; for in decking out *Tristram* with feathers from the history of Gargantua he was pillaging a homogeneous work. Nor can it be pleaded in extenuation that he improved upon his originals—though it can, I think, be pleaded that he made his borrowings his own. I do not think much of Mr. Whibley's instance of Servius Sulpicius' letter. No doubt Sterne took his translation of it from Burton ; but the letter is a very well known one, and Burton's translation happened to be uncommonly good, and the borrowing of a good rendering without acknowledgment was not, as far as I know, then forbidden by custom. In any case, the whole passage is intended merely to lead up to the beautiful perplexity of My Uncle Toby. And that is Sterne's own, and could never have been another man's. "After all," says Mr.

Whibley, " all the best in Sterne is still Sterne's own."

But the more I agree with Mr. Whibley's strictures the more I desire to remove them from an Introduction to *Tristram Shandy*, and to read them in a volume of Mr. Whibley's collected essays. Were it not better, in reading *Tristram Shandy*, to take Sterne for once (if only for a change) at his own valuation, or at least to accept the original postulates of the story? If only for the entertainment he provides we owe him the effort. There will be time enough afterwards to turn to the cold judgment of this or that critic, or to the evidence of this or that thief-taker. For the moment he claims to be heard without prejudice; he has genius enough to make it worth our while to listen without prejudice; and the most lenient "appreciation" of his sins, if we read it beforehand, is bound to raise prejudice and infect our enjoyment as we read. And, as a corollary of this demand, let us ask that he shall be allowed to present his book to us exactly as he chooses. Mr. Whibley says, " He set out upon the road of authorship with a false ideal : ' Writing,' said he, ' when properly managed, is but a different name for conversation.' It would be juster to assert that writing is never properly managed, unless it be removed from conversation as far as possible." Very true; or, at least, very likely. But since Sterne *had* this ideal, let us grant him full liberty to make his spoon or spoil his horn, and let us judge afterwards concerning the result. The famous blackened page and the empty pages (all omitted in this new edition) are part of Sterne's method. They may seem to us trick-work and foolery; but, if we consider, they link on to his notion that writing is but a name for conversation; they are included in his demand that in writing a book a man should be allowed to "go cluttering away like hey-go mad." "You may take my word"— it is Sterne who speaks, and in his very first chapter—

"You may take my word that nine parts in ten of a man's sense or his nonsense, his success and miscarriages in this world, depend upon their motions and activity, and the different tracks and trains you put them into, so that when they are once set going— whether right or wrong, 'tis not a halfpenny matter— away they go cluttering like hey-go mad ; and by treading the same steps over and over again, they presently make a road of it, as plain and smooth as a garden walk, which, when once they are used to, the devil himself sometimes shall not be able to drive them off it."

This, at any rate, is Sterne's own postulate. And I had rather judge him with all his faults after reading the book than be prepared beforehand to make allowances.

Let one thing be recorded to the credit of this much-abused man. He wrote two master-pieces of fiction (one of them a work of considerable length), and in neither will you find an ill-natured character or an ill-natured word. On the admission of all critics My Father, My Mother, My Uncle Toby, Corporal Trim, and Mrs. Wadman are immortal creations. To the making of them there has gone no single sour or uncharitable thought. They are essentially amiable : and the same may be said of all the minor characters and of the author's disquisitions. Sterne has given us a thousand occasions to laugh, but never an occasion to laugh on the wrong side of the mouth. For savagery or bitterness you will search his books in vain. He is obscene, to be sure. But who, pray, was ever the worse for having read him? Alas, poor Yorick! He had his

Nov. 12, 1895. Sterne's Good-nature.

obvious and deplorable failings.   I never heard that he communicated them.   Good-humor he has been communicating now for a hundred and fifty years.

SCOTT AND BURNS

" All Balzac's novels occupy one shelf,
The new edition fifty volumes long,"

Dec. 9,
1893.
Scott's
Letters.

—says Bishop Blougram.   But for Scott the
student will soon have to hire a room.   The
novels and poems alone stretch away into just
sixty volumes in Cadell's edition ; and this is
only the beginning.   At this very moment two
new editions (one of which, at least, is indispensable) are unfolding their magnificent lengths,
and report says that Messrs. Hodder and Stough-
ton already project a third, with introductory
essays by Mr. Barrie.   Then the Miscellaneous
Prose Works by that untiring hand extend to
some twenty-eight or thirty volumes.   And
when Scott stops, his biographer and his commentators begin, and all with like liberal notions of space and time.   Nor do they deceive
themselves.   We take all they give, and call for
more.   Three years ago, and fifty-eight from
the date of Scott's death, his Journal was pub-

lished; and although Lockhart had drawn upon it for one of the fullest biographies in the language, the little that Lockhart had left unused was sufficient to make its publication about the most important literary event of the year 1890.

And now Mr. David Douglas, the publisher of the "Journal," gives us in two volumes a selection from the familiar letters preserved at Abbotsford. The period covered by this correspondence is from 1797, the year of Sir Walter's marriage, to 1825, when the "Journal" begins—"covered," however, being too large a word for the first seven years, which are represented by seven letters only; it is only in 1806 that we start upon something like a consecutive story. Mr. Douglas speaks modestly of his editorial work. "I have done," he says, "little more than arrange the correspondence in chronological order, supplying where necessary a slight thread of continuity by annotation and illustration." It must be said that Mr. Douglas has done this exceedingly well. There is always a note where a note is wanted, and never where information would be superfluous. On the taste and judgment of his se-

lection one who has not examined the whole
mass of correspondence at Abbotsford can only
speak on *a priori* grounds. But it is unlikely
that the writer of these exemplary footnotes has
made many serious mistakes in compiling his
text.

Man's perennial and pathetic curiosity about
virtue has no more striking example than the
public eagerness to be acquainted with every
detail of Scott's life. For what, as a mere
story, is that life?—a level narrative of many
prosperous years; a sudden financial crash;
and the curtain falls on the struggle of a tired
and dying gentleman to save his honor. Scott
was born in 1771 and died in 1832, and all
that is special in his life belongs to the last six
years of it. Even so the materials for the story
are of the simplest—enough, perhaps, under the
hand of an artist to furnish forth a tale of the
length of Trollope's *The Warden*. In pictur-
esqueness, in color, in wealth of episode and
περιπέτεια, Scott's career will not compare for a
moment with the career of Coleridge, for instance. Yet who could endure to read the life
of Coleridge in six volumes? De Quincey, in
an essay first published the other day by Dr.

Japp, calls the story of the Coleridges " a perfect romance   .   .   .   a romance of beauty,
of intellectual power, of misfortune suddenly
illuminated from heaven, of prosperity suddenly
overcast by the waywardness of the individual."
But the "romance" has been written twice
and thrice, and desperately dull reading it
makes in each case.   Is it then an accident
that Coleridge has been unhappy in his biographers, while Lockhart succeeded once for
all, and succeeded so splendidly?

It is surely no accident.   Coleridge is an ill
man to read about just as certainly as Scott is
a good man to read about ; and the secret is
just that Scott had character and Coleridge had
not.   In writing of the man of the " graspless
hand," the biographer's own hand in time
grows graspless on the pen ; and in reading
of him our hands too grow graspless on the
page.   We pursue the man and come upon
group after group of his friends ; and each
as we demand " What have you done with
Coleridge ? " answers " He was here just now,
and we helped him forward a little way."
Our best biographies are all of men and
women of character — and, it may be added,

of beautiful character—of Johnson, Scott, and Charlotte Brontë.

There are certain people whose biographies *ought* to be long. Who could learn too much concerning Lamb? And concerning Scott, who will not agree with Lockhart's remark in the preface to his abridged edition of 1848:— " I should have been more willing to produce an enlarged edition ; for the interest of Sir Walter's history lies, I think, peculiarly in its minute details " ? You may explore here, and explore there, and still you find pure gold ; for the man was gold right through.

So in the present volume every line is of interest because we refer it to Scott's known character and test it thereby. The result is always the same ; yet the employment does not weary. In themselves the letters cannot stand, as mere writing, beside the letters of Cowper, or of Lamb. They are just the common-sense epistles of a man who to his last day remained too modest to believe in the extent of his own genius. The letters in this collection which show most acuteness on literary matters are not Scott's, but Lady Louisa Stuart's, who appre-

ciated the Novels on their appearance (their
faults as well as their merits) with a judicious-
ness quite wonderful in a contemporary. Scott's
literary observations (with the exception of one
passage where the attitude of an English gentleman towards literature is stated thus—" he asks
of it that it shall arouse him from his habitual
contempt of what goes on about him ") are
much less amusing ; and his letters to Joanna
Baillie the dullest in the volume, unless it be
the answers which Joanna Baillie sent. Best
of all, perhaps, is the correspondence (scarcely
used by Lockhart) between Scott and Lady
Abercorn, with its fitful intervals of warmth
and reserve. This alone would justify Mr.
Douglas's volumes. But, indeed, while nothing
can be found now to alter men's conception of
Scott, any book about him is justified, even if
it do no more than heap up superfluous testimony to the beauty of his character.

*June 15.
1895.
A racial
disability.*

Since about one-third of the number of my
particular friends happen to be Scotsmen, it
has always distressed and annoyed me that,
with the best will in the world, I have never
been able to understand on what principle that

perfervid race conducts its enthusiasms. Mine
is a racial disability, of course; and the converse has been noted by no less a writer than
Stevenson, in the story of his journey " Across
the Plains " :—

> " There were no emigrants direct from Europe—save
> one German family and a knot of Cornish miners who
> kept grimly by themselves, one reading the New Testa-
> ment all day long through steel spectacles, the rest dis-
> cussing privately the secrets of their old-world mysteri-
> ous race. Lady Hester Stanhope believed she could
> make something great of the Cornish ; for my part I
> can make nothing of them at all. A division of races,
> older and more original than that of Babel, keeps this
> close, esoteric family apart from neighbouring English-
> men."

The loss on my side, to be sure, would be
immensely the greater, were it not happily certain that I *can* make something of Scotsmen ;
can, and indeed do, make friends of them.

All the same, this disability weighs me down *The Cult of*
with a sense of hopeless obtuseness when I con- *Burns.*
sider the deportment of the average intelligent
Scot at a Burns banquet, or a Burns *conversa-
zione*, or a Burns festival, or the unveiling of
a Burns statue, or the putting up of a pillar on

some spot made famous by Burns. All over the
world—and all under it, too, when their time
comes—Scotsmen are preparing after - dinner
speeches about Burns.   The great globe
swings round out of the sun into the dark;
there is always midnight somewhere; and always in this shifting region the eye of imagination sees orators gesticulating over Burns;
companies of heated exiles with crossed arms
shouting " Auld Lang Syne " ; lesser groups—
if haply they be lesser—reposing under tables,
still in honor of Burns.   And as the vast con-
tinents sweep " eastering out of the high shadow which reaches beyond the moon," and as
new nations, with *their* cities and villages, their
mountains and seashores, rise up on the morn-
ing-side, lo ! fresh troops, and still fresh troops,
and yet again fresh troops, wend or are carried
out of action with the dawn.

*Scott and
Burns.*

None but a churl would wish this enthusiasm
abated.   But why is it all lavished on Burns ?
That is what gravels the Southron.   Why Burns?
Why not Sir Walter ?   Had I the honor to
be a fellow - countryman of Scott, and had I
command of the racial tom-tom, it seems to me
that I would tund upon it in honor of that

great man until I dropped. To me, a Southron, Scott is the most imaginative, and at the
same time the justest, writer of our language
since Shakespeare died. To say this is not to
suggest that he is comparable with Shakespeare.
Scott himself, sensible as ever, wrote in his
Journal, " The blockheads talk of my being
like Shakespeare — not fit to tie his brogues."
" But it is also true," said Mr. Swinburne, in
his review of the *Journal*, " that if there were
or could be any man whom it would not be a
monstrous absurdity to compare with Shakespeare as a creator of men and inventor of circumstance, that man could be none other than
Scott. Greater poems than his have been
written ; and, to my mind, one or two novels
better than his best. But when one considers
the huge mass of his work, and its quality in
the mass ; the vast range of his genius, and its
command over that range ; who shall be compared with him ?

These are the reflections which occur, somewhat obviously, to the Southron. As for character, it is enough to say that Scott was one of
the best men who ever walked on this planet ;
and that Burns was not. But Scott was not

merely good: he was winningly good: of a
character so manly, temperate, courageous that
men read his Life, his Journal, his Letters with
a thrill, as they might read of Rorke's Drift or
Chitral. How then are we to account for the
undeniable fact that his countrymen, in public
at any rate, wax more enthusiastic over Burns?
Is it that the *homeliness* of Burns appeals to
them as a wandering race? Is it because, in
farthest exile, a line of Burns takes their hearts
straight back to Scotland?—as when Luath the
collie, in "The Twa Dogs," describes the cot-
ters' New Year's Day: —

> " That merry day the year begins,
>   They bar the door on frosty winds ;
>   The nappy reeks wi' mantling ream,
>   An' sheds a heart-inspirin' steam ;
>   The luntin' pipe an' sneeshin' mill
>   Are handed round wi' richt guid will ;
>   The cantie auld folks crackin' crouse,
>   The young anes rantin' through the house,—
>   My heart has been sae fain to see them,
>   That I for joy hae barkit wi' them."

That is one reason, no doubt. But there is
another, I suspect. With all his immense range
Scott saw deeply into character; but he did
not, I think, see very deeply into feeling. You

may extract more of the *lacrimæ rerum* from
the story of his own life than from all his published works put together. The pathos of Lam-
mermoor is taken-for-granted pathos. If you
deny this, you will not deny, at any rate, that
the pathos of the last scene of *Lear* is quite
beyond his scope. Yet this is not more certainly beyond his scope than is the feeling in
many a single line or stanza of Burns'. Verse
after verse, line after line, rise up for quotation—

> " Thou'lt break my heart, thou bonnie bird
>   That sings beside thy mate ;
> For sae I sat, and sae I sang,
>   And wist na o' my fate."

Or,

> " O pale, pale now, those rosy lips
>   I aft hae kissed sae fondly !
> And closed for aye the sparkling glance
>   That dwelt on me sae kindly !
> And mouldering now in silent dust
>   The heart that lo'ed me dearly—
> But still within my bosom's core
>   Shall live my Highland Mary."

Or,

> " Had we never loved sae kindly,
>   Had we never loved sae blindly,
> Never met—or never parted,
>   We had ne'er been broken-hearted."

Scott left an enormous mass of writing behind him, and almost all of it is good.   Burns
left very much less, and among it a surprising
amount of inferior stuff.   But such pathos as
the above Scott cannot touch.   I can understand the man who holds that these deeps of
pathos should not be probed in literature: and
am not sure that I wholly disagree with him.
The question certainly is discutable and worth
discussing.   But such pathos, at any rate, is
immensely popular: and perhaps this will account for the hold which Burns retains on the
affections of a race which has a right to be at
least thrice as proud of Scott.

However, if Burns is honored at the feast,
Scott is read by the fireside.   Hardly have the
rich Dryburgh and Border editions issued from
the press before Messrs. Archibald Constable
and Co. are bringing out their reprint of the
famous 48-volume edition of the Novels; and
Mr. Barrie is supposed to be meditating another, with introductory notes of his own upon
each Novel.   In my own opinion nothing has
ever beaten, or come near to beat, the 48-
volume "Waverley" of 1829; and Messrs.
Constable and Co. were happily inspired when

they decided to make this the basis of their new edition. They have improved upon it in two respects. The paper is lighter and better. And each novel is kept within its own covers, whereas in the old editions a volume would contain the end of one novel and beginning of another. The original illustrations, by Wilkie, Landseer, Leslie, Stanfield, Bonington, and the rest, have been retained, in order to make the reprint complete. But this seems to me a pity; for a number of them were bad to begin with, and will be worse than ever now, being reproduced (as I understand) from impressions of the original plates. To do without illustrations were a counsel of perfection. But now that the novels have become historical, surely it were better to illustrate them with authentic portraits of Scott, pictures of scenery, facsimiles of MSS., and so on, than with (*e.g.*) a worn reproduction of what Mr. F. P. Stephanoff thought that Flora Mac-Ivor looked like while playing the harp and introducing a few irregular strains which harmonized well with the distant waterfall and the soft sigh of the evening breeze in the rustling leaves of an aspen which overhung the fair harpress— especially as F. P. Stephanoff does not seem to have known the difference between an aspen and a birch.

In short, did it not contain the same illustrations, this edition would probably excel even that of 1828. As it is, after many disappointments, we now have a cheap Waverley on what has always been the best model.

A Protest. ' SIR,—In your ' Literary Causerie' of last week . . . the question is discussed why the name of Burns raises in Scotsmen such unbounded enthusiasm while that of Scott falls comparatively flat. This question has puzzled many another Englishman besides 'A. T. Q. C.' And yet the explanation is not far to seek : Burns appeals to the hearts and feelings of the masses in a way Scott never does. 'A. T. Q. C.' admits this, and gives quotations in support. These quotations, however excellent in their way, are not those that any Scotsman would trust to in support of the above proposition. A Scotsman would at once appeal to ' Scots wha hae,' 'Auld Lang Syne,' and 'A man's a man for a' that.' The very familiarity of these quotations has bred the proverbial contempt. Think of the soul-inspiring, ' fire-eyed fury' of ' Scots wha hae '; the glad, kind, ever fresh greeting of ' Auld Lang Syne '; the manly, sturdy independence of ' A man's a man for a' that,' and who can wonder at the ever-increasing enthusiasm for Burns' name ?

> ' Is there for honest poverty
>   That hangs his head and a' that ?

116

> The coward slave we pass him by—
> We dare be poor for a' that.'

.   .   .   .

> ' The rank is but the guinea stamp—
> The man's the gowd for a' that.'

" Nor is it in his patriotism, independence, and conviviality alone that Burns touches every mood of a Scotsman's heart. There is an enthusiasm of humanity about Burns which you will hardly find equalled in any other author, and which most certainly does not exist in Scott.

> ' Man's inhumanity to man
> Makes countless thousands mourn.'

.   .   .   .

> ' Why has man this will and power
> To make his fellow mourn ? '

" These quotations might be multiplied were it necessary ; but I think enough has been said to explain what puzzles ' A. T. Q. C.' I have an unbounded admiration of Sir W. Scott—quite as great as ' A. T. Q. C.' Indeed, I think him the greatest of all novelists ; but, as a Scot, somewhat Anglicised by a residence in London of more than a quarter of a century, I unhesitatingly say that I would rather be the author of the above three lyrics of Burns' than I would be the author of all Scott's novels. Certain I am that if immortality were my aim I should be much surer of it in the one case than the other. I cannot conceive ' Scots wha hae,' ' Auld Lang Syne,' etc., ever dying. Are there any of Scott's writings of which the same could be said ? I doubt it. . . . .
—I am yours, etc.,   " J. B.

  " London, June 18th, 1895."

The hopelessness of the difficulty is amusingly, if rather distressingly, illustrated by this letter. Here again you have the best will in the world. Nothing could be kindlier than "J. B.'s" tone. As a Scot he has every reason to be impatient of stupidity on the subject of Burns: yet he takes real pains to set me right. Alas! his explanations leave me more than ever at sea, more desperate than ever of understanding *what exactly it is* in Burns that kindles this peculiar enthusiasm in Scotsmen and drives them to express it in feasting and oratory.

After casting about for some time, I suggested that Burns—though in so many respects immeasurably inferior to Scott—frequently wrote with a depth of feeling which Scott could not command. On second thoughts, this was wrongly put. Scott may have *possessed* the feeling, together with notions of his own, on the propriety of displaying it in his public writings. Indeed, after reading some of his letters again, I am sure he did possess it. Hear, for instance, how he speaks of Dalkeith Palace, in one of his letters to Lady Louisa Stuart:—

"I am delighted my dear little half god-daughter is turning out beautiful. I was at her christening, poor soul, and took the oaths as representing I forget whom. That was in the time when Dalkeith was Dalkeith ; how changed alas ! I was forced there the other day by some people who wanted to see the house, and I felt as if it would have done me a great deal of good to have set my manhood aside, to get into a corner and cry like a schoolboy. Every bit of furniture, now looking old and paltry, had some story and recollections about it, and the deserted gallery, which I have seen so happily filled, seemed waste and desolate like Moore's

> ' Banquet hall deserted,
>   Whose flowers are dead,
>   Whose odours fled,
> And all but I departed.'

But it avails not either sighing or moralising ; to have known the good and the great, the wise and the witty, is still, on the whole, a pleasing reflection, though saddened by the thought that their voices are silent and their halls empty."

Yes, indeed, Scott possessed deep feelings, though he did not exhibit them to the public.

Now Burns does exhibit his deep feelings, as I demonstrated by quotations. And I suggested that it is just his strength of emotion, his command of pathos and readiness to employ it, by which Burns appeals to the mass of his countrymen. On this point " J. B." expressly agrees with me ; but—he will have nothing to do with my quotations ! " However excellent in their way " these quotations may be, they " are not those that any Scotsman would trust to in support of the above proposition " ; the above proposition being that " Burns appeals to the hearts and feelings of the masses in a way that Scott never does."

You see, I have concluded rightly ; but on wrong evidence. Let us see, then, what evidence a Scotsman will call to prove that Burns is a writer of deep feeling. " A Scotsman," says " J. B." " would at once appeal to " Scots wha hae," " Auld Lang Syne," and " A man's a man for a' that.' . . . Think of the soul-inspiring, ' fire-eyed fury ' of 'Scots wha hae ' ; the glad, kind, ever fresh greeting of ' Auld Lang Syne '; the manly, sturdy independence of ' A man's a man for a' that,' and who can wonder at the ever-increasing enthusiasm for Burns' name ? . . . . . . I would rather," says " J. B.," " be the author of the above three lyrics than I would be the author of all Scott's novels."

Here, then, is the point at which I give up my attempts, and admit my stupidity to be

incurable.   I grant " J. B." his " Auld Lang
Syne."   I grant the poignancy of—

> " We twa hae paidl't i' the burn,
>   Frae morning sun till dine :
> But seas between us braid hae roar'd
>   Sin auld lang syne."

I see poetry and deep feeling in this.   I can
see exquisite poetry and deep feeling in " Mary
Morison "—

> " Yestreen when to the trembling string,
>   The dance ga'ed thro' the lighted ha',
> To thee my fancy took its wing,
>   I sat, but neither heard nor saw :
> Tho' this was fair, and that was braw,
>   And yor the toast a' the town,
> I sigh'd and said amang them a'
>   ' Ye are na Mary Morison.' "

I see exquisite poetry and deep feeling in the
Lament for the Earl of Glencairn—

> " The bridegroom may forget the bride
>   Was made his wedded wife yestreen ;
> The monarch may forget the crown
>   That on his head an hour has been ;
> The mother may forget the child
>   That smiles sae sweetly on her knee ;
> But I'll remember thee, Glencairn,
>   And a' that thou hast done for me ! "

But—it is only honest to speak one's opinion
and to hope, if it be wrong, for a better mind—

I do *not* find poetry of any high order either in "Scots wha hae" or "A man's a man for a' that." The former seems to me to be very fine rant—inspired rant, if you will—hovering on the borders of poetry. The latter, to be frank, strikes me as rather poor rant, neither inspired nor even quite genuine, and in no proper sense poetry at all. And "J. B." simply bewilders my Southron intelligence when he quotes it as an instance of deeply emotional song.

> " Ye see yon birkie, ca'd a lord,
>   Wha struts, and stares, and a' that ;
> Tho' hundreds worship at his word,
>   He's but a coof for a' that :
> For a' that, and a' that,
>   His riband, star and a' that,
> The man of independent mind,
>   He looks and laughs at a' that."

The proper attitude, I should imagine, for a man " of independent mind " in these circumstances—assuming for the moment that ribands and stars *are* bestowed on imbeciles—would be a quiet disdain. The above stanza reminds me rather of ill-bred barking. People of assured self-respect do not call other people " birkies " and " coofs," or " look and *laugh* at a' that "—at least, not so loudly.

Compare these verses of Burns with Samuel Daniel's " Epistle to the Countess of Cumberland," and you will find a higher manner altogether—

" He that of such a height hath built his mind,
  And reared the dwelling of his thoughts so strong,
  As neither fear nor hope can shake the frame
  Of his resolved powers ; nor all the wind
  Of vanity and malice pierce to wrong
  His settled peace, or to disturb the same ;
  What a fair seat hath he, from whence he may
  The boundless wastes and wilds of men survey ?

" And with how free an eye doth he look down
  Upon these lower regions of turmoil ? "   .   .   .

As a piece of thought, " A man's a man for a' that " unites the two defects of obviousness and inaccuracy. As for the deep feeling, I hardly see where it comes in—unless it be a feeling of wounded and blatant but militant self-esteem. As for the *poetry*—well, " J. B." had rather have written it than have written one-third of Scott's novels. Let us take him at less than his word : he would rather have written " A man's a man for a' that " than " Ivanhoe," " Redgauntlet," and " The Heart of Midlothian."

Ma sonties !

CHARLES READE

March 10, 1894. " The Cloister and the Hearth."

THERE is a venerable proposition—I never heard who invented it—that an author is finally judged by his best work. This would be comforting to authors if true: but is it true? A day or two ago I picked up on a railway bookstall a copy of Messrs. Chatto & Windus's new sixpenny edition of *The Cloister and the Hearth*, and a capital edition it is. I think I must have worn out more copies of this book than of any other; but somebody robbed me of the pretty " Elzevir edition " as soon as it came out, and so I have only just read Mr. Walter Besant's Introduction, which the publishers have considerately reprinted and thrown in with one of the cheapest sixpennyworths that ever came from the press. Good wine needs no bush, and the bush which Mr. Besant hangs out is a very small one. But one sentence at least has challenged attention.

" I do not say that the whole of life, as it was at the end of the fourteenth century, may be found in the

Cloister and the Hearth; but I do say that there is portrayed so vigorous, lifelike, and truthful a picture of a time long gone by, and differing in almost every particular from our own, that the world has never seen its like. To me it is a picture of the past more faithful than anything in the works of Scott."

This last sentence—if I remember rightly—was called a very bold one when it first appeared in print. To me it seems altogether moderate. Go steadily through Scott, and which of the novels can you choose to compare with the *Cloister* as a "vigorous, lifelike, and truthful picture of a time long gone by"?

Is it *Ivanhoe?*—a gay and beautiful romance, no doubt; but surely, as the late Mr. Freeman was at pains to point out, not a "lifelike and truthful picture" of any age that ever was. Is it *Old Mortality?* Well, but even if we here get something more like a "vigorous, lifelike, and truthful picture of a time gone by," we are bound to consider the scale of the two books. Size counts, as Aristotle pointed out, and as we usually forget. It is the whole of Western Europe that Reade reconstructs for the groundwork of his simple story.

Mr. Besant might have said more. He might have pointed out that no novel of

Scott's approaches the *Cloister* in lofty humanity, in sublimity of pathos. The last fifty pages of the tale reach an elevation of feeling that Scott never touched or dreamed of touching. And the sentiment is sane and honest, too: the author reaches to the height of his great argument easily and without strain. It seems to me that, as an appeal to the feelings, the page that tells of Margaret's death is the finest thing in fiction. It appeals for a score of reasons, and each reason is a noble one. We have brought together in that page extreme love, self-sacrifice, resignation, courage, religious feeling: we have the end of a beautiful love-tale, the end of a good woman, and the last earthly trial of a good man. And with all this, there is no vulgarization of sacred ground, no cheap parade of the heart's secrets; but a deep sobriety relieved with the most delicate humor. Moreover, the language is Charles Reade's at its best—which is almost as good as at its worst it is abominable.

That Scott could never reach the emotional height of Margaret's death-scene, or of the scene in Clement's cave, is certain. Moreover in the *Cloister* Reade challenges comparison with

Scott on Scott's own ground—the ground of sustained adventurous narrative—and the advantage is not with Scott. Once more, take all the Waverley Novels and search them through for two passages to beat the adventures of Gerard and Denis the Burgundian (1) with the bear and (2) at "The Fair Star" Inn, by the Burgundian Frontier. I do not think you will succeed, even then. Indeed, I will go so far as to say that to match these adventures of Gerard and Denis you must go again to Charles Reade, to the homeward voyage of the *Agra* in *Hard Cash*. For these and for sundry other reasons which, for lack of space, cannot be unfolded here, *The Cloister and the Hearth* seems to me a finer achievement than the finest novel of Scott's.

And now we come to the proposition that an author must be judged by his best work. If this proposition be true, then I must hold Reade to be a greater novelist than Scott. But do I hold this? Does anyone hold this? Why, the contention would be an absurdity.

Reade wrote some twenty novels beside *The Cloister and the Hearth*, and not one of the twenty approaches it. One only — *Griffith Gaunt*—is fit to be named in the same day with it ; and *Griffith Gaunt* is marred by an insincerity in the plot which vitiates, and is at once felt to vitiate, the whole work. On everything he wrote before and after *The Cloister* Reade's essential vulgarity of mind is written large. That he shook it off in that great instance is one of the miracles of literary history. It may be that the sublimity of his theme kept him throughout in a state of unnatural exaltation. If the case cannot be explained thus, it cannot be explained at all. Other of his writings display the same, or at any rate a like, capacity for sustained narrative. *Hard Cash* displays it ; parts of *It is Never Too Late to Mend* display it. But over much of these two novels lies the trail of that defective taste which makes *A Simpleton*, for instance, a prodigy of cheap ineptitude.

But if Reade be hopelessly Scott's inferior in manner and taste, what shall we say of the invention of the two men ? Mr. Barrie once affirmed very wisely in an essay on Robert Louis Stevenson, " Critics have said enthusiastically—for it is difficult to write of Mr. Steven-

son without enthusiasm—that Alan Breck is as
good as anything in Scott.   Alan Breck is certainly a masterpiece, quite worthy of the greatest
of all story-tellers, *who, nevertheless, it should be
remembered, created these rich side characters by
the score, another before dinner-time."*   Inven-
tiveness, is, I suppose, one of the first qualities
of a great novelist : and to Scott's invention
there was no end.   But set aside *The Cloister*,
and Reade's invention will be found to be extraordinarily barren.   Plot after plot turns on
the same old tiresome trick.   Two young people are in love : by the villainy of a third person they are separated for a while, and one
of the lovers is persuaded that the other is dead.
The missing one may be kept missing by various devices ; but always he is supposed to be
dead, and always evidence is brought of his
death, and always he turns up in the end.   It is
the same in *The Cloister*, in *It is Never Too
Late to Mend*, in *Put Yourself in His Place*,
in *Griffith Gaunt*, in *A Simpleton*. Sometimes,
as in *Hard Cash* and *A Terrible Temptation*,
he is wrongfully incarcerated as a madman ;
but this is obviously a variant only on the favorite trick.   Now the device is good enough
in a tale of the fourteenth century, when news

travelled slowly, and when by the suppression
of a letter, or by a piece of false news, two
lovers, the one in Holland, the other in
Rome, could easily be kept apart. But in a
tale of modern life no trick could well be
stagier. Besides the incomparable Margaret—
of whom it does one good to hear Mr. Besant
say, " No heroine in fiction is more dear to
me "—Reade drew some admirable portraits of
women ; but his men, to tell the truth—and
especially his priggish young heroes—seem remarkably ill invented. Again, of course, I
except *The Cloister*. Omit that book, and you
would say that such a character as Bailie Nicol
Jarvie or Dugald Dalgetty were altogether beyond Reade's range. Open *The Cloister* and
you find in Denis the Burgundian a character
as good as the Bailie and Dalgetty rolled into
one.

Other authors have been lifted above themselves. But was there ever a case of one sustained at such an unusual height throughout a
long, intricate and arduous work ?

HENRY KINGSLEY

M R. SHORTER begins his Memoir of the author of *Ravenshoe* with this paragraph :— *Feb. 9, 1895. Henry Kingsley.*

"The story of Henry Kingsley's life may well be told in a few words, because that life was on the whole a failure. The world will not listen very tolerantly to a narrative of failure unaccompanied by the halo of remoteness. To write the life of Charles Kingsley would be a quite different task. Here was success, victorious success, sufficient indeed to gladden the heart even of Dr. Smiles—success in the way of Church preferment, success in the way of public veneration, success, above all, as a popular novelist, poet, and preacher. Canon Kingsley's life has been written in two substantial volumes containing abundant letters and no indiscretions. In this biography the name of Henry Kingsley is absolutely ignored. And yet it is not too much to say that, when time has softened his memory for us, as it has softened for us the memories of Marlowe and Burns and many another, the public interest in Henry Kingsley will be stronger than in his now more famous brother." *

* *The Recollections of Geoffry Hamlyn.* By Henry Kingsley. New Edition, with a Memoir by Clement Shorter. London : Ward, Lock & Bowden.

A prejudice confessed.

I almost wish I could believe this. If one cannot get rid of a prejudice, the wisest course is to acknowledge it candidly : and therefore I confess myself as capable of jumping over the moon as of writing fair criticism on Charles or Henry Kingsley. As for Henry, I worshipped his books as a boy ; to-day I find them full of faults—often preposterous, usually ill-constructed, at times unnatural beyond belief. John Gilpin never threw the Wash about on both sides of the way more like unto a trundling mop or a wild goose at play than did Henry Kingsley the decent flow of fiction when the mood was on him. His notion of constructing a novel was to take equal parts of wooden melodrama and low comedy and stick them boldly together in a paste of impertinent drollery and serious but entirely irrelevant moralizing. And yet each time I read *Ravenshoe*—and I must be close upon " double figures "—I like it better. Henry did my green unknowing youth engage, and I find it next to impossible to give him up, and quite impossible to choose the venerated Charles as a substitute in my riper age. For here crops up a prejudice I find quite ineradicable. To put it plainly, I cannot like Charles Kingsley. Those who have had

opportunity to study the deportment of a certain class of Anglican divine at a foreign *table
d'hôte* may perhaps understand the antipathy.
There was almost always a certain sleek offensiveness about Charles Kingsley when he sat
down to write. He had a knack of using the
most insolent language, and attributing the
vilest motives to all poor foreigners and Roman
Catholics and other extra-parochial folk, and
would exhibit a pained and completely ludicrous surprise on finding that he had hurt the
feelings of these unhappy inferiors—a kind of
indignant wonder that Providence should have
given them any feelings to hurt. At length,
encouraged by popular applause, this very sec-
ond-rate man attacked a very first-rate man.
He attacked with every advantage and with
utter unscrupulousness; and the first-rate man
handled him; handled him gently, scrupu-
lously, decisively; returned him to his parish;
and left him there, a trifle dazed, feeling his
muscles.

Still, one may dislike the man and his books *Charles*
without thinking it probable that his brother *and*
Henry will supersede him in the public inter- *Henry.*
est; nay, without thinking it right that he

should. Dislike him as you will, you must acknowledge that Charles Kingsley had a lyrical gift that—to set all his novels aside—carries him well above Henry's literary level. It is sufficient to say that Charles wrote "The Pleasant Isle of Avès" and "When all the world is young, lad," and the first two stanzas of "The Sands of Dee." Neither in prose nor in verse could Henry come near such excellence. But we may go farther. Take the novels of each, and, novel for novel, you must acknowledge—I say it regretfully—that Charles carries the heavier guns. If you ask me whether I prefer *Westward Ho!* or *Ravenshoe*, I answer without difficulty that I find *Ravenshoe* almost wholly delightful, and *Westward Ho!* as detestable in some parts as it is admirable in others; that I have read *Ravenshoe* again and again merely for pleasure, and that I can never read a dozen pages of *Westward Ho!* without wishing to put the book in the fire. But if you ask me which I consider the greater novel, I answer with equal readiness that *Westward Ho!* is not only the greater, but much the greater. It is a truth too seldom recognized that in literary criticism, as in politics, one may detest a man's work while admitting his greatness. Even

134

in his episodes it seems to me that Charles
stands high above Henry. Sam Buckley's gal-
lop on Widderin in *Geoffry Hamlyn* is (I imagine) Henry Kingsley's finest achievement in
vehement narrative : but if it can be compared
for one moment with Amyas Leigh's quest of
the Great Galleon then I am no judge of narrative. The one point—and it is an important
one — in which Henry beats Charles as an artist is his sustained vivacity. Charles soars far
higher at times ; but Charles is often profoundly
dull. Now, in all Henry's books I have not
found a single dull page. He may be trivial,
inconsequent, irrelevant, absurd ; but he never
wearies. It is a great merit : but it is not
enough in itself to place a novelist even in the
second rank. In a short sketch of Henry
Kingsley, contributed by his nephew, Mr.
Maurice Kingsley, to Messrs. Scribner's paper,
The Bookbuyer, I find that the younger brother
was considered at home "undoubtedly the
novelist of the family ; the elder being more of
the poet, historian, and prophet." (Prophet !)
"My father only wrote one novel pure and
simple—viz. *Two Years Ago*—his other works
being either historical novels or ' signs of the
times.' " Now why an "historical novel"

should not be a "novel pure and simple," and what kind of literary achievement a "sign of the times" may be, I leave the reader to guess. The whole passage seems to suggest a certain confusion in the Kingsley family with regard to the fundamental divisions of literature. And it seems clear that the Kingsley family considered novel-writing "pure and simple"—in so far as they differentiated this from other kinds of novel-writing—to be something not entirely respectable.

Their opinion of Henry Kingsley in particular is indicated in no uncertain manner. In Mrs. Charles Kingsley's life of her husband, Henry's existence is completely ignored. The briefest biographical note was furnished forth for Mr. Leslie Stephen's *Dictionary of National Biography*: and Mr. Stephen dismisses our author with a few curt lines. This disposition to treat Henry as an awful warning and nothing more, while sleek Charles is patted on the back for a saint, inclines one to take up arms on the other side and assert, with Mr. Shorter, that "when time has softened his memory for us, the public interest in Henry Kingsley will be stronger than in his now more famous brother."

But can we look forward to this reversal of the public verdict ? Can we consent with it if it ever comes ? The most we can hope is that future generations will read Henry Kingsley, and will love him in spite of his faults.

Henry, the third son of the Rev. Charles Kingsley, was born in Northamptonshire on the 2nd of January, 1830, his brother Charles being then eleven years old. In 1836 his father became rector of St. Luke's Church, Chelsea—the church of which such effective use is made in *The Hillyars and the Burtons*—and his boyhood was passed in that famous old suburb. He was educated at King's College School and Worcester College, Oxford, where he became a famous oarsman, rowing bow of his College boat; also bow of a famous light-weight University " four," which swept everything before it in its time. He wound up his racing career by winning the Diamond Sculls at Henley. From 1853 to 1858 his life was passed in Australia, whence after some variegated experiences he returned to Chelsea in 1858, bringing back nothing but good " copy," which he worked into *Geoffry Hamlyn*, his first romance. *Ravenshoe* was written in 1861; *Austin Elliot* in

137

1863; *The Hillyars and the Burtons* in 1865; *Silcote of Silcotes* in 1867; *Mademoiselle Mathilde* (admired by few, but a favorite of mine) in 1868. He was married in 1864, and settled at Wargrave-on-Thames. In 1869 he went north to edit the *Edinburgh Daily Review*, and made a mess of it; in 1870 he represented that journal as field-correspondent in the Franco-Prussian War, was present at Sedan, and claimed to have been the first Englishman to enter Metz. In 1872 he returned to London and wrote novels in which his powers appeared to deteriorate steadily. He removed to Cuckfield, in Sussex, and there died in May, 1876. Hardly a man of letters followed him to the grave, or spoke, in print, a word in his praise.

And yet, by all accounts, he was a wholly amiable ne'er-do-well—a wonderful flyfisher, an extremely clever amateur artist, a lover of horses and dogs and children (surely, if we except a chapter of Victor Hugo's, the children in *Ravenshoe* are the most delightful in fiction), and a joyous companion.

"To us children," writes Mr. Maurice Kingsley, "Uncle Henry's settling in Eversley was a great event. . . . At times he fairly bubbled over with humour ; while his knowledge of slang—Burschen, Bargee, Parisian, Irish, Cockney, and English pro-vincialisms—was awful and wonderful. Nothing was better than to get our uncle on his ' genteel behavi-our,' which, of course, meant exactly the opposite, and brought forth inimitable stories, scraps of old songs and impromptu conversations, the choicest of which were between children, Irishwomen, or cock-neys. He was the only man, I believe, who ever knew by heart the famous *Irish Court Scenes*—naught-iest and most humorous of tales—unpublished, of course, but handed down from generation to generation of the faithful. Most delightful was an interview between his late Majesty George the Fourth and an itinerant show-man, which ended up with, ' No, George the Fourth, you shall not have my Rumptifoozle !' What said animal was, or the authenticity of the story, he never would divulge."

I think it is to the conversational quality of their style—its ridiculous and good-humored impertinences and surprises—that his best books owe a great deal of their charm. The foot-notes are a study in themselves, and range from the mineral strata of Australia to the best way of sliding down banisters. Of the three tales already republished in this pleasant edition, *Ravenshoe* has always seemed to me the best in every respect ; and in spite of its feeble plot and its impossible lay-figures—Erne, Sir George

139

Hillyar, and the painfully inane Gerty—I should rank *The Hillyars and the Burtons* above the more terrifically imagined and more neatly constructed *Geoffry Hamlyn*.   But this is an opinion on which I lay no stress.

ALEXANDER WILLIAM
KINGLAKE

ALEXANDER WILLIAM KINGLAKE *January 10, 1891.*
was born in 1812, the son of a country *His Life.*
gentleman—Mr. W. Kinglake, of Wilton House,
Taunton—and received a country gentleman's
education at Eton and Trinity College, Cambridge. From college he went to Lincoln's
Inn, and in 1837 was called to the Chancery
Bar, where he practised with fair but not eminent success. In 1844 he published *Eothen*,
and having startled the town, quietly resumed
his legal work and seemed willing to forget the
achievement. Ten years later he accompanied
his friend, Lord Raglan, to the Crimea. He
retired from the Bar in 1856, and entered Parliament next year as member for Bridgwater.
Re-elected in 1868, he was unseated on peti-
tion in 1869, and thenceforward gave himself
up to the work of his life. He had consented,
after Lord Raglan's death, to write a history of

the Invasion of the Crimea. The two first volumes appeared in 1863; the last was published but two years before he succumbed, in the first days of 1891, to a slow incurable disease. In all, the task had occupied thirty years. Long before these years ran out, the world had learnt to regard the Crimean struggle in something like its true perspective; but over Kinglake's mind it continued to loom in all its original proportions. To adapt a phrase of M. Jules Lemaître's, " *le monde a changé en trente ans : lui ne bouge ; il ne lève plus de dessus son papier à copie sa face congestionné.*' And yet Kinglake was no cloistered scribe. Before his last illness he dined out frequently, and was placed by many among the first half-a-dozen talkers in London. His conversation, though delicate and finished, brimmed full of interest in life and affairs : but let him enter his study, and its walls became a hedge. Without, the world was moving: within, it was always 1854, until by slow toiling it turned into 1855.

Style.   His style is hard, elaborate, polished to brilliance. Its difficult labor recalls Thucydides. In effect it charms at first by its accuracy and vividness : but with continuous perusal it be-

gins to weigh upon the reader, who feels the
strain, the unsparing effort that this glittering
fabric must have cost the builder, and at length
ceases to sympathize with the story and begins to sympathize with the author.   Kinglake
started by disclaiming " composition."   " My
narrative," he says, in the famous preface to
Eothen, " conveys not those impressions which
ought to have been produced upon any well-
constituted mind, but those which were really
and truly received, at the time of his ram-
bles, by a headstrong and not very amiable
traveller.   .   .   .   As I have felt, so I have
written."

For all this, page after page of *Eothen* gives   *" Eothen."*
evidence of deliberate calculation of effect.
That book is at once curiously like and curiously unlike Borrows' *Bible in Spain*.   The
two belong to the same period and, in a sense,
to the same fashion.   Each combines a tanta-
lizing personal charm with a strong, almost
fierce, coloring of circumstance.   The central
figure in each is unmistakably an Englishman,
and quite as unmistakably a singular Englishman.   Each bears witness to a fine eye for
theatrical arrangement.   But whereas Borrow

143

stood for ever fortified by his wayward nature and atrocious English against the temptation of writing as he ought, Kinglake commenced author with a respect for "composition," ingrained perhaps by his Public School and University training. Borrow arrays his page by instinct, Kinglake by study. His irony (as in the interview with the Pasha) is almost too elaborate; his artistic judgment (as in the Plague chapter) almost too sure; the whole book almost too clever. The performance was wonderful; the promise a trifle dangerous.

The "Invasion."

"Composition" indeed proved the curse of the *Invasion of the Crimea* : for Kinglake was a slow writer, and composed with his eye on the page, the paragraph, the phrase, rather than on the whole work. Force and accuracy of expression are but parts of a good prose style; indeed are, strictly speaking, inseparable from perspective, balance, logical connection, rise and fall of emotion. It is but an indifferent landscape that contains no pedestrian levels : and his desire for the immediate success of each paragraph as it came helped Kinglake to miss the broad effect. He must always be vivid; and when the strain told, he exaggerated and

sounded—as Matthew Arnold accused him of
sounding—the note of provinciality. There
were other causes. He was, as we have seen,
an English country gentleman—*avant tout je
suis gentilhomme anglais*, as the Duke of Wel-
lington wrote to Louis XVIII. His admiration
of the respectable class to which he belonged is
revealed by a thousand touches in his narrative
—we can find half a score in the description of
Codrington's assault on the Great Redoubt in
the battle of the Alma ; nor, when some high
heroic action is in progress, do we often miss
an illustration, or at least a metaphor, from the
hunting-field. Undoubtedly he had the distinction of his class ; but its narrowness was his
as surely. Also the partisanship of the eight
volumes grows into a weariness. The longev-
ity of the English Bench is notorious ; but it
comes of hearing both sides of every question.

After all, he was a splendid artist. He tamed
that beautiful and dangerous beast, the English
sentence, with difficulty indeed, but having
tamed, worked it to high achievements. The
great occasion always found him capable, and
his treatment of it is not of the sort to be forgotten : witness the picture of the Prince

President cowering in an inner chamber during the bloodshed of the *Coup d'État*, the short speech of Sir Colin Campbell to his Highlanders before the Great Redoubt (given in the exact manner of Thucydides), or the narrative of the Heavy Brigade's charge at Balaclava, culminating thus—

" The difference that there was in the temperaments of the two comrade regiments showed itself in the last moments of the onset. The Scots Greys gave no utterance except to a low, eager, fierce moan of rapture—the moan of outbursting desire. The Inniskillings went in with a cheer. With a rolling prolongation of clangour which resulted from the bends of a line now deformed by its speed, the ' three hundred ' crashed in upon the front of the column."

C. S. C. and J. K. S.

WHAT I am about to say will, no doubt, *Dec. 5, 1891.* be set down to tribal malevolence; but *Cambridge Baras.* I confess that if Cambridge men appeal to me less at one time than another it is when they begin to talk about their poets. The grievance is an old one, of course—at least as old as Mr. Birrell's " *Obiter Dicta* " : but it has been revived by the little book of verse (" *Quo Musa Tendis?* ") that I have just been read ing. I laid it down and thought of Mr. Birrell's essay on Cambridge Poets, as he calls them : and then of another zealous gentleman, hailing from the same University, who arranged all the British bards in a tripos and brought out the Cambridge men at the top. This was a very characteristic performance : but Mr. Birrell's is hardly less so in these days when (to quote the epistolary parent) so much prominence is given to athleticism in our seats of learning. For he picks out a team of light-blue singers as though he meant to play an inter-University match, and challenges Oxford to "come on." He gives Milton a "blue," and says we oughtn't to play Shelley because Shelley isn't in residence.

Now to me this is as astonishing as if my butcher were to brag about Kirke White. My doctor might retort with Keats; and my scrivener—if I had one—might knock them both down with the name of Milton. It would be a pretty set-to; but I cannot see that it would affect the relative merits of mutton and laudanum and the obscure products of scriven-age. Nor, conversely (as they say at Cambridge), is it certain, or even likely, that the difference between a butcher or a doctor is the difference between Kirke White and Keats. And this talk about "University" poets seems somewhat otiose unless it can be shown that Cambridge and Oxford directly encourage poesy, or aim to do so. I am aware that somebody wins the Newdigate every year at Oxford, and that the same thing happens annually at Cambridge with respect to the Chancellor's Prize. But—to hark back to the butcher and apothecary—verses are perennially made upon

Mr. Lipton's Hams and Mrs. Allen's Hair Restorer. Obviously some incentive is needed beyond a prize for stanzas on a given subject. I can understand Cambridge men when they assert that they produce more Wranglers than Oxford : that is a justifiable boast. But how does Cambridge encourage poets ?

Oxford expelled Shelley : Cambridge whipped Milton.* *Facit indignatio versus.* If we press this misreading of Juvenal, Oxford erred only on the side of thoroughness. But that, notoriously, is Oxford's way. She expelled Landor, Calverley, and some others. My contention is that to expel a man is—however you look at it —better for his poesy than to make a don of him. Oxford says, " You are a poet ; therefore this is no place for you. Go elsewhere ; we set your aspiring soul at large." Cambridge says : " You are a poet. Let us employ you to fulfil other functions. Be a don." She made a don *Calverley.* of Gray, of Calverley. Cambridge men are for ever casting Calverley in our teeth ; whereas, in truth, he is specially to be quoted against them. As everybody knows, he was at both Universi-

* I am bound to admit that the only authority for this is a note written into the text of Aubrey's *Lives.*

ties, so over him we have a fair chance of comparing methods. As everybody knows, he went to Balliol first, and his ample cabin'd spirit led him to climb a wall, late at night. Something else caused him to be discovered, and Blaydes —he was called Blaydes then—was sent down.

Nobody can say what splendid effect this might have had upon his poetry. But he changed his name and went to Cambridge. And Cambridge made a don of him. If anybody thinks this was an intelligent stroke, let him consider the result. Calverley wrote a small amount of verse that, merely as verse, is absolutely faultless. To compare great things with little, you might as well try to alter a line of Virgil's as one of Calverley's. Forget a single epithet and substitute another, and the result is certain disaster. He has the perfection of the phrase—and there it ends. I cannot remember a single line of Calverley's that contains a spark of human feeling. Mr. Birrell himself has observed that Calverley is just a bit inhuman. But the cause of it does not seem to have occurred to him. Nor does the biography explain it. If we are to believe the common report of all who knew Calverley, he was a man of simple mind and sincere, of quick and generous emotions. His biographers tell us also that he was one who seemed to have the world at his feet, one who had only to choose a calling to excel in it. Yet he never fulfilled his friends' high expectations. What was the reason of it all?

The accident that cut short his career is not wholly to blame, I think. At any rate, it will not explain away the exception I have taken to his verse. Had that been destined to exhibit the humanity which we seek, some promise of it would surely be discoverable; for he was a full-grown man at the time of that unhappy tumble on the ice. But there is none. It is all sheer wit, impish as a fairy changeling's, and always barren of feeling. Mr. Birrell has not supplied the explanatory epithet, so I will try to do so. It is "donnish." Cambridge, fondly imagining that she was showing right appreciation of Calverley thereby, gave him a Fellowship. Mr. Walter Besant, another gentleman from Calverley's college, complained, the other day, that literary distinction was never marked with a peerage. It is the same sort of error. And now Cambridge, having made

Calverley a don, claims him as a Cambridge
poet; and the claim is just, if the epithet be
intended to mark the limitations imposed by
that University on his achievement.

"J. K. S."   Of " J. K. S.," whose second volume, *Quo
Musa Tendis?* (Macmillan & Bowles), has just
come from the press, it is fashionable to say
that he follows after Calverley, at some distance. To be sure, he himself has encouraged
this belief by coming from Cambridge and
writing about Cambridge, and invoking C. S. C.
on the first page of his earlier volume, *Lapsus
Calami.* But, except that J. K. S. does his
talent some violence by constraining it to imi-
tate Calverley's form, the two men have little
in common. The younger has a very different
wit. He is more than academical. He thinks
and feels upon subjects that were far outside
Calverley's scope. Among the dozen themes
with which he deals under the general heading
of *Paullo Majora Canamus*, there is not one
which would have interested his " master " in
the least. Calverley appears to have invited
his soul after this fashion—" Come, let us go
into the King's Parade and view the undergraduate as he walks about having no knowledge of

good or evil. Let us make a jest of the books he admires and the schools for which he is reading." And together they manage it excellently. They talk Cambridge "shop" in terms of the wittiest scholarship. But of the very existence of a world of grown-up men and women they seem to have no inkling, or, at least, no care.

The problems of J. K. S. are very much more grown-up. You have only to read *Paint and Ink* (a humorous, yet quite serious, address to a painter upon the scope of his art) or *After the Golden Wedding* (wherein are given the soliloquies of the man and the woman who have been married for fifty years) to assure yourself that if J. K. S. be not Calverley's equal, it is only because his mind is vexed with problems bigger than ever presented themselves to the Cambridge don. To C. S. C., Browning was a writer of whose eccentricities of style delicious sport might be made. J. K. S. has parodied Browning too; but he has also perpended Browning, and been moulded by him. There are many stanzas in this small volume that, had Browning not lived, had never been written. Take this, from a writer to a painter :—

" So I do dare claim to be kin with you,
    And I hold you higher than if your task
Were doing no more than you say you do :
    We shall live, if at all, we shall stand or fall,
As men before whom the world doffs its mask
And who answer the questions our fellows ask."

Many such lines prove our writer's emancipation from servitude to the Calverley fetish, a fetish that, I am convinced, has done harm to many young men of parts. It is pretty, in youth, to play with style as a puppy plays with a bone, to cut teeth upon it. But words are, after all, a poor thing without matter. J. K. S.'s emancipation has come somewhat late ; but he has depths in him which he has not sounded yet, and it is quite likely that when he sounds them he may astonish the world rather considerably. Now, if we may interpret the last poem in his book, he is turning towards prose. "I go," he says—

    " I go to fly at higher game :
        At prose as good as I can make it ;
    And though it brings nor gold nor fame,
        I will not, while I live, forsake it."

It is no disparagement to his verse to rejoice over this resolve of his. For a young man who begins with epic may end with good epic ; but

a young man who begins with imitating Calverley will turn in time to prose if he means to
write in earnest. And J. K. S. may do well
or ill, but that he is to be watched has been
evident since the days when he edited the *Re-
flector*.*

* The reader will refer to the date at the head of this
paper :—

"Heu miserande puer ! signa fata aspera rumpas,
   Tu Marcellus eris.

  .   .   .   .

   Sed nox atra caput tristi circumvolat umbra."

ROBERT LOUIS STEVENSON

*April 15, 1893.
The
" Island
Nights'
Entertain-
ments."*

I WISH Mr. Stevenson had given this book
another title. It covers but two out of the
three stories in the volume ; and, even so, it
has the ill-luck to be completely spoilt by its
predecessor, the *New Arabian Nights*.

The *New Arabian Nights* was in many respects a parody of the Eastern book. It had, if
we make a few necessary allowances for the
difference between East and West, the same, or
very near the same, atmosphere of gallant, extravagant, intoxicated romance. The characters had the same adventurous irresponsibility,
and exhibit the same irrelevancies and futilities.
The Young Man with the Cream Cakes might
well have sprung from the same brain as the
facetious Barmecide, and young Scrymgeour
sits helpless before his destiny as sat that other
young man while the inexorable Barber sang
the song and danced the dance of Zantout.

Indeed Destiny in these books resembles nothing so much as a Barber with forefinger and thumb nipping his victims by the nose. It is as omnipotent, as irrational, as humorous and almost as cruel in the imitation as in the original. Of course I am not comparing these in any thing but their general presentment of life, or holding up *The Rajah's Diamond* against *Aladdin*. I am merely pointing out that life is presented to us in Galland and in Mr. Stevenson's first book of tales under very similar conditions—the chief difference being that Mr. Stevenson has to abate something of the supernatural, or to handle it less frankly.

But several years divide the *New Arabian Nights* from the *Island Nights' Entertainments*; and in the interval our author has written *The Master of Ballantrae* and his famous *Open Letter* on Father Damien. That is to say, he has grown in his understanding of the human creature and in his speculations upon his creature's duties and destinies. He has travelled far, on shipboard and in emigrant trains; has passed through much sickness; has acquired property and responsibility; has mixed in public affairs; has written *A Footnote to History*, and sundry

letters to the *Times* ; and even, as his latest letter shows, stands in some danger of imprison-
ment. Therefore, while the title of his new
volume would seem to refer us once more to
the old Arabian models, we are not surprised
to find this apparent design belied by the contents. The third story, indeed, *The Isle of
Voices*, has affinity with some of the Arabian
tales—with Sindbad's adventures, for instance.
But in the longer *Beach of Falesá* and *The
Bottle Imp* we are dealing with no debauch of
fancy, but with the problems of real life.

For what is the knot untied in the *Beach of
Falesá?* If I mistake not, our interest centres
neither in Case's dirty trick of the marriage,
nor in his more stiff-jointed trick of the devil-
contraptions. The first but helps to construct
the problem, the second seems a superfluity.
The problem is (and the author puts it before
us fair and square), How is Wiltshire a fairly
loose moralist with some generosity of heart,
going to treat the girl he has wronged? And
I am bound to say that as soon as Wiltshire answers that question before the missionary—an
excellent scene and most dramatically managed
—my interest in the story, which is but half-

told at this point, begins to droop. As I said, the " devil-work " chapter strikes me as stiff, and the conclusion but rough - and - tumble. And I feel certain that the story itself is to blame, and neither the scenery nor the persons, being one of those who had as lief Mr. Stevenson spake of the South Seas as of the Hebrides, so that he speak and I listen. Let it be granted that the Polynesian names are a trifle hard to distinguish at first—they are easier than Russian by many degrees—yet the difficulty vanishes as you read the *Song of Rahéro*, or the *Footnote to History*. And if it comes to habits, customs, scenery, etc., I protest a man must be exacting who can find no romance in these while reading Melville's *Typee*. No, the story itself is to blame.

But what is the human problem in *The Bottle Imp ?* (Imagine Schcherazadé with a human problem !) Nothing less, if you please than the problem of Alcestis—nothing less and even something more ; for in this case when the wife has made her great sacrifice of self, it is no fortuitous god but her own husband who wins her release, and at a price no less fearful than she herself has paid. Keawe being in possession of a bottle which must infallibly bring him to hell-flames unless he can dispose of it at a certain price, Kokua his wife by a stratagem purchases the bottle from him, and stands committed to the doom he has escaped. She does her best to hide this from Keawe, but he, by accident discovering the truth, by another stratagem wins back the curse upon his own head, and is only rescued by a *deus ex machinâ* in the shape of a drunken boatswain.

Two or three reviewers have already given utterance upon this volume ; and they seem strangely unable to determine which is the best of its three tales. I vote for *The Bottle Imp* without a second's doubt ; and, if asked my reasons, must answer (1), that it deals with a high and universal problem, whereas in *The Isle of Voices* there is no problem at all, and in the *Beach of Falesá* the problem is less momentous and perhaps (though of this I won't be sure) more closely restricted by the accidents of circumstance and individual character ; (2) as I have hinted, the *Beach of Falesá* has faults of construction, one of which is serious, if not vital, while *The Isle of Voices*, though beautifully composed, is tied down by the triviality of

its subject. But *The Bottle Imp* is perfectly
constructed: the last page ends the tale, and
the tale is told with a light grace, sportive
within restraint, that takes nothing from the
seriousness of the subject. Some may think
this extravagant praise for a little story which,
after all (they will say), is flimsy as a soap bub-
ble. But let them sit down and tick off on
their fingers the names of living authors who
could have written it, and it may begin to dawn
on them that a story has other dimensions than
length and thickness.

Some while ago Mr. Barrie put together in
a little volume eleven sketches of eleven men
whose fame has travelled far beyond the University of Edinburgh. For this reason, I believe, he called them "An Edinburgh Eleven"
—as fond admirers speak of Mr. Arthur Shrews-
bury (upon whose renown it is notorious that
the sun never sets) as "the Notts Professional,"
and of a yet more illustrious cricketer by his
paltry title of "Doctor"—

Sept. 9, 1893. First Thoughts on "Catriona."

> "Not so much honouring thee,
>   As giving it a hope that there
>   It could not wither'd be."

Of the Eleven referred to, Mr. Robert Louis Stevenson was sent in at eighth wicket down to face this cunning "delivery" :—"He experiments too long; he is still a boy wondering what he is going to be.   With Cowley's candor he tells us that he wants to write something by which he may be for ever known.   His attempts in this direction have been in the nature of trying different ways, and he always starts off whistling.   Having gone so far without losing himself, he turns back to try another road. Does his heart fail him, despite his jaunty bearing, *or is it because there is no hurry ?*   .   .   . But it is quite time the great work was begun."

I have taken the liberty to italicise a word or two, because in them Mr. Barrie supplied an answer to his question.   "The lyf so short, the craft so long to lerne ! " is not an exhortation to hurry : and in Mr. Stevenson's case, at any rate, there was not the least need to hurry. There was, indeed, a time when Mr. Stevenson had not persuaded himself of this.   In *Across the Plains* he tells us how, at windy Anstruther and an extremely early age, he used to draw his chair to the table and pour forth literature " at such a speed, and with such intimations of early death and immortality, as I now look back upon with wonder. Then it was that I wrote *Voces Fidelium*, a series of dramatic monologues in verse; then that I indited the bulk of a Covenanting novel—like so many others, never finished. Late I sat into the night, toiling (as I thought) under the very dart of death, toiling to leave a memory behind me. I feel moved to thrust aside the curtain of the years, to hail that poor feverish idiot, to bid him go to bed and clap *Voces Fidelium* on the fire before he goes, so clear does he appear to me, sitting there between his candles in the rose-scented room and the late night; so ridiculous a picture (to my elderly wisdom) does the fool present ! ''

There was no hurry then, as he now sees: and there never was cause to hurry, I repeat. '' But how is this ? Is, then, the great book written ? '' I am sure I don't know. Probably not: for human experience goes to show that *The* Great Book (like *The* Great American Novel) never gets written. But that *a* great story has been written is certain enough: and one of the curious points about this story is its title.

It is not *Catriona ;* nor is it *Kidnapped.*
Kidnapped is a taking title, and *Catriona* beautiful in sound and suggestion of romance : and
Kidnapped (as everyone knows) is a capital
tale, though imperfect ; and *Catriona* (as the
critics began to point out, the day after its
issue) a capital tale with an awkward fissure
midway in it. " It is the fate of sequels "—
thus Mr. Stevenson begins his Dedication—
" to disappoint those who have waited for
them " ; and it is possible that the boys of
Merry England (who, it may be remembered,
thought more of *Treasure Island* than of *Kidnapped*) will take but lukewarmly to *Catriona,*
having had five years in which to forget its
predecessor. No : the title of the great story
is *The Memoirs of David Balfour.* Catriona
has a prettier name than David, and may give
it to the last book of her lover's adventures :
but the Odyssey was not christened after Pene-
lope.

Put *Kidnapped* and *Catriona* together within
the same covers, with one title-page, one dedication (here will be the severest loss) and one
table of contents, in which the chapters are
numbered straight away from I. to LX. : and

—this above all things—read the tale right through from David's setting forth from the garden gate at Essendean to his homeward voyage, by Catriona's side, on the Low Country ship. And having done this, be so good as to perceive how paltry are the objections you raised against the two volumes when you took them separately. Let me raise again one or two of them.

(1.) *Catriona* is just two stories loosely hitched together — the one of David's vain attempt to save James Stewart, the other of the loves of David and Catriona: and in case the critic should be too stupid to detect this, Mr. Stevenson has been at the pains to divide his book into Part I. and Part II. Now this, which is a real fault in a book called *Catriona*, is no fault at all in *The Memoirs of David Balfour*, which by its very title claims to be constructed loosely. In an Odyssey the road taken by the wanderer is all the nexus required; and the continuity of his presence (if the author know his business) is warrant enough for the continuity of our interest in his adventures. That the history of Gil Blas of Santillane consists chiefly of episodes is not a serious criticism upon Lesage's novel.

(2.) In *Catriona* more than a few of the
characters are suffered to drop out of sight just
as we have begun to take an interest in them.
There is Mr. Rankeillor, for instance, whose
company in the concluding chapter of *Kidnapped* was too good to be spared very easily;
and there is Lady Allardyce — a wonderfully
clever portrait; and Captain Hoseason — we
tread for a moment on the verge of re-acquaint-
ance, but are disappointed; and Balfour of
Pilrig; and at the end of Part I. away into
darkness goes the Lord Advocate Preston-
grange, with his charming womenkind.

Well, if this be an objection to the tale, it is
one urged pretty often against life itself—that
we scarce see enough of the men and women we
like. And here again that which may be a
fault in *Catriona* is no fault at all in *The Memoirs of David Balfour*. Though novelists
may profess in everything they write to hold a
mirror up to life, the reflection must needs be
more artificial in a small book than in a large.
In the one, for very clearness, they must isolate
a few human beings and cut off the currents (so
to speak) bearing upon them from the outside
world : in the other, with a larger canvas they

are able to deal with life more frankly. Were
the Odyssey cut down to one episode—say that
of Nausicäa — we must round it off and have
everyone on the stage and provided with his
just portion of good and evil before we ring the
curtain down. As it is, Nausicäa goes her way.
And as it is, Barbara Grant must go her way at
the end of Chapter XX.; and the pang we feel
at parting with her is anything rather than a
reproach against the author.

(3.) It is very certain, as the book stands,
that the reader must experience some shock of
disappointment when, after 200 pages of the
most heroical endeavoring, David fails in the
end to save James Stewart of the Glens. Were
the book concerned wholly with James Stewart's
fate, the cheat would be intolerable : and as a
great deal more than half of *Catriona* points
and trembles towards his fate like a magnetic
needle, the cheat is pretty bad if we take *Catriona* alone. But once more, if we are dealing with *The Memoirs of David Balfour*—if
we bear steadily in mind that David Balfour is
our concern — not James Stewart — the disappointment is far more easily forgiven. Then,
and then only, we get the right perspective of

David's attempt, and recognize how inevitable
was the issue when this stripling engaged to turn
back the great forces of history.

It is more than a lustre, as the Dedication reminds us, since David Balfour, at the end of
the last chapter of *Kidnapped*, was left to kick
his heels in the British Linen Company's office.
Five years have a knack of making people five
years older; and the wordy, politic intrigue
of *Catriona* is at least five years older than the
rough-and-tumble intrigue of *Kidnapped*; of
the fashion of the *Vicomte de Bragelonne*
rather than of the *Three Musketeers*. But this
is as it should be; for older and astuter heads
are now mixed up in the case, and Preston-
grange is a graduate in a very much higher
school of diplomacy than was Ebenezer Balfour.
And if no word was said in *Kidnapped* of the love
of women, we know now that this matter was
held over until the time came for it to take its
due place in David Balfour's experience. Everyone knew that Mr. Stevenson would draw a
woman beautifully as soon as he was minded.
Catriona and her situation have their foreshad-
owing in *The Pavilion on the Links*. But for
all that she is a surprise. She begins to be a

surprise—a beautiful surprise—when in Chapter X. she kisses David's hand "with a higher passion than the common kind of clay has any sense of;" and she is a beautiful surprise to the end of the book. The loves of these two make a moving story—old, yet not old: and I pity the heart that is not tender for Catriona when she and David take their last walk together in Leyden, and "the knocking of her little shoes upon the way sounded extraordinarily pretty and sad."

A certain Oxford lecturer, whose audience demurred to some trivial mistranslation from the Greek, remarked: "I perceive, gentlemen, that you have been taking a mean advantage of me. You have been looking it out in the Lexicon." *Nov. 3, 1894. "The Ebb Tide,"*

The pleasant art of reasoning about literature on internal evidence suffers constant discouragement from the presence and activity of those little people who insist upon "looking it out in the Lexicon." Their brutal methods will upset in two minutes the nice calculations of months. Your logic, your taste, your palpitating sense of style, your exquisite ear for rhythm and cadence—what do these avail against the man who goes straight to Stationers' Hall or the Parish Register?

> " Two thousand pounds of education
>   Drops to a ten-rupee jezail,"

as Mr. Kipling sings.   The answer, of course, is that the beauty of reasoning upon internal evidence lies in the process rather than the results.   You spend a month in studying a poet, and draw some conclusion which is entirely wrong : within a week you are set right by some fellow with a Parish Register.   Well, but meanwhile you have been reading poetry, and he has not.   Only the uninstructed judge criticism by its results alone.

If, then, after studying Messrs. Stevenson and Osbourne's *The Ebb-Tide* (London : Heinemann) I hazard a guess or two upon its authorship ; and if somebody take it into his head to write out to Samoa and thereby elicit the information that my guesses are entirely wrong— why then we shall have been performing each of us his proper function in life ; and there's an end of the matter.

Let me begin though—after reading a number of reviews of the book — by offering my sympathy to Mr. Lloyd Osbourne. Very possibly he does not want it. I guess him to be a gentleman of uncommonly cheerful heart. I hope so, at any rate: for it were sad to think that indignation had clouded even for a minute the gay spirit that gave us *The Wrong Box*— surely the funniest book written in the last ten years. But he has been most shamefully served. Writing with him, Mr. Stevenson has given us *The Wrecker* and *The Ebb-Tide*. Faults may be found in these, apart from the criticism that they are freaks in the development of Mr. Stevenson's genius. Nobody denies that they are splendid tales: nobody (I imagine) can deny that they are tales of a singular and original pattern. Yet no reviewer praises them on their own merits or points out their own defects. They are judged always in relation to Mr. Stevenson's previous work, and the reviewers concentrate their censure upon the point that they are freaks in Mr. Stevenson's development—that he is not continuing as the public expected him to continue.

Now there are a number of esteemed novel-

ists about the land who earn comfortable in-
comes by doing just what the public expects of
them. But of Mr. Stevenson's genius—always
something wayward—freaks might have been
predicted from the first. A genius so consciously artistic, so quick in sympathy with
other men's writings, however diverse, was
bound from the first to make many experiments. Before the public took his career in
hand and mapped it out for him, he made such
an experiment with *The Black Arrow ;* and it
was forgiven easily enough. But because he
now takes Mr. Osbourne into partnership for a
new set of experiments, the reviewers—not considering that these, whatever their faults, are vast
improvements on *The Black Arrow* — ascribe
all those faults to the new partner.

But that is rough criticism. Moreover it is
almost demonstrably false. For the weakness
of *The Wrecker*, such as it was, lay in the
Paris and Barbizon business and the author's
failure to make this of one piece with the main
theme, with the romantic histories of the *Currency Lass* and the *Flying Scud*. But which
of the two partners stands responsible for this
Pais-Barbizon business? Mr. Stevenson be-

yond a doubt. If you shut your eyes to Mr.
Stevenson's confessed familiarity with the Paris
and the Barbizon of a certain era; if you
choose to deny that he wrote that chapter on
Fontainebleau in *Across the Plains ;* if you go
on to deny that he wrote the opening of Chapter XXI. of *The Wrecker ;* why then you are
obliged to maintain that it was Mr. Osbourne,
and not Mr. Stevenson, who wrote that famous
chapter on the Roussillon Wine—which is absurd.
And if, in spite of its absurdity, you stick to this
also, why, then you are only demonstrating that
Mr. Lloyd Osbourne is one of the greatest living writers of fiction : and your conception of
him as a mere imp of mischief jogging the
master's elbow is wider of the truth than ever.

No ; the vital defect of *The Wrecker* must
be set down to Mr. Stevenson's account. Fine
story as that was, it failed to assimilate the Paris-
Barbizon business. *The Ebb-Tide*, on the other
hand, is all of one piece. It has at any rate
one atmosphere, and one only. And who can
demand a finer atmosphere of romance than
that of the South Pacific ?

The Ebb-Tide, so far as atmosphere goes, is

173

all of one piece.   And the story, too, is all of one piece — until we come to Attwater: I own Attwater beats me.   As Mr. Osbourne might say, "I have no use for" that monstrous person.   I wish, indeed, Mr. Osbourne *had* said so: for again I cannot help feeling that the offence of Attwater lies at Mr. Stevenson's door.   He strikes me as a bad dream of Mr. Stevenson's—a General Gordon out of the *Arabian Nights*.   Do you remember a drawing of Mr. du Maurier's in *Punch*, wherein, seizing upon a locution of Miss Rhoda Broughton's, he gave us a group of "magnificently ugly" men?   I seem to see Attwater in that group.

But if Mr. Stevenson is responsible for Attwater, surely also he contributed the two splendid surprises of the story.   I am the more certain because they occur in the same chapter, and within three pages of each other.   I mean, of course, Captain Davis's sudden confession about his "little Adar," and the equally startling discovery that the cargo of the *Farallone* schooner, supposed to be champagne, is mostly water.   These are the two triumphant surprises of the book: and I shall continue to be-

lieve that only one living man could have con-
trived them, until somebody writes to Samoa
and obtains the assurance that they are among
Mr. Osbourne's contributions to the tale.

Two small complaints I have to make.   The
first is of the rather inartistically high level of
profanity maintained by the speech of Davis
and Huish.   It is natural enough, of course ;
but that is no excuse if the frequency of the
swearing prevent its making its proper impression in the right place.   And the name
" Robert Herrick," bestowed on one of the
three beach-loafers, might have been shunned.
You may call an ordinary negro " Julius Cæsar " :
for out of such extremes you get the legitimately grotesque.   But the Robert Herrick, loose
writer of the lovely *Hesperides*, and the Robert
Herrick, shameful haunter of Papeete beach,
are not extremes : and it was so very easy to
avoid the association of ideas.

The Editor asks me to speak of Stevenson *Dec. 22,*
this week : because, since the foundation of *1894.*
R. L. S.
THE SPEAKER, as each new book of Stevenson's *In*
Memoriam.
appeared, I have had the privilege of writing

175

about it here. So this column, too, shall be filled ; at what cost ripe journalists will understand, and any fellow-cadet of letters may guess.

For when the telegram came, early on Monday morning, what was our first thought, as soon as the immediate numbness of sorrow passed and the selfish instinct began to reassert itself (as it always does) and whisper "What have *I* lost? What is the difference to *me* ?" Was it not something like this—"Put away books and paper and pen. Stevenson is dead. Stevenson is dead, and now there is nobody left to write for." Our children and grandchildren shall rejoice in his books ; but we of this generation possessed in the living man something that they will not know. So long as he lived, though it were far from Britain— though we had never spoken to him and he, perhaps, had barely heard our names—we always wrote our best for Stevenson. To him each writer amongst us — small or more than small—had been proud to have carried his best. That best might be poor enough. So long as it was not slipshod, Stevenson could forgive. While he lived, he moved men to put their utmost even into writings that quite certainly would never meet his eye. Surely another age will wonder over this curiosity of letters—that for five years the needle of literary endeavor in Great Britain has quivered towards a little island in the South Pacific, as to its magnetic pole.

Yet he founded no school, though most of us from time to time have poorly tried to copy him. He remained altogether inimitable, yet never seemed conscious of his greatness. It was native in him to rejoice in the successes of other men at least as much as in his own triumphs. One almost felt that, so long as good books were written, it was no great concern to him whether he or others wrote them. Born with an artist's craving for beauty of expression, he achieved that beauty with infinite pains. Confident in romance and in the beneficence of joy, he cherished the flame of joyous romance with more than Vestal fervor, and kept it ardent in a body which Nature, unkind from the beginning, seemed to delight in visiting with more unkindness—a " soul's dark cottage, battered and decayed " almost from birth. And his books leave the impression that he did this chiefly from a sense of duty: that he labored and kept

177

the lamp alight chiefly because, for the time, other and stronger men did not.

Had there been another Scott, another Dumas—if I may change the image—to take up the torch of romance and run with it, I doubt if Stevenson would have offered himself. I almost think in that case he would have consigned with Nature and sat at ease, content to read of new Ivanhoes and new D'Artagnans: for —let it be said again—no man had less of the ignoble itch for merely personal success. Think, too, of what the struggle meant for him: how it drove him unquiet about the world, if somewhere he might meet with a climate to repair the constant drain upon his feeble vitality; and how at last it flung him, as by a "sudden freshet," upon Samoa—to die "far from Argos, dear land of home."

And then consider the brave spirit that carried him—the last of a great race—along this far and difficult path; for it is the man we must consider now, not, for the moment, his writings. Fielding's voyage to Lisbon was long and tedious enough; but almost the whole of Stevenson's life has been a voyage to Lisbon, a voyage in the very penumbra of death. Yet Stevenson spoke always as gallantly as his great predecessor. Their "cheerful stoicism," which allies his books with the best British breeding, will keep them classical as long as our nation shall value breeding. It shines to our dim eyes now, as we turn over the familiar pages of *Virginibus Puerisque*, and from page after page—in sentences and fragments of sentences—"It is not altogether ill with the invalid after all" . . . "Who would project a serial novel after Thackeray and Dickens had each fallen in mid-course." [*He* had two books at least in hand and uncompleted, the papers say.] "Who would find heart enough to begin to live, if he dallied with the consideration of death?" . . . "What sorry and pitiful quibbling all this is!" . . . "It is better to live and be done with it, than to die daily in the sick-room. By all means begin your folio; even if the doctor does not give you a year, even if he hesitates over a month, make one brave push and see what can be accomplished in a week. . . . For surely, at whatever age it overtake the man, this is to die young. . . . The noise of the mallet and chisel is scarcely quenched, the trumpets are hardly done blowing, when, trailing with him clouds of glory, this happy-starred, full-blooded spirit shoots into the spiritual land.''

As it was in *Virginibus Puerisque*, so is it in the last essay in his last book of essays :—

" And the Kingdom of Heaven is of the childlike, of those who are easy to please, who love and who give pleasure. Mighty men of their hands, the smiters, and the builders, and the judges, have lived long and done sternly, and yet preserved this lovely character ; and among our carpet interests and two-penny concerns, the shame were indelible if *we* should lose it. *Gentleness and cheerfulness, these come before all morality ; they are the perfect duties.* . . . "

I remember now (as one remembers little things at such times) that, when first I heard of his going to Samoa, there came into my head (Heaven knows why) a trivial, almost ludicrous passage from his favorite, Sir Thomas Browne : a passage beginning " He was fruitlessly put in hope of advantage by change of Air, and imbibing the pure Aerial Nitre of those Parts ; and therefore, being so far spent, he quickly found Sardinia in Tivoli, and the most healthful air of little effect, where Death had set her Broad Arrow. . . ." A statelier sentence of the same author occurs to me now—

"To live indeed, is to be again ourselves, which being not only a hope, but an evidence in noble believers, it is all one to lie in St. Innocent's Churchyard, as in the sands of Egypt. Ready to be anything in the ecstacy of being ever, and as content with six foot as the *moles* of Adrianus."

This one lies, we are told, on a mountain-top, overlooking the Pacific. At first it seemed so much easier to distrust a News Agency than to accept Stevenson's loss. "O captain, my captain!" . . . One needs not be an excellent writer to feel that writing will be thankless work, now that Stevenson is gone. But the papers by this time leave no room for doubt. "A grave was dug on the summit of Mount Vaea, 1,300 feet above the sea. The coffin was carried up the hill by Samoans with great difficulty, a track having to be cut through the thick bush which covers the side of the hill from the base to the peak." For the good of man, his father and grandfather planted the high sea-lights upon the Inchcape and the Tyree Coast. He, the last of their line, nursed another light and tended it. Their lamps still shine upon the Bell Rock and the Skerryvore;

and—though in alien seas, upon a rock of exile
—this other light shall continue, unquenchable
by age, beneficent, serene.

Nov. 2, 1895.
The " Vailima Letters."

Eagerly as we awaited this volume, it has
proved a gift exceeding all our hopes—a gift, I
think, almost priceless. It unites in the rarest
manner the value of a familiar correspondence
with the value of an intimate journal : for these
Samoan letters to his friend Mr. Sidney Colvin
form a record, scarcely interrupted, of Stevenson's thinkings and doings from month to
month, and often from day to day, during the
last four romantic years of his life. The first is
dated November 2nd, 1890, when he and his
household were clearing the ground for their
home on the mountain-side of Vaea : the last,
October 6th, 1894, just two months before his
grave was dug on Vaea top. During his Odyssey
in the South Seas (from August, 1888, to the
spring of 1890) his letters, to Mr. Colvin at
any rate, were infrequent and tantalizingly
vague ; but soon after settling on his estate
in Samoa, " he for the first time, to my infinite
gratification, took to writing me long and regu-
lar monthly budgets as full and particular as

heart could wish; and this practice he maintained until within a few weeks of his death.''
These letters, occupying a place quite apart in
Stevenson's correspondence, Mr. Colvin has
now edited with pious care and given to the
public.

But the great, the happy surprise of the
Vailima Letters is neither their continuity nor
their fulness of detail — although on each of
these points they surpass our hopes. The great,
the entirely happy surprise is their intimacy.
We all knew — who could doubt it? — that
Stevenson's was a clean and transparent mind.
But we scarcely allowed for the innocent zest
(innocent, because wholly devoid of vanity or
selfishness) which he took in observing its
operations, or for the child-like confidence with
which he held out the crystal for his friend to
gaze into.

One is at first inclined to say that had these
letters been less open-hearted they had made
less melancholy reading—the last few of them,
at any rate. For, as their editor says, '' the
tenor of these last letters of Stevenson's to me,
and of others written to several of his friends at

the same time, seemed to give just cause for anxiety. Indeed, as the reader will have perceived, a gradual change had during the past months been coming over the tone of his correspondence. . . . To judge by these letters, his old invincible spirit of cheerfulness was beginning to give way to moods of depression and overstrained feeling, although to those about him, it seems, his charming, habitual sweetness and gaiety of temper were undiminished." Mr. Colvin is thinking, no doubt, of passages such as this, from the very last letter :—

" I know I am at a climacteric for all men who live by their wits, so I do not despair. But the truth is, I am pretty nearly useless at literature. . . . Were it not for my health, which made it impossible, I could not find it in my heart to forgive myself that I did not stick to an honest, commonplace trade when I was young, which might have now supported me during these ill years. But do not suppose me to be down in anything else ; only, for the nonce, my skill deserts me, such as it is, or was. It was a very little dose of inspiration, and a pretty little trick of style, long lost, improved by the most heroic industry. So far, I have managed to please the journalists. But I am a fictitious article, and have long known it. I am read by journalists, by my fellow-novelists, and by boys ; with these *incipit et explicit* my vogue."

I appeal to all who earn their living by pen or brush—Who does not know moods such as this? Who has not experience of those dark days when the ungrateful canvas refuses to come right, and the artist sits down before it and calls himself a fraud? We may even say that these fits of incapacity and blank despondency are part of the cost of all creative work. They may be intensified by terror for the family exchequer. The day passes in strenuous but futile effort, and the man asks himself, " What will happen to me and mine if this kind of thing continues?" Stevenson, we are allowed to say (for the letters tell us), did torment himself with these terrors. And we may say further that, by whatever causes impelled, he certainly worked too hard during the last two years of his life. With regard to the passage quoted, what seems to me really melancholy is not the baseless self-distrust, for that is a transitory malady most incident to authorship ; but that, could a magic carpet have transported Stevenson at that moment to the side of the friend he addressed—could he for an hour or two have visited London—all this apprehension had been at once dispelled. He left England before achieving his full conquest of the public heart, and the extent of that conquest he, in his exile, never quite realized. When he visited Sydney, early in 1893, it was to him a new and disconcerting experience—but not, I fancy altogether unpleasing—*digito monstrari*, or, as he puts it elsewhere, to " do the affable celebrity life-sized." Nor do I think he quite realized how large a place he filled in the education, as in the affections, of the younger men—the Barries and Kiplings, the Weymans, Doyles and Crocketts—whose courses began after he had left these shores. An artist gains much by working alone and away from chatter and criticism and adulation : but his gain has this corresponding loss, that he must go through his dark hours without support. Even a master may take benefit at times—if it be only a physical benefit—from some closer and handier assurance than any letters can give of the place held by his work in the esteem of " the boys."

We must not make too much of what he wrote in this dark mood. A few days later he was at work on *Weir of Hermiston*, laboring " at the full pitch of his powers and in the conscious happiness of their exercise." Once more he felt himself to be working at his best.

The result the world has not yet been allowed
to see : for the while we are satisfied and com-
forted by Mr. Colvin's assurances. "The
fragment on which he wrought during the last
month of his life gives to my mind (as it did
to his own) for the first time the true measure
of his powers ; and if in the literature of romance there is to be found work more masterly, of more piercing human insight and more
concentrated imaginative wisdom, I do not
know it."

On the whole, these letters from Vailima give
a picture of a serene and — allowance being
made for the moods—a contented life. It is, I
suspect, the genuine Stevenson that we get in
the following passage from the letter of March,
1891 :—

" Though I write so little, I pass all my hours of field-
work in continual converse and imaginary correspondence. I scarce pull up a weed, but I invent a sentence
on the matter to yourself ; it does not get written ; *au-
tant en emportent les vents ;* but the intent is there, and
for me (in some sort) the companionship. To-day, for
instance, we had a great talk. I was toiling, the sweat
dripping from my nose, in the hot fit after a squall of
rain ; methought you asked me—frankly, was I happy ?
Happy (said I) ; I was only happy once ; that was at

Hyères ; it came to an end from a variety of reasons—decline of health, change of place, increase of money, age with his stealing steps ; since then, as before then, I know not what it means.   But I know pleasures still ; pleasure with a thousand faces and none perfect, a thousand tongues all broken, a thousand hands, and all of them with scratching nails.   High among these I place the delight of weeding out here alone by the garrulous water, under the silence of the high wood, broken by incongruous sounds of birds.   And take my life all through, look at it fore and back, and upside down—I would not change my circumstances, unless it were to bring you here.   And yet God knows perhaps this intercourse of writing serves as well ; and I wonder, were you here indeed, would I commune so continually with the thought of you.   I say ' I wonder' for a form ; I know, and I know I should not."

In a way the beauty of these letters is this, that they tell us so much of Stevenson that is new, and nothing that is strange—nothing that we have difficulty in reconciling with the picture we had already formed in our own minds. Our mental portraits of some other writers, drawn from their deliberate writings, have had to be readjusted, and sometimes most cruelly readjusted, as soon as their private correspondence came to be published.   If any of us dreamed of this danger in Stevenson's case (and I doubt if anyone did), the danger at any

188

rate is past. The man of the letters is the man of the books—the same gay, eager, strenuous, lovable spirit, curious as ever about life and courageous as ever in facing its chances. Profoundly as he deplores the troubles in Samoa, when he hears that war has been declared he can hardly repress a boyish excitement. " War is a huge *entraînement*," he writes in June, 1893 ; " there is no other temptation to be compared to it, not one. We were all wet, we had been five hours in the saddle, mostly riding hard ; and we came home like schoolboys, with such a lightness of spirits, and I am sure such a brightness of eye, as you could have lit a candle at."

And that his was not by any means mere " literary "courage one more extract will prove. One of his boys, Paatalise by name, had suddenly gone mad :—

" I was busy copying David Balfour, with my left hand—a most laborious task—Fanny was down at the native house superintending the floor, Lloyd down in Apia, and Bella in her own house cleaning, when I heard the latter calling on my name. I ran out on the verandah ; and there on the lawn beheld my crazy boy with an axe in his hand and dressed out in green ferns, dancing. I ran downstairs and found all my house boys on the back verandah, watching him through the dining-room. I asked what it meant?—'Dance belong his place,' they said.—'I think this is no time to dance,' said I. 'Has he done his work?'—'No,' they told me, 'away bush all morning.' But there they all stayed in the back verandah. I went on alone through the dining-room and bade him stop. He did so, shouldered the axe, and began to walk away; but I called him back, walked up to him, and took the axe out of his unresist-ing hands. The boy is in all things so good, that I can scarce say I was afraid; only I felt it had to be stopped ere he could work himself up by dancing to some crazi-ness. Our house boys protested they were not afraid; all I know is they were all watching him round the back door, and did not follow me till I had the axe. As for the out-boys, who were working with Fanny in the native house, they thought it a bad business, and made no secret of their fears."

But indeed all the book is manly, with the manliness of Scott's *Journal* or of Fielding's *Voyage to Lisbon*. "To the English-speaking world," concludes Mr. Colvin, "he has left behind a treasure which it would be vain as yet to attempt to estimate; to the profession of letters one of the most ennobling and inspirit-ing of examples; and to his friends an image of memory more vivid and more dear than are the presences of almost any of the living." Very few men of our time have been followed

out of this world with the same regret. None
have repined less at their own fate—

> " This be the verse you grave for me :—
> ' Here he lies where he longed to be ;
>   Home is the sailor, home from the sea,
>   And the hunter home from the hill.' "

M. ZOLA

Sept. 23, 1892.
La Débâcle.

TO what different issues two men will work the same notion! Imagine this world to be a flat board accurately parcelled out into squares, and you have the basis at once of *Alice through the Looking-Glass* and of *Les Rougon-Macquart*. But for the mere fluke that the Englishman happened to be whimsical and the Frenchman entirely without humor (and the chances were perhaps against this), we might have had the Rougon-Macquart family through the looking-glass, and a natural and social history of Alice in *parterres* of existence labelled *Drink, War, Money,* etc. As it is, in drawing up any comparison of these two writers we should remember that Mr. Carroll sees the world in sections because he chooses, M. Zola because he cannot help it.

If life were a museum, M. Zola would stand a reasonable chance of being a Balzac. But I invite the reader who has just laid down *La*

Débâcle to pick up *Eugénie Grandet* again and say if that little Dutch picture has not more sense of life, even of the storm and stir and big furies of life, than the detonating *Débâcle*. The older genius

" Saw life steadily and saw it whole "

—No matter how small the tale, he draws no curtain around it; it stands in the midst of a real world, set in the white and composite light of day. M. Zola sees life in sections and by one or another of those colors into which daylight can be decomposed by the prism. He is like a man standing at the wings with a lime-light apparatus. The rays fall now here, now there, upon the stage; are luridly red or vividly green; but neither mix nor pervade.

I am aware that the tone of the above paragraph is pontifical and its substance a trifle obvious, and am eager to apologize for both. Speaking as an impressionist, I can only say that *La Débâcle* stifles me. And this is the effect produced by all his later books. Each has the exclusiveness of a dream; its subject— be it drink or war or money — possesses the reader as a nightmare possesses the dreamer.

For the time this place of wide prospect, the world, puts up its shutters ; and life becomes all drink, all war, all money, while M. Zola (adaptable Bacchanal !) surrenders his brain to the intoxication of his latest theme. He will drench himself with ecclesiology, or veterinary surgery, or railway technicalities—everything by turns and everything long ; but, like the gentleman in the comic opera, he "never mixes." Of late he almost ceased to add even a dash of human interest.

Mr. George Moore, reviewing *La Débâcle* in the *Fortnightly* last month, laments this. He reminds us of the splendid opportunity M. Zola has flung away in his latest work.

"Jean and Maurice," says Mr. Moore, "have fought side by side ; they have alternately saved each other's lives ; war has united them in a bond of inseparable friendship ; they have grasped each other's hands, and looked in each other's eyes, overpowered with a love that exceeds the love that woman ever gave to man ; now they are ranged on different sides, armed one against the other. The idea is a fine one, and it is to be deeply regretted that M. Zola did not throw history to the winds and develop the beautiful human story of the division of friends in civil war. Never would history have tempted Balzac away from the human passion of such a subject. . . ."

But it is just fidelity to the human interest of
every subject that gives the novelist his rank;
that makes—to take another instance—a page
or two of Balzac, when Balzac is dealing with
money, of more value than the whole of
l'Argent.

Of Burke it has been said by a critic with
whom it is a pleasure for once in a way to agree,
that he knew how the whole world lived.

" It was Burke's peculiarity and his glory to apply the
imagination of a poet of the first order to the facts and
business of life. . . . Burke's imagination led him
to look over the whole land : the legislator devising new
laws, the judge expounding and enforcing old ones, the
merchant despatching all his goods and extending his
credit, the banker advancing the money of his customers
upon the credit of the merchant, the frugal man slowly
accumulating the store which is to support him in old
age, the ancient institutions of Church and University
with their seemly provisions for sound learning and true
religion, the parson in his pulpit, the poet pondering his
rhymes, the farmer eyeing his crops, the painter cov-
ering his canvases, the player educating the feelings.
Burke saw all this with the fancy of a poet, and dwelt
on it with the eye of a lover."

Now all this, which is true of Burke, is true
of the very first literary artists—of Shakespeare

and Balzac. All this, and more—for they not only see all this immense activity of life, but the emotions that animate each of the myriad actors.

Suppose them to treat of commerce: they see not only the goods and money changing hands, but the ambitions, dangers, fears, delights, the fierce adventures by desert and seas, the slow toil at home, upon which the foundations of commerce are set. Like the Gods,

> " They see the ferry
>   On the broad, clay-laden
>   Lone Chorasmian stream ;—thereon,
>   With snort and strain,
>   Two horses, strongly swimming, tow
>   The ferry-boat, with woven ropes
>   To either bow
>   Firm-harness'd by the mane ; a chief,
>   With shout and shaken spear,
>   Stands at the prow, and guides them ; but astern
>   The cowering merchants, in long robes,
>   Sit pale beside their wealth.   .   .   ."

Like the Gods, they see all this; but, unlike the Gods, they must feel also :—

> " They see the merchants
>   On the Oxus stream ;—*but care*
>   *Must visit first them too, and make them pale.*
>   Whether, through whirling sand,

> A cloud of desert robber-horse have burst
> Upon their caravan : or greedy kings,
> In the wall'd cities the way passes through,
> Crush'd them with tolls ; or fever-airs,
> On some great river's marge,
> Mown them down, far from home."

Mr. Moore speaks of M. Zola's vast imagination. It is vast in the sense that it sees one thing at a time, and sees it a thousand times as big as it appears to most men. But can the imagination that sees a whole world under the influence of one particular fury be compared with that which surveys this planet and sees its inhabitants busy with a million diverse occupations? Drink, Money, War—these may be usefully personified as malignant or beneficent angels, for pulpit purposes. But the employment of these terrific spirits in the harrying of the Rougon-Macquart family recalls the announcement that

" The Death-Angel smote Alexander McGlue, . . ."

while the methods of the *Roman Expérimental* can hardly be better illustrated than by the rest of the famous stanza—

> " —And gave him protracted repose :
> He wore a check shirt and a Number 9 shoe,
> And he had a pink wart on his nose."

SELECTION

May 4,
1895.
Hazlitt.

"COMING forward and seating himself on
the ground in his white dress and
tightened turban, the chief of the Indian jugglers begins with tossing up two brass balls,
which is what any of us could do, and concludes
with keeping up four at the same time, which is
what none of us could do to save our lives."
. . . You remember Hazlitt's essay on the
Indian Jugglers, and how their performance
shook his self-conceit. "It makes me ashamed
of myself. I ask what there is that I can do
as well as this. Nothing. . . . Is there
no one thing in which I can challenge compe-
tition, that I can bring as an instance of exact
perfection, in which others cannot find a flaw?
The utmost I can pretend to is to write a description of what this fellow can do. I can
write a book; so can many others who have not
even learned to spell. What abortions are these
essays! What errors, what ill - pieced transi-

198

tions, what crooked reasons, what lame conclusions! How little is made out, and that little how ill! Yet they are the best I can do."

Nevertheless a play of Shakespeare's, or a painting by Reynolds, or an essay by Hazlitt, imperfect though it be, is of more rarity and worth than the correctest juggling or tight-rope walking. Hazlitt proceeds to examine why this should be, and discovers a number of good reasons. But there is one reason, omitted by him, or perhaps left for the reader to infer, on which we may profitably spend a few minutes. It forms part of a big subject, and tempts to much abstract talk on the universality of the Fine Arts; but I think we shall be putting it simply enough if we say that an artist is superior to an "artiste" because he does well what ninety - nine people in a hundred are doing poorly all their lives.

When people compare fiction with "real life," they start with asserting "real life" to be a conglomerate of innumerable details of all possible degrees of pertinence and importance, and go on to show that the novelist selects from this mass those which are the most important and pertinent to his purpose. (I speak here particularly of the novelist, but the same is alleged of all practitioners of the fine arts.) And, in a way, this is true enough. But who (unless in an idle moment, or with a view to writing a treatise in metaphysics) ever takes this view of the world? Who regards it as a conglomerate of innumerable details? Critics say that the artist's difficulty lies in selecting the details proper to his purpose, and his justification rests on the selection he makes. But where lives the man whose difficulty and whose justification do not lie just here?—who is not

Selection. consciously or unconsciously selecting from morning until night? You take the most ordinary country walk. How many millions of leaves and stones and blades of grass do you pass without perceiving them at all? How many thousands of others do you perceive, and at once allow to slip into oblivion? Suppose you have walked four miles with the express object of taking pleasure in country sights. I dare wager the objects that have actually engaged your attention for two seconds are less than five hundred, and those that remain in your memory, when you reach home, as few as a dozen. All the way you have been, quite unconsciously, selecting and rejecting. And it is the brain's bedazzlement over this work, I suggest, and not merely the rhythmical physical exertion, that lulls the more ambitious walker and induces that phlegmatic mood so prettily described by Stevenson—the mood in which

" we can think of this or that, lightly or laughingly, as a child thinks, or as we think in a morning doze ; we can make puns or puzzle out acrostics, and trifle in a thousand ways with words and rhymes ; but when it comes to honest work, when we come to gather ourselves together for an effort, we may sound the trumpet as long and loud as we please ; the great barons of the mind will not rally to the standard, but sit, each one at home, warming his hands over his own fire and brooding on his own private thought ! "

Again, certain critics never seem tired of pelting the novelist with comparisons drawn between painting and photography. " Mr. So-and-So's fidelity to life suggests the camera rather than the brush and palette " ; and the implication is that Mr. So-and-So and the camera resemble each other in their tendency to reproduce irrelevant detail. The camera, it is assumed, repeats this irrelevant detail. The photographer does not select. But is this true ? I have known many enthusiasts in photography whose enthusiasm I could not share. But I never knew one, even among amateurs, who wished to photograph everything he saw, from every possible point of view. Even the amateur selects—wrongly as a rule: still he selects. The mere act of setting up a camera in any particular spot implies a process of selection. And when the deed is done, the scenery has been libelled. Our eyes behold the photograph, and go through another process of selection. In short, whatever they look upon, men and women are selecting ceaselessly.

The artist therefore does well and consciously, and for a particular end, what every man or woman does poorly, and unconsciously, and casually. He differs in the photographer in that he has more licence to eliminate. When once the camera is set up, it's owner's power over the landscape has come to an end. The person who looks on the resultant photograph must go through the same process of choosing and rejecting that he would have gone through in contemplating the natural landscape. The sole advantage is that the point of view has been selected for him, and that he can enjoy it without fatigue in any place and at any time.

The truth seems to be that the human brain abhors the complexity—the apparently aimless complexity—of nature and real life, and is for ever trying to get away from it by selecting this and ignoring that. And it contrives so well that I suppose the average man is not consciously aware twice a year of that conglomerate of details which the critics call real life. He holds one stout thread, at any rate, to guide him through the maze—the thread of self-interest.

The justification of the poet or the novelist is that he discovers a better thread. He follows up a universal where the average man follows only a particular. But in following it, he does but use those processes by which the average man arrives, or attempts to arrive, at pleasure.

EXTERNALS

Nov. 18, 1893.
Story and Anecdote.

I SUPPOSE I am no more favored than most people who write stories in receiving from unknown correspondents a variety of suggestions, outlines of plots, sketches of situations, characters, and so forth. One cannot but feel grateful for all this spontaneous beneficence. The mischief is that in ninety-nine cases out of a hundred (the fraction is really much smaller) these suggestions are of no possible use.

Why should this be? Put briefly, the reason is that a story differs from an anecdote. I take the first two instances that come into my head: but they happen to be striking ones, and, as they occur in a book of Mr. Kipling's, are safe to be well known to all my correspondents. In Mr. Kipling's fascinating book, *Life's Handicap*, *On Greenhow Hill* is a story; *The Lang Men o' Larut* is an anecdote. *On Greenhow Hill* is founded on a study of the human heart, and it is upon the human heart

204

that the tale constrains one's interest. *The Lang Men o' Larut* is just a yarn spun for the yarn's sake : it informs us of nothing, and is closely related (if I may use some of Mr. Howells' expressive language for the occasion) to " the lies swapped between men after the ladies have left the table." And the reason why the story-teller, when (as will happen at times) his invention runs dry, can take no comfort in the generous outpourings of his unknown friends, is just this — that the plots are merely plots, and the anecdotes merely anecdotes, and the difference between these and a story that shall reveal something concerning men and women is just the difference between bad and good art.

Let us go a step further. At first sight it seems a superfluous contention that a novelist's rank depends upon what he can see and what he can tell us of the human heart. But, as a matter of fact, you will find that four-fifths at least of contemporary criticism is devoted to matters quite different—to what I will call Externals, or the Accidents of Story-telling : and that, as a consequence, our novelists are spending a quite unreasonable proportion of their labor upon Externals. I wrote "as a consequence" hastily, because it is always easier to blame the critics. If the truth were known, I dare say the novelists began it with their talk about "documents," "the scientific method," "observation and experiment," and the like.

The Fallacy of "Documents."

Now you may observe a man until you are tired, and then you may begin and observe him over again : you may photograph him and his surroundings : you may spend years in studying what he eats and drinks : you may search out what his uncles died of, and the price he pays for his hats, and—know nothing at all about him. At least, you may know enough to insure his life or assess him for Income Tax : but you are not even half-way towards writing a novel about him. You are still groping among externals. His unspoken ambitions ; the stories he tells himself silently, at midnight, in his bed ; the pain he masks with a dull face and the ridiculous fancies he hugs in secret—these are the Essentials, and you cannot get them by Observation. If you can discover these, you are a Novelist born : if not, you may as well shut up your note-book and turn to some more remunerative trade. You will never surprise the secret of a soul by accumulating notes upon Externals.

Then, again, we have Local Color, an article inordinately bepraised just now ; and yet an External.   For human nature, when every possible allowance has been made for geographical conditions, undergoes surprisingly little change as we pass from one degree of latitude or longitude to another.   The Story of Ruth is as intelligible to an Englishman as though Ruth had gleaned in the stubble behind Tess Durbeyfield.   Levine toiling with the mowers, Achilles sulking in his tent, Iphigeneia at the altar, Gil Blas before the Archbishop of Granada have as close a claim on our sympathy as if they lived but a few doors from us.   Let me be understood.   I hold it best that a novelist should be intimately acquainted with the country in which he lays his scene.   But, none the less, the study of local color is not of the first importance.   And the critic who lavishes praise upon a writer for " introducing us to an entirely new atmosphere," for " breaking new ground," and " wafting us to scenes with which the jaded novel-reader is scarcely acquainted," and for " giving us work which bears every

Local Color.

trace of minute local research," is praising that which is of secondary importance. The works of Richard Jefferies form a considerable museum of externals of one particular kind ; and this is possibly the reason why the Cockney novelist waxes eloquent over Richard Jefferies. He can now import the breath of the hay-field into his works at no greater expense of time and trouble than taking down the *Gamekeeper at Home* from his club bookshelf and perusing a chapter or so before settling down to work. There is not the slightest harm in his doing this : the mistake lies in thinking local color (however acquired) of the first importance.

In judging fiction there is probably no safer rule than to ask one's self, How far does the pleasure excited in me by this book depend upon the transitory and trivial accidents that distinguish this time, this place, this character, from another time, another place, another character ? And how far upon the abiding elements of human life, the constant temptations, the constant ambitions, and the constant nobility and weakness of the human heart ? These are the essentials, and no amount of documents or local color can fill their room.

Sept. 30,
1893.
The
Country as
" Copy."

The case of a certain small volume of verse in which I take some interest, and its treatment at the hands of the reviewers, seems to me to illustrate in a sufficiently amusing manner a trick that the British critic has been picking up of late. In a short account of Mr. Hosken, the postman poet, written by way of preface to his *Verses by the Way* (Methuen & Co.), I took occasion to point out that he is not what is called in the jargon of these days a "nature-poet"; that his poetic bent inclines rather to meditation than to description; and that though his early struggles in London and elsewhere have made him acquainted with many strange people in abnormal conditions of life, his interest has always lain, not in these striking anomalies, but in the destiny of humanity as a whole and its position in the great scheme of things.

These are simple facts. I found them, easily enough, in Mr. Hosken's verse—where anybody else may find them. They also seem to me to be, for a critic's purpose, ultimate facts. It is an ultimate fact that Publius Virgilius Maro wore his buskins somewhat higher in the heel than did Quintus Horatius Flaccus: and no

critic, to my knowledge, has been impertinent
enough to point out that, since Horace had
some experience of the tented field, while Virgil
was a stay-at-home courtier, therefore Horace
should have essayed to tell the martial exploits
of Trojan and Rutulian while Virgil contented
himself with the gossip of the Via Sacra. Yet—
to compare small things with great—this is the
mistake into which our critics have fallen in
Mr. Hosken's case; and I mention it because
the case is typical. They try to get behind the
ultimate facts and busy themselves with questions they have no proper concern with. Some
ask petulantly why Mr. Hosken is not a "nature-poet." Some are gravely concerned that
"local talent" (*i.e.* the talent of a man who
happens to dwell in some locality other than
the critic's) should not concern itself with local affairs; and remind him—

> " To thine orchard edge belong
>   All the brass and plume of song."

As if a man may not concern himself with the
broader problems of life and attack them with
all the apparatus of recorded experience, unless
he happen to live on one bank or other of the
Fleet Ditch! If a man have the gift, he can

find all the "brass and plume of song" in his orchard edge. If he have not, he may (provided he be a *bonâ fide* traveller) find it elsewhere. What, for instance, were the use of telling Keats : "To thy surgery belong all the brass and plume of song"? He couldn't find it there, so he betook himself to Chapman and Lempriere. If you ask, "What right has a country postman to be handling questions that vexed the brain of Plato?" — I ask in return, "What right had John Keats, who knew no Greek, to busy himself with Greek mythology?" And the answer is that each has a perfect right to follow his own bent.

The assumption of many critics that only within the metropolitan cab radius can a comprehensive system of philosophy be constructed, and that only through the plate-glass windows of two or three clubs is it possible to see life steadily, and see it whole, is one that I have before now had occasion to dispute. It is joined in this case to another yet more preposterous— that from a brief survey of an author's circumstances we can dictate to him what he ought to write about, and how he ought to write it. And I have observed particularly that if a writer be a countryman, or at all well acquainted with country life, all kinds of odd entertainment is expected of him in the way of notes on the habits of birds, beasts, and fishes, on the growth of all kinds of common plants, on the proper way to make hay, to milk a cow, and so forth.

Now it is just the true countryman who would no more think of noting these things down in a book than a Londoner would think of stating in a novel that Bond Street joins Oxford Street and Piccadilly : simply because they have been familiar to him from boyhood. And to my mind it is a small but significant sign of a rather lamentable movement—of none other, indeed, than the " Rural Exodus," as Political Economists call it—that each and every novelist of my acquaintance, while assuming as a matter of course that his readers are tolerably familiar with the London Directory, should, equally as a matter of course, assume them to be ignorant of the commonest features of open-air life. I protest there are few things more pitiable than the transports of your Cockney critic over Richard Jefferies. Listen, for instance, to this kind of thing :—

Richard Jefferies.

" Here and there upon the bank wild gooseberry and currant bushes may be found, planted by birds carrying off ripe fruit from the garden. A wild gooseberry may sometimes be seen growing out of the decayed ' touch-wood ' on the top of a hollow withy-pollard. Wild apple-trees, too, are not uncommon in the hedges.

" The beautiful rich colour of the horse-chestnut, when quite ripe and fresh from its prickly green shell, can hardly be surpassed ; underneath the tree the grass is strewn with shells where they have fallen and burst. Close to the trunk the grass is worn away by the rest-less trampling of horses, who love the shade its foliage gives in summer. The oak apples which appear on the oaks in spring—generally near the trunk—fall off in summer, and lie shrivelled on the ground, not unlike rotten cork, or black as if burned. But the oak-galls show thick on some of the trees, light green, and round as a ball ; they will remain on the branches after the leaves have fallen, turning brown and hard, and hang-ing there till the spring comes again."—*Wild Life in a Southern County*, pp. 224–5.

I say it is pitiable that people should need to read these things in print. Let me apply this method to some district of south-west Lon-don—say the Old Brompton Road :—

" Here and there along the street Grocery Stores and shops of Italian Warehousemen may be observed, opened here as branches of bigger establishments in the City. Three gilt balls may occasionally be seen hanging out under the first-floor windows of a ' pawnbroker's ' res-

idence. House-agents, too, are not uncommon along
the line of route.

"The appearance of a winkle, when extracted from
its shell with the aid of a pin, is extremely curious.
There is a winkle-stall by the South Kensington Station
of the Underground Railway. Underneath the stall the
pavement is strewn with shells, where they have fallen
and continue to lie. Close to the stall is a cab-stand,
paved with a few cobbles, lest the road be worn over-
much by the restless trampling of cab-horses, who stand
here because it is a cab-stand. The thick woollen goods
which appear in the haberdashers' windows through the
winter—generally *inside* the plate glass—give way to
garments of a lighter texture as the summer advances,
and are put away or exhibited at decreased prices. But
collars continue to be shown, quite white and circular in
form; they will probably remain, turning grey as the
dust settles on them, until they are sold."

This is no travesty. It is a hasty, but I believe a pretty exact application of Jefferies'
method. And I ask how it would look in a
book. If the critics really enjoy, as they profess to, all this trivial country lore, why on
earth don't they come into the fresh air and
find it out for themselves? There is no imperative call for their presence in London.
Ink will stain paper in the country as well as
in town, and the Post will convey their articles to their editors. As it is, they do but

overheat already overheated clubs. Mr. Henley has suggested concerning Jefferies' works that

" in years to be, when the whole island is one vast congeries of streets, and the fox has gone down to the bustard and the dodo, and outside museums of comparative anatomy the weasel is not, and the badger has ceased from the face of the earth, it is not doubtful that the *Gamekeeper* and *Wild Life* and the *Poacher*—epitomising, as they will, the rural England of certain centuries before—will be serving as material authority for historical descriptions, historical novels, historical epics, historical pictures, and will be honoured as the most useful stuff of their kind in being."

Let me add that the movement has begun. These books are already supplying the club-novelist with his open-air effects : and, therefore, the club-novelist worships them. From them he gathers that "wild apple-trees, too, are not uncommon in the hedges," and straightway he informs the public of this wonder. But it is hard on the poor countryman who, for the benefit of a street-bred reading public, must cram his books with solemn recitals of his A, B, C, and impressive announcements that two and two make four and a hedge-sparrow's egg is blue.

Aug. 18,
1894.
A Defence
of " Local
Fiction."

Under the title " Three Years of American Copyright " the *Daily Chronicle* last Tuesday published an account of an interview with Mr. Brander Matthews, who holds (among many titles to distinction) the Professorship of Literature in Columbia College, New York. Mr. Matthews is always worth listening to, and has the knack of speaking without offensiveness even when chastising us Britons for our national peculiarities. His conversation with the *Daily Chronicle's* interviewer contained a number of good things ; but for the moment I am occupied with his answer to the question " What form of literature should you say is at present in the ascendant in the United States ? " " Undoubtedly," said Mr. Matthews, " what I may call local fiction."

" Every district of the country is finding its ' sacred poet.' Some of them have only a local reputation, but all possess the common characteristic of starting from fresh, original, and loving study of local character and manners. You know what Miss Mary E. Wilkins has done for New England, and you probably know, too, that she was preceded in the same path by Miss Sarah Orne Jewett and the late Mrs. Rose Terry Cooke. Mr. Harold Frederic is performing much the same service for rural New York, Miss Murfree (Charles Egbert Craddock) for the mountains of Tennessee, Mr. James Lane

Allen for Kentucky, Mr. Joel Chandler Harris for
Georgia, Mr. Cable for Louisiana, Miss French (Octave
Thanet) for Iowa, Mr. Hamlin Garland for the western prairies, and so forth. Of course, one can trace
the same tendency, more or less clearly, in English
fiction. . . . ."

And Mr. Matthews went on to instance
several living novelists, Scotch, Irish, and
English to support this last remark.

The matter, however, is not in doubt.
With Mr. Barrie in the North, and Mr.
Hardy in the South; with Mr. Hall Caine
in the Isle of Man, Mr. Crockett in Gallo-
way, Miss Barlow in Lisconnell; with Mr.
Gilbert Parker in the territory of the H.B.C.,
and Mr. Hornung in Australia; with Mr.
Kipling scouring the wide world, but returning always to India when the time comes to
him to score yet another big artistic success;
it hardly needs elaborate proof to arrive at the
conclusion that 'locality' is playing a strong
part in current fiction.

The thing may possibly be overdone.
Looking at it from the artistic point of view
as dispassionately as I may, I think we are

overdoing it. But that, for the moment, is
not the point of view I wish to take. If
for the moment we can detach ourselves from
the prejudice of fashion and look at the
matter from the historical point of view—if
we put ourselves into the position of the conscientious gentleman who, fifty or a hundred
years hence, will be surveying us and our
works—I think we shall find this elaboration
of " locality " in fiction to be but a swing-
back of the pendulum, a natural revolt from
the thin-spread work of the " carpet-bagging "
novelist who takes the whole world for his
province, and imagines he sees life steadily
and sees it whole when he has seen a great
deal of it superficially.

The " carpet-bagger " still lingers among
us. We know him, with his " tourist's return " ticket, and the ready-made " plot "
in his head, and his note-book and pencil
for jotting down " local color." We still
find him working up the scenery of Bolivia
in the Reading Room of the British Museum.
But he is going rapidly out of fashion ; and
it is as well to put his features on record and
pigeon-hole them, if only that we may recog-

nize him on that day when the pendulum shall swing him triumphantly back into our midst, and "locality" shall in its turn pass out of vogue.

I submit this simile of the pendulum with some diffidence to those eager theorists who had rather believe that their art is advancing steadily, but at a fair rate of speed, towards perfection. My own less cheerful—yet not altogether cheerless view—is that the various fashions in art swing to and fro upon intersecting curves. Some of the points of intersection are fortunate points—others are obviously the reverse; and generally the fortunate points lie near the middle of each arc, or the mean; while the less fortunate ones lie towards the ends, that is, towards excess upon one side or another. I have already said that, in the amount of attention they pay to locality just now, the novelists seem to be running into excess. If I must choose between one excess and the other—between the carpet-bagger and the writer of "dialect-stories," each at his worst—I unhesitatingly choose the latter. But that is probably because I happened to be born in the 'sixties.

Let us get back (I hear you implore) to the
historical point of view, if possible : anywhere,
anywhere, out of the *Poetics !* And I admit
that a portion of the preceding paragraph reads
like a bad parody of that remarkable work.
Well, then, I believe that our imaginary historian—I suppose he will be a German : but
we need not let our imagination dwell upon
that—will find a dozen reasons in contemporary life to account for the attention now paid
by novelists to " locality." He will find one
of them, no doubt, in the development of loco-
motion by steam. He will point out that any
cause which makes communication easier between two given towns is certain to soften the
difference in the characteristics of their inhabitants : that the railway made communication
easier and quicker year by year ; and its tendency was therefore to obliterate local peculiarities. He will describe how at first the carpet-
bagger went forth in railway-train and steam-
boat, rejoicing in his ability to put a girdle
round the world in a few weeks, and disposed
to ignore those differences of race and region
which he had no time to consider and which
he was daily softening into uniformity. He
will then relate that towards the close of the

nineteenth century, when these differences were rapidly perishing, people began to feel the loss of them and recognize their scientific and romantic value ; and that a number of writers entered into a struggle against time and the carpet-bagger, to study these differences and place them upon record, before all trace of them should disappear. And then I believe our historian, though he may find that in 1894 we paid too much attention to the *minutiæ* of dialect, folk-lore and ethnic differences, and were inclined to overlay with these the more catholic principles of human conduct, will acknowledge that in our hour we did the work that was most urgent. Our hour, no doubt, is not the happiest ; but, since this is the work it brings, there can be no harm in going about it zealously.

CLUB TALK

Nov. 12,
1892.
Mr. Gilbert
Parker.

MR. GILBERT PARKER'S book of Canadian tales, "Pierre and His People" (Methuen and Co.), is delightful for more than one reason. To begin with, the tales themselves are remarkable, and the language in which they are told, though at times it overshoots the mark by a long way and offends by what I may call an affected virility, is always distinguished. You feel that Mr. Parker considers his sentences, not letting his bolts fly at a venture, but aiming at his effects deliberately. It is the trick of promising youth to shoot high and send its phrases in parabolic curves over the target. But a slight wildness of aim is easily corrected, and to see the target at all is a more conspicuous merit than the public imagines. Now Mr. Parker sees his target steadily; he has a thoroughly good notion of what a short story ought to be : and more than two or three stories in his book are as good as can be.

But to me the most pleasing quality in the book is its open-air flavor. Here is yet another young author, and one of the most promising, joining the healthy revolt against the workshops. Though for my sins I have to write criticism now and then, and use the language of the workshops, I may claim to be one of the rebels, having chosen to pitch a small tent far from cities and to live out of doors : and it rejoices me to see the movement growing, as it undoubtedly has grown during the last few years, and find yet one more of the younger men refusing, in Mr. Stevenson's words, to cultivate restaurant fat, to fall in mind " to a thing perhaps as low as many types of *bourgeois*—the implicit or exclusive artist." London is an alluring dwelling-place for an author, even for one who desires to write about the country. He is among the paragraph-writers, and his reputation swells as a cucumber under glass. Being in sight of the newspaper men, he is also in their mind. His prices will stand higher than if he go out into the wilderness. Moreover, he has there the stimulating talk of the masters in his profession, and will be apt to think that his intelligence is developing amazingly, whereas in fact he is developing all

223

on one side; and the end of him is—the Exclusive Artist:—

" When the flicker of London sun falls faint on the
  Club-room's green and gold,
The sons of Adam sit them down and scratch with
  their pens in the mould—
They scratch with their pens in the mould of their
  graves and the ink and the anguish start,
For the Devil mutters behind the leaves: ' It's pretty,
  but is it Art?'"

The spirit of our revolt is indicated clearly enough on that page of Mr. Stevenson's
" Wrecker," from which I have already quoted
a phrase:—

" That was a home word of Pinkerton's, deserving to
be writ in letters of gold on the portico of every School
of Art: ' What I can't see is why you should want to
do nothing else.' The dull man is made, not by the nature, but by the degree of his immersion in a single business. And all the more if that be sedentary, unevent-
ful, and ingloriously safe. More than half of him will
then remain unexercised and undeveloped; the rest will
be distended and deformed by over-nutrition, over-cere-
bration and the heat of rooms. And I have often mar-
velled at the impudence of gentlemen who describe and
pass judgment on the life of man, in almost perfect ig-
norance of all its necessary elements and natural careers.
Those who dwell in clubs and studios may paint excellent
pictures or write enchanting novels. There is one thing
that they should not do: they should pass no judgment

on man's destiny, for it is a thing with which they are unacquainted. Their own life is an excrescence of the moment, doomed, in the vicissitude of history, to pass and disappear. The eternal life of man, spent under sun and rain and in rude physical effort, lies upon one side, scarce changed since the beginning."

A few weeks ago our novelists were discussing the reasons why they were novelists and not playwrights. The discussion was sterile enough, in all conscience : but one contributor—it was " Lucas Malet "—managed to make it clear that English fiction has a character to lose. " If there is one thing," she said, " which as a nation we understand, it is *out-of-doors* by land and sea." Heaven forbid that, with only one Atlantic between me and Mr. W. D. Howells, I should enlarge upon any merit of the English novel : but I do suggest that this open-air quality is a characteristic worth preserving, and that nothing is so likely to efface it as the talk of workshops. It is worth preserving because it tends to keep us in sight of the elemental facts of human nature. After all, men and women depend for existence on the earth and on the sky that makes earth fertile ; and man's last act will be, as it was his first, to till the soil. All empires, cities, tumults, civil and religious wars, are transitory in comparison. The slow toil of the farm-laborer, the endurance of the seaman, outlast them all.

That studio-talk tends to deaden this sense *Open Air* of the open-air is just as certain. It runs not *in Criticism.* upon Nature, but upon the presentation of Nature. I am almost ready to assert that it injures a critic as surely as it spoils a creative writer. Certainly I remember that the finest appreciation of Carlyle—a man whom every critic among English-speaking races had picked to pieces and discussed and reconstructed a score of times—was left to be uttered by an inspired loafer in Camden, New Jersey. I love to read of Whitman dropping the newspaper that told him of Carlyle's illness, and walking out under the stars—

" Every star dilated, more vitreous, larger than usual. Not as in some clear nights when the larger stars entirely outshine the rest. Every little star or cluster just as distinctly visible and just as high. Berenice's hair showing every gem, and new ones. To the north-east and north the Sickle, the Goat and Kids, Cassiopeia, Castor and Pollux, and the two Dippers. While through the whole of this silent indescribable show, inclosing and bathing my whole receptivity, ran the thought of Carlyle dying."

226

In such a mood and place—not in a club
after a dinner unearned by exercise—a man is
likely, if ever, to utter great criticism as well as
to conceive great poems. It is from such a
mood and place that we may consider the following fine passage fitly to issue :—

> " The way to test how much he has left his country
> were to consider, or try to consider, for a moment the
> array of British thought, the resultant *ensemble* of the
> last fifty years, as existing to-day, *but with Carlyle left
> out.* It would be like an army with no artillery. The
> show were still a gay and rich one—Byron, Scott, Ten-
> nyson, and many more—horsemen and rapid infantry,
> and banners flying—but the last heavy roar so dear to
> the ear of the trained soldier, and that settles fate and
> victory, would be lacking."

For critic and artist, as for their fellow-
creatures, I believe an open-air life to be the
best possible. And that is why I am glad to
read in certain newspaper paragraphs that Mr.
Gilbert Parker is at this moment on the wide
seas, and bound for Quebec, where he starts to
collect material for a new series of short stories.
His voyage will loose him, in all likelihood,
from the little he retains of club art.

Of course, a certain proportion of our novelists must write of town life: and to do this

fitly they must live in town. But they must study in the town itself, not in a club. Before anyone quotes Dickens against me, let him reflect, first on the immensity of Dickens' genius, and next on the conditions under which Dickens studied London. If every book be a part of its writer's autobiography I invite the youthful author who now passes his evenings in swapping views about Art with his fellow cockneys to pause and reflect if he is indeed treading in Dickens' footsteps or stands in any path likely to lead him to results such as Dickens achieved.

EXCURSIONISTS IN POETRY

BESIDES the glorious exclusiveness of it, Nov. 5, 1892. there is a solid advantage just now, in not An Itinerary. being an aspirant for the Laureateship. You can go out into the wilderness for a week without troubling to leave an address. A week or so back I found with some difficulty a friend who even in his own judgment has no claim to the vacant office, and we set out together across Dartmoor, Exmoor, the Quantocks, by eccentric paths over the southern ranges of Wales to the Wye, and homewards by canoe between the autumn banks of that river. The motto of the voyage was Verlaine's line—

" Et surtout ne parlons pas littérature "

—especially poetry. I think we felt inclined to congratulate each other after passing the Quantocks in heroic silence ; but were content to read respect in each other's eyes.

On our way home we fell across a casual

copy of the *Globe* newspaper, and picked up a scrap of information about the Blorenge, a mountain we had climbed three days before. It is (said the *Globe*) the only thing in the world that rhymes with orange. From this we inferred that the Laureate had not been elected during our wanderings, and that the Anglo-Saxon was still taking an interest in poetry. It was so.

Public Excursions in Verse. The progress of this amusing epidemic may be traced in the *Times*. It started mildly and decorously with the death of a politician. The writer of Lord Sherbrooke's obituary notice happened to remember and transcribe the rather flat epigram beginning—

" Here lie the bones of Robert Lowe,
  Where he's gone to I don't know. . . ."

with Lowe's own Latin translation of the same. At once the *Times* was flooded with other versions by people who remembered the lines more or less imperfectly, who had clung each to his own version since childhood, who doubted if the epigram were originally written on Lord Sherbrooke, who had seen it on an eighteenth-century tombstone in several parts of England, and so on. London Correspondents took up the game and carried it into the provincial press. Then country clergymen bustled up and tried to recall the exact rendering; while others who had never heard of the epigram waxed emulous and produced translations of their own, with the Latin of which the local compositor made sport after his kind. For weeks there continued quite a pretty rivalry among these decaying scholars.

The gentle thunders of this controversy had scarcely died down when the *Times* quoted a four-lined epigram about Mr. Leech making a speech, and Mr. Parker making something darker that was dark enough without; and another respectable profession, which hitherto had remained cold, began to take fire and dispute with ardor. The Church, the Legislature, the Bar, were all excited by this time. They strained on the verge of surpassing feats, should the occasion be given. From men in this mood the occasion is rarely withheld. Lord Tennyson died. He had written at Cambridge a prize poem on Timbuctoo. Somebody else, at Cambridge or elsewhere, had also written about Timbuctoo and a Cassowary that ate a mission-

ary with his this and his that and his hymn-
book too.   Who was this somebody ?   Did he
write it at Cambridge (home of poets) ?   And
what were the "trimmings," as Mr. Job Trot-
ter would say, with which the missionary was
eaten ?

Poetry was in the air by this time.   It would
seem that those treasures which the great Laureate had kept close were by his death unlocked
and spread over England, even to the most
unexpected corners.   "All have got the seed,"
and already a dozen gentlemen were busily
growing the flower in the daily papers.   It was
not to be expected that our senators, barristers,
stockbrokers, having proved their strength,
would stop short at Timbuctoo and the Cassowary.   Very soon a bold egregious wether
jumped the fence into the Higher Criticism,
and gave us a new and amazing interpretation
of the culminating line in *Crossing the Bar*.
The whole flock was quick upon his heels.
" Allow me to remind the readers of your valuable paper that there are *two* kinds of pilot "
is the sentence that now catches our eyes as we
open the *Times*.   And according to the *Globe*
if you need a rhyme for orange you must use

Blorenge.   And the press exists to supply the
real wants of the public.*

They talk of decadence.   But who will deny
the future to a race capable of producing, on
the one hand, *Crossing the Bar*—and on the
other, this comment upon it, signed "T. F.
W." and sent to the *Times* from Cambridge,
October 27th, 1892?—

". . . a poet so studious of fitness of language as
Tennyson would hardly, I suspect, have thrown off such
words on such an occasion haphazard.   If the analogy
is to be inexorably criticised, may it not be urged that,
having in his mind not the mere passage 'o'er life's
solemn main,' which we all are taking, with or without
reflection, but the near approach to an unexplored

* *Note*, Oct. 21, 1893.—The nuisance revived again when
Mr. Nettleship the younger perished on Mont Blanc.   And
again, the friend of Lowe and Nettleship, the great Master
of Balliol, had hardly gone to his grave before a dispute
arose, not only concerning his parentage (about which any
man might have certified himself at the smallest expense
of time and trouble), but over an unusually pointless epigram that was made at Cambridge many years ago, and
neither on him, nor on his father, but on an entirely
different Jowett, *Semper ego auditor tantum?*—

If a funny "Cantab" write a dozen funny rhymes,
Need a dozen "Cantabs" write about it to the *Times?*
Need they write, at any rate, a generation after,
Stating cause and date of joke and reasons for their laughter?

ocean beyond it, he was mentally assigning to the pilot
in whom his confidence was fast the *status* of the navi-
gator of old days, the sailing-master, on whose knowledge
and care crews and captains engaged in expeditions
alike relied ? Columbus himself married the daughter
of such a man, *un piloto Italiano famoso navigante*.
Camoens makes the people of Mozambique offer Vasco
da Gama a *piloto* by whom his fleet shall be deftly
(*sabiamente*) conducted across the Indian Ocean. In
the following century (1520–30) Sebastian Cabot, then
in the service of Spain, commanded a squadron which
was to pass through the Straits of Magellan to the Mo-
luccas, having been appointed by Charles V. Grand
Pilot of Castile. The French still call the mates of
merchant vessels — that is, the officers who watch
about, take charge of the deck—*pilotes*, and this desig-
nation is not impossibly reserved to them as representing
the *pilote hauturier* of former times, the scientific guide
of ships *dans la haute mer*, as distinguished from the
pilote côtier, who simply hugged the shore. The last
class of pilot, it is almost superfluous to observe, is still
with us and does take our ships, inwards or outwards,
across the bar, if there be one, and does no more. The
hauturier has long been replaced in all countries by the
captain, and it must be within the experience of some
of us that when outward bound the captain as often as
not has been the last man to come on board. We did
not meet him until the ship, which until his arrival was
in the hands of the *côtier*, was well out of harbour. Then
our *côtier* left us."

Prodigious !

234

THE POPULAR CONCEP-
TION OF A POET

WHAT seems to me chiefly remarkable in
the popular conception of a Poet is its
unlikeness to the truth.   Misconception in this
case has been flattered, I fear, by the poets
themselves :—

" The poet in a golden clime was born,
    With golden stars above ;
Dowered with the hate of hate, the scorn of scorn,
    The love of love.
He saw thro' life and death, thro' good and ill ;
He saw thro' his own soul.
The marvel of the Everlasting Will,
    An open scroll,
Before him lay. . . ."

I should be sorry to vex any poet's mind
with my shallow wit ; but this passage always
reminds me of the delusions of the respectable
Glendower :—

" At my birth
The frame and huge foundation of the earth
Shak'd like a coward."

June 24,
1893.
March 3,
1894.
In what
respect
Remark-
able.

235

—and Hotspur's interpretation (slightly petulant, to be sure), " Why, so it would have done at the time if your mother's cat had but kittened, though you yourself had never been born." I protest that I reverence poetry and the poets : but at the risk of being warned off the holy ground as a " dark-browed sophist," must declare my plain opinion that the above account of the poet's birth and native gifts does not consist with fact.

Yet it consents with the popular notion, which you may find presented or implied month by month and week by week, in the reviews ; and even day by day—for it has found its way into the newspapers. Critics have observed that considerable writers fall into two classes—

Two lines of Poetic Development.

(1) Those who start with their heads full of great thoughts, and are from the first occupied rather with their matter than with the manner of expressing it.

(2) Those who begin with the love of expression and intent to be artists in words, *and come through expression to profound thought.*

236

Now, for some reason it is fashionable just now to account Class 1 the more respectable; a judgment to which, considering that Virgil and Shakespeare belong to Class 2, I refuse my assent. It is fashionable to construct an imaginary figure out of the characteristics of Class 1, and set him up as the Typical Poet. *The Popular Type.* The poet at whose nativity Tennyson assists in the above verses of course belongs to Class 1. A babe so richly dowered can hardly help his matter overcrowding his style; at least, to start with.

But this is not all. A poet who starts with this tremendous equipment can hardly help being something too much for the generation in which he is born. Consequently, the Typical Poet is misunderstood by his contemporaries, and probably persecuted. In his own age his is a voice crying in the wilderness; in the wilderness he speeds the "viewless arrows of his thought"; which fly far, and take root as they strike earth, and blossom; and so Truth multiplies, and in the end (most likely after his death) the Typical Poet comes by his own.

Such is the popular conception of the Typi-

cal Poet, and I observe that it fascinates even
educated people. I have in mind the recent
unveiling of Mr. Onslow Ford's Shelley Me-
morial at University College, Oxford. Those
who assisted at that ceremony were for the
most part men and women of high culture.
Excesses such as affable Members of Parliament commit when distributing school prizes
or opening free public libraries were clearly out
of the question. Yet even here, and almost
within the shadow of Bodley's great library,
speaker after speaker assumed as axiomatic this
curious fallacy — that a Poet is necessarily a
thinker in advance of his age, and therefore
peculiarly liable to persecution at the hands of
his contemporaries.

How sup-
ported by
History.

But logic, I believe, still flourishes in Oxford ;
and induction still has its rules. Now, however many different persons Homer may have
been, I cannot remember that one of him suffered martyrdom, or even discomfort, on account of his radical doctrine. I seem to remember that Æschylus enjoyed the esteem of
his fellow-citizens, sided with the old aristocratic party, and lived long enough to find his
own tragedies considered archaic ; that Soph-

238

ocles, towards the end of a very prosperous life, was charged with senile decay and consequent inability to administer his estates—two infirmities which even his accusers did not seek to connect with advanced thinking; and that Euripides, though a technical innovator, stood hardly an inch ahead of the fashionable dialectic of his day, and suffered only from the ridicule of his comic contemporaries and the disdain of his wife — misfortunes incident to the most respectable. Pindar and Virgil were court favorites, repaying their patrons in golden song. Dante, indeed, suffered banishment; but his banishment was just a move in a political (or rather a family) game. Petrarch and Ariosto were not uncomfortable in their generations. Chaucer and Shakespeare lived happy lives and sang in the very key of their own times. Puritanism waited for its hour of triumph to produce its great poet, who lived unmolested when the hour of triumph passed and that of reprisals succeeded. Racine was a royal pensioner; Goethe a chamberlain and the most admired figure of his time. Of course, if you hold that these poets one and all pale their ineffectual fires before the radiant Shelley, our argument must go a few steps farther back. I

239

have instanced them as acknowledged kings of song.

The Case of Tennyson. Tennyson was not persecuted. He was not (and more honor to him for his clearness) even misunderstood. I have never met with the contention that he stood an inch ahead of the thought of his time. As for seeing through death and life and his own soul, and having the marvel of the everlasting will spread before him like an open scroll,—well, to begin with, I doubt if these things ever happened to any man. Heaven surely has been, and is, more reticent than the verse implies. But if they ever happened, Tennyson most certainly was not the man they happened to. What Tennyson actually sang, till he taught himself to sing better, was:—

> " Airy, fairy Lilian,
>   Flitting fairy Lilian,
>   When I ask her if she love me,
>   Claps her tiny hands above me,
>   Laughing all she can ;
>   She'll not tell me if she love me,
>   Cruel little Lilian."

There is not much of the scorn of scorn, or the love of love, or the open scroll of the everlasting will, about *Cruel Little Lilian*. But there *is* a distinct striving after style—a striving that, as everyone knows, ended in mastery: and through style Tennyson reached such heights of thought as he was capable of. To the end his thought remained inferior to his style: and to the end the two in him were separable, whereas in poets of the very first rank they are inseparable. But that towards the end his style lifted his thought to heights of which even *In Memoriam* gave no promise cannot, I think, be questioned by any student of his collected works.

Tennyson belongs, if ever poet belonged, to Class 2 : and it is the prettiest irony of fate that, having unreasonably belauded Class 1, he is now being found fault with for not conforming to the supposed requirements of that Class. He, who spoke of the poet as of a seër " through life and death," is now charged with seeing but a short way beyond his own nose. The Rev. Stopford Brooke finds that he had little sympathy with the aspirations of the struggling poor ; that he bore himself coldly towards the burning questions of the hour ; that, in short, he stood anywhere but in advance of his age. As if plenty of people were not interested in these things ! Why, I cannot step out into the street without running against somebody who is in advance of the times on some point or another.

Of Virgil and Shakespeare.

Virgil and Shakespeare were neither martyrs nor preachers despised in their generation. I have said that as poets they also belong to Class 2. Will a champion of the Typical Poet (new style) dispute this, and argue that Virgil and Shakespeare, though they escaped persecution, yet began with matter that overweighted their style—with deep stuttered thoughts—in fine, with a Message to their Time? I think that view can hardly be maintained. We have the *Eclogues* before the *Æneid ;* and *The Comedy of Errors* before *As You Like It.* Expression comes first ; and through expression, thought. These are the greatest names, or of the greatest : and they belong to Class 2.

Of Milton.

Again, no English poetry is more thoroughly informed with thought than Milton's Did he find big thoughts hustling within him for utterance? And did he at an early age stutter in numbers till his oppressed soul found relief? And was it thus that he attained the glorious manner of

"Seasons return, but not to me returns
    Day, or the sweet approach of even or morn. . . ."

—and so on. No, to be short, it was not. At the age of twenty-four, or thereabouts, he deliberately proposed to himself to be a great poet. To this end he practised and studied, and travelled unweariedly until his thirty-first year. Then he tried to make up his mind what to write about. He took some sheets of paper —they are to be seen at this day in the Library of Trinity College, Cambridge—and set down no less than ninety-nine subjects for his proposed *magnum opus*, before he could decide upon *Paradise Lost*. To be sure, when the *magnum opus* was written it fetched £5 only. But even this does not prove that Milton was before his age. Perhaps he was behind it. *Paradise Lost* appeared in 1667: in 1657 it might have fetched considerably more than £5.

If the Typical Poet have few points in common with Shakespeare or Milton, I fear that the Typical Poet begins to be in a bad way.

Shall we try Coleridge? He had " great thoughts "—thousands of them. On the other hand, he never had the slightest difficulty in

Of Coleridge.

uttering them, in prose. His great achievements in verse—his *Genevieve*, his *Christabel*,
his *Kubla Khan*, his *Ancient Mariner*—are
achievements of expression. When they appeal
from the senses to the intellect their appeal is
usually quite simple.

> " He prayeth best who loveth best
>   All things both great and small."

No, I am afraid Coleridge is not the Typical
Poet.

On the whole I suspect the Typical Poet to
be a hasty generalization from Shelley.

POETS ON THEIR OWN ART

May 11, 1895.
A Prelude to Poetry.

" TO those who love the poets most, who care most for their ideals, this little book ought to be the one indispensable book of devotion, the *credo* of the poetic faith." " This little book " is the volume with which Mr. Ernest Rhys prefaces the pretty series of Lyrical Poets which he is editing for Messrs. Dent & Co. He calls it *The Prelude to Poetry*, and in it he has brought together the most famous arguments stated from time to time by the English poets in defence and praise of their own art. Sidney's magnificent " Apologie " is here, of course, and two passages from Ben Jonson's " Discoveries," Wordsworth's preface to the second edition of " Lyrical Ballads," the fourteenth chapter of the " Biographia Literaria," and Shelley's " Defence."

What admirable prose these poets write!

Southey, to be sure, is not represented in this volume. Had he written at length upon his art—in spite of his confession that, when writing prose, "of what is now called style not a thought enters my head at any time"—we may be sure the reflection would have been even more obvious than it is. But without him this small collection makes out a splendid case against all that has been said in disparagement of the prose style of poets. Let us pass what Hazlitt said of Coleridge's prose ; or rather let us quote it once again for its vivacity, and so pass on—

"One of his (Coleridge's) sentences winds its 'forlorn way obscure' over the page like a patriarchal procession with camels laden, wreathed turbans, household wealth, the whole riches of the author's mind poured out upon the barren waste of his subject. The palm tree spreads its sterile branches overhead, and the land of promise is seen in the distance."

All this is very neatly malicious, and particularly the last co-ordinate sentence. But in the chapter chosen by Mr. Rhys from the " Biographia Literaria " Coleridge's prose is seen at its best—obedient, pertinent, at once imaginative and restrained—as in the conclusion—

" Finally, good sense is the body of poetic genius, fancy its drapery, motion its life, and imagination the soul that is everywhere, and in each ; and forms all into one graceful and intelligent whole."

The prose of Sidney's *Apologie* is Sidney's best ; and when that has been said, nothing remains but to economize in quoting. I will take three specimens only. First then, for beauty :—

" Nature never set forth the earth in so rich tapistry, as divers Poets have done, neither with plesant rivers, fruitful trees, sweet-smelling flowers : nor whatsoever else may make the too much loved earth more lovely. Her world is brasen, the Poets only deliver a golden : but let those things alone and goe to man, for whom as the other things are, so it seemeth in him her uttermost cunning is imployed, and know whether shee have brought forth so true a lover as *Theagines*, so constant a friende as *Pilades*, so valiant a man as *Orlando*, so right a Prince as *Xenophon's Cyrus ;* so excellent a man every way as *Virgil's Aeneas.* . . ."

Next for wit—roguishness, if you like the term better :—

" And therefore, if *Cato* misliked *Fulvius*, for carrying *Ennius* with him to the field, it may be answered, that if *Cato* misliked it, the noble *Fulvius* liked it, or else he had not done it."

And lastly for beauty and wit combined :—

247

" For he (the Poet) doth not only show the way, but giveth so sweete a prospect into the way, as will intice any man to enter into it. Nay he doth, as if your journey should lye through a fayre Vineyard, at the first give you a cluster of Grapes : that full of that taste, you may long to passe further. He beginneth not with obscure definitions, which must blur the margent with interpretations, and load the memory with doubtfulnesse : but he cometh to you with words set in delightful proportion, either accompanied with or prepared for the well inchanting skill of Musicke : and with a tale forsooth he cometh unto you : with a tale which holdeth children from play, and old men from the chimney corner."

" Is not this a glorious way to talk ? " demanded the Rev. T. E. Brown of this last passage, when he talked about Sidney, the other day, in Mr. Henley's *New Review*. " No one can fail," said Mr. Brown, amiably assuming the fineness of his own ear to be common to all mankind—" no one can fail to observe the sweetness and the strength, the outspokenness, the downrightness, and, at the same time, the nervous delicacy of pausation, the rhythm all ripple and suspended fall, the dainty *but*, the daintier *and forsooth*, as though the pouting of a proud reserve curved the fine lip of him, and had to be atoned for by the homeliness of *the chimney-corner*."

Everybody admires Sidney's prose. But how of this?—

" Poetry is the breath and finer spirit of all knowledge ; it is the impassioned expression which is in the countenance of all science. Emphatically it may be said of the Poet, as Shakespeare has said of man, ' that he looks before and after.' He is the rock of defence of human nature ; an upholder and preserver, carrying everywhere with him relationship and love. In spite of difference of soil and climate, of language and manners, of laws and customs, *in spite of things silently gone out of mind, and things violently destroyed*, the Poet binds together by passion and knowledge the vast empire of human society, as it is spread over the whole earth, and over all time."

It is Wordsworth who speaks—too rhetorically, perhaps. At any rate, the prose will not compare with Sidney's. But it is good prose, nevertheless ; and the phrase I have ventured to italicise is superb.

As might be expected, the poets in this volume agree in pride of their calling. We have just listened to Wordsworth. Shelley quotes Tasso's proud sentence—" Non c'è in mondo chi merita nome di creatore, se non Iddio ed il Poeta " : and himself says, ' The jury which sits in judgment upon a poet, belonging as he

Their high claims for Poesy.

249

does to all time, must be composed of his peers : it must be impanelled by Time from the selectest of the wise of many generations.'' Sidney exalts the poet above the historian and the philosopher ; and Coleridge asserts that "no man was ever yet a great poet without being at the same time a profound philosopher.'' Ben Jonson puts it characteristically : " Every beggarly corporation affords the State a mayor or two bailiffs yearly ; but *Solus rex, aut poeta, non quotannis nascitur*.'' The longer one lives, the more cause one finds to rejoice that different men have different ways of saying the same thing.

Inspiration not Improvisation. The agreement of all these poets on some other matters is more remarkable. Most of them claim *inspiration* for the great practitioners of their art ; but wonderful is the unanimity with which they dissociate this from *improvisation*. They are sticklers for the rules of the game. The Poet does not pour his full heart

" In profuse strains of *unpremeditated* art."

On the contrary, his rapture is the sudden result of long premeditation. The first and most conspicuous lesson of this volume seems to be that Poetry is an *art*, and therefore has rules. Next after this, one is struck with the careful-ness with which these practitioners, when it comes to theory, stick to their Aristotle.

For instance, they are practically unanimous in accepting Aristotle's contention that it is not the metrical form that makes the poem. "Verse," says Sidney, " is an ornament and no cause to poetry, since there have been many most excellent poets that never versified, and now swarm many versifiers that need never answer to the name of poets." Wordsworth apologizes for using the word " Poetry " as syn-onymous with metrical composition. "Much confusion," he says, "has been introduced into criticism by this contradistinction of Poetry and Prose, instead of the more philo-sophical one of Poetry and Matter of Fact or Science. The only strict antithesis to Prose is Metre : nor is this, in truth, a *strict* anti-thesis, because lines and passages of metre so naturally occur in writing prose that it would be scarcely possible to avoid them, even were it desirable." And Shelley—"It is by no means essential that a poet should accom-

Poetry not mere Met-rical Com-position.

251

modate his language to this traditional form, so that the harmony, which is its spirit, be observed. . . . The distinction between poets and prose writers is a vulgar error.'' Shelley goes on to instance Plato and Bacon as true poets, though they wrote in prose. '' The popular division into prose and verse,'' he repeats, '' is inadmissible in accurate philosophy.'' Then again, upon what Wordsworth calls '' the more philosophical distinction '' between Poetry and Matter of Fact—quoting, *Its philo-sophic function.* of course, the famous '' Φιλοσοφώτερον καὶ σπουδαιότερον '' passage in the *Poetics*—it is wonderful with what hearty consent our poets pounce upon this passage, and paraphrase it, and expand it, as the great justification of their art : which indeed it is. Sidney gives the passage at length. Wordsworth writes, '' Aristotle, I have been told, hath said that Poetry is the most philosophic of all writings : it is so.'' Coleridge quotes Sir John Davies, who wrote of Poesy (surely with an eye on the *Poetics*) :

> '' From their gross matter she abstracts their forms,
>   And draws a kind of quintessence from things ;
> Which to her proper nature she transforms
>   To bear them light on her celestial wings.

" Thus does she, when from individual states
    She doth abstract the universal kinds ;
Which then reclothed in divers names and fates
    Steal access through our senses to our minds."

And Shelley has a remarkable paraphrase, ending, " The story of particular facts is as a mirror which obscures and distorts that which should be beautiful : poetry is a mirror which makes beautiful that which is distorted."

In fine, this book goes far to prove of poetry, as it has been proved over and over again of other arts, that it is the men big enough to break the rules who accept and observe them most cheerfully.

THE ATTITUDE OF THE PUBLIC TOWARDS LETTERS

Sept. 29, 1894.
The " Great Heart" of the Public.

I OBSERVE that our hoary friend, the Great Heart of the Public, has been taking his annual outing in September. Thanks to the German Emperor and the new head of the House of Orleans, he has had the opportunity of a stroll through the public press arm in arm with his old crony and adversary, the Divine Right of Kings. And the two have gone once more a-roaming by the light of the moon, to drop a tear, perchance, on the graves of the Thin End of the Wedge and the Stake in the Country. You know the unhappy story?— how the Wedge drove its thin end into the Stake, with fatal results: and how it died of remorse and was buried at the cross-roads with the Stake in its inside! It is a pathetic tale, and the Great Heart of the Public can always be trusted to discriminate true pathos from false.

It was Mr. G. B. Burgin, in the September number of the *Idler*, who let the Great Heart loose this time—unwittingly, I am sure ; for Mr. Burgin, when he thinks for himself (as he usually does), writes sound sense and capital English.   But in the service of Journalism Mr. Burgin called on Miss Marie Corelli, the authoress of *Barabbas,* and asked what she thought of the value of criticism.   Miss Corelli " idealised the subject by the poetic manner in which she mingled tea and criticism together." She said—

Miss Marie Corelli's Opinion of it.

" I think authors do not sufficiently bear in mind the important fact that, in this age of ours, the public *thinks for itself* much more extensively than we give it credit for. It is a cultured public, and its great brain is fully capable of deciding things. It rather objects to be treated like a child and told ' what to read and what to avoid ' ; and, moreover, we must not fail to note that it mistrusts criticism generally, and seldom reads ' reviews.'   And why? Simply because it recognises the existence of ' logrolling.'   It is perfectly aware, for instance, that Mr. Theodore Watts is logroller-in-chief to Mr. Swinburne ; that Mr. Le Gallienne ' rolls' greatly for Mr. Norman Gale ; and that Mr. Andrew Lang tumbles his logs along over everything for as many as his humour fits. . . ."

—I don't know the proportion of tea to criticism in all this : but Miss Corelli can hardly be said to " idealise the subject " here :—

". . . The public is the supreme critic ; and though it does not write in the *Quarterly* or the *Nineteenth Century*, it thinks and talks independently of everything and everybody, and on its thought and word alone depends the fate of any piece of literature."

Mr. Hall Caine's View.

Then Mr. Burgin called on Mr. Hall Caine, who " had just finished breakfast." Mr. Hall Caine gave reasons which compelled him to believe that " for good or bad, criticism is a tremendous force." But he, too, confessed that in his opinion the public is the " ultimate critic." " It often happens that the public takes books on trust from the professed guides of literature, but if the books are not *right*, it drops them." And he proceeded to make an observation, with which we may most cordially agree. " I am feeling," he said, " increasingly, day by day, that *rightness* in imaginative writing is more important than subject, or style, or anything else. If a story is right in its theme, and the evolution of its theme, it will live; if it is not right, it will die, whatever its secondary literary qualities."

I say that we may agree with this most cordially : and it need not cost us much to own that the public is the "ultimate critic," if we mean no more than this, that, since the public holds the purse, it rests ultimately with the public to buy, or neglect to buy, an author's books.   That, surely, is obvious enough without the aid of fine language.   But if Mr. Hall Caine mean that the public, without instruction from its betters, is the best judge of a book ; if he consent with Miss Corelli that the general public is a cultured public with a great brain, and by the exercise of that great brain approves itself an infallible judge of the rightness or wrongness of a book, then I would respectfully ask for evidence.   The poets and critics of his time united in praising Campion as a writer of lyrics : the Great Brain and Heart of the Public neglected him utterly for three centuries : then a scholar and critic arose and persuaded the public that Campion was a great lyrical writer : and now the public accepts him as such.   Shall we say, then, the Great Heart of the Public is the "ultimate judge" of Campion's lyrics ?   Perhaps : but we might as well praise for his cleanliness a boy who has been held under the pump.   When Martin Farquhar Tupper wrote, the Great Heart of the Public

In what sense the Public is the "Ultimate Critic."

257

expanded towards him at once. The public bought his effusions by tens of thousands. Gradually the small voice of skilled criticism made itself heard, and the public grew ashamed of itself; and, at length, laughed at Tupper. Shall we, then, call the public the ultimate judge of Tupper? Perhaps: but we might as well praise the continence of a man who turns in disgust from drink on the morning after a drunken fit. *

* In a private letter, from which I am allowed to quote, Mr. Hall Caine (October 2nd, 1894) explains and (as I think) amends his position :—"If I had said *time* instead of *the public*, I should have expressed myself exactly. It is impossible for me to work up any enthusiasm for the service done to literature by criticism as a whole. I have, no doubt, the unenviable advantage over you of having wasted three mortal months in reading all the literary criticism extant of the first quarter of this century. It would be difficult to express my sense of its imbecility, its blundering, and its bad passions. But the good books it assailed are not lost, and the bad ones it glorified do not survive. It is not that the public has been the better judge, but that good work has the seeds of life, while bad work carries with it the seeds of dissolution. This is the key to the story of Wordsworth on the one hand, and to the story of Tupper on the other. Tupper did not topple down because James Hannay smote him. Fifty James Hannays had shouted him up before. And if there had not been a growing sense that the big mountain was a mockery, five hundred James Hannays would not have brought it down. The truth is that it is not the ' critic

The proposition that the Man in the Street is a better judge of literature than the Critic— the man who knows little than the man who knows more—wears (to my mind, at least) a slightly imbecile air on the face of it. It also appears to me that people are either confusing thought or misusing language when they confer the title of " supreme critic " on the last person to be persuaded. And, again, what is " the public ? " I gather that Miss Corelli's story of *Barabbas* has had an immense popular success. *What is " The Public " ?*

who knows ' or the public which does not know that determines the ultimate fate of a book—the immediate fate they may both influence. The book must do that for itself. If it is right, it lives ; if it is wrong, it dies. And the critic who re-establishes a neglected poet is merely articulating the growing sense. There have always been a few good critics, thank God . . . but the finest critic is the untutored sentiment of the public, not of to-day or to-morrow or the next day, but of all days together—a sentiment which tells if a thing is right or wrong by holding on to it or letting it drop."

Of course, I agree that a book must ultimately depend for its fate upon its own qualities. But when Mr. Hall Caine talks of " a growing sense," I ask, In whom does this sense first grow ? And I answer, In the cultured few who enforce it upon the many—as in this very case of Wordsworth. And I hold the credit of the result (apart from the author's share) belongs rather to those few persistent advocates than to those judges who are only " ultimate " in the sense that they are the last to be convinced.

But so, I believe, has the *Deadwood Dick* series of penny dreadfuls. And the gifted author of *Deadwood Dick* may console himself (as I daresay he does) for the neglect of the critics by the thought that the Great Brain * of the Public is the supreme judge of literature. But obviously he and Miss Corelli will not have the same Public in their mind. If for "the Great Brain of the Public" we substitute "the Great Brain of that Part of the Public which subscribes to Mudie's," we may lose something of impressiveness, but we shall at least know what we are talking about.

June 17, 1893. Mr. Gosse's View.

Astounding as the statement must appear to any constant reader of the Monthly Reviews, it is mainly because Mr. Gosse happens to be a man of letters that his opinion upon literary questions is worth listening to. In his new book † he discusses a dozen or so : and one of

---

* If the reader object that I am using the Great Heart and Great Brain of the Public as interchangeable terms, I would refer him to Mr. Du Maurier's famous Comic Alphabet, letter Z :—

"Z is a Zoophyte, whose heart's in his head,
And whose head's in his tum—rudimentary Z !"

† *Questions at Issue:* by Edmund Gosse. London: William Heinemann.

them — the question, "What Influence has Democracy upon Literature?"—not only has a chapter to itself, but seems to lie at the root of all the rest. I may add that Mr. Gosse's answer is a trifle gloomy.

"As we filed slowly out of the Abbey on the afternoon of Wednesday, the 12th of October, 1892, there must have occurred to others, I think, as to myself, a whimsical and half - terrifying sense of the symbolic contrast between what we had left and what we had emerged upon. Inside, the grey and vitreous atmosphere, the reverberations of music moaning somewhere out of sight, the bones and monuments of the noble dead, reverence, antiquity, beauty, rest. Outside, in the raw air, a tribe of hawkers urging upon the edges of a dense and inquisitive crowd a large sheet of pictures of the pursuit of a flea by a 'lady,' and more insidious salesmen doing a brisk trade in what they falsely pretended to be 'Tennyson's last poem.' Next day we read in our newspapers affecting accounts of the emotion displayed by the vast crowd outside the Abbey—horny hands dashing away the tear, seamstresses holding 'the little green volumes' to their faces to hide their agitation. Happy for those who could see these with their fairy telescopes out of the garrets of Fleet Street. I, alas!—though I sought assiduously—could mark nothing of the kind."

Nothing of the kind was there. Why should anything of the kind be there? Her poetry has been one of England's divinest treasures:

261

but of her population a very few understand it;
and the shrine has always been guarded by the
elect who happen to possess, in varying degrees, certain qualities of mind and ear.   It is,
as Mr. Gosse puts it, by a sustained effort of
bluff on the part of these elect that English
poetry is kept upon its high pedestal of hon-
or.   The worship of it as one of the glories
of our birth and state is imposed upon the
masses by a small aristocracy of intelligence
and taste.

Mr. Giss-
ing's Testi-
mony.

What do the "masses" care for poetry?
In an appendix Mr. Gosse prints a letter from
Mr. George Gissing, who, as everyone knows,
has studied the popular mind assiduously, and
with startling results.   Here are a few sentences
from his letter:—

(1) "After fifteen years' observation of the poorer
classes of English folk, chiefly in London and the south,
I am pretty well assured that, whatever civilising agen-
cies may be at work among the democracy, poetry is not
one of them."

(2) "The custodian of a Free Library in a southern
city informs me that 'hardly once in a month' does a
volume of verse pass over his counter; that the excep-
tional applicant (seeking Byron or Longfellow) is generally 'the wife of a tradesman;' and that an offer of

verse to man or woman who comes simply for ' a book ' is invariably rejected ; ' they won't even look at it.' "

(3) " It was needless folly to pretend that, because one or two of Tennyson's poems became largely known through popular recitation, therefore Tennyson was dear to the heart of the people, a subject of their pride whilst he lived, of their mourning when he died. My point is that *no* poet holds this place in the esteem of the English lower orders."

(4) " Some days before (the funeral) I was sitting in a public room, where two men, retired shopkeepers, exchanged an occasional word as they read the morning's news. ' A great deal here about Lord Tennyson ' said one. The ' Lord ' was significant. I listened anxiously for his companion's reply. ' Ah, yes.' The man moved uneasily, and added at once : ' What do you think about this long-distance ride ? ' In that room (I frequented it on successive days with this object) not a syllable did I hear regarding Tennyson save the sentence faithfully recorded."

Mr. Gissing, be it observed, speaks only of the class which he has studied : but in talking of " demos," or, more loosely, of " democracy," we must be careful not to limit these terms to the " lower " and " lower-middle " classes. For Poetry, who draws her priests and warders from all classes of society, is generally beloved of none. The average country magnate, the average church dignitary, the average professional man, the average commer-

Poetry not beloved by any one Class.

cial traveller—to all these she is alike unknown : at least, the insensibility of each is differentiated by shades so fine that we need not trouble ourselves to make distinctions. A public school and university education does as little for the Squire Westerns one meets at country dinnertables as a three-guinea subscription to a circulating library for the kind of matron one comes upon at a *table d'hôte*. Five minutes after hearing the news of Browning's death I stopped an acquaintance in the street, a professional man of charming manner, and repeated it to him. He stared for a moment, and then murmured that he was sorry to hear it. Clearly he did not wish to hurt my feelings by confessing that he hadn't the vaguest idea who Browning might be. And if anybody think this an extreme case, let him turn to the daily papers and read the names of those who were at Newmarket on that same afternoon when our great poet was laid in the Abbey with every pretence of national grief. The pursuit of one horse by another is doubtless a more elevating spectacle than " the pursuit of a flea by a ' lady,' " but on that afternoon even a tepid lover of letters must have found an equal incongruity in both entertainments.

I do not say that the General Public hates
Poetry. But I say that those who care about it
are few, and those who know about it are fewer.
Nor do these assert their right of interference
as often as they might. Just once or twice in
the last ten or fifteen years they have pulled up
some exceptionally coarse weed on which the
General Public had every disposition to graze,
and have pitched it over the hedge to Lethe
wharf, to root itself and fatten there ; and terrible as those of Polydorus have been the shrieks
of the avulsed root. But as a rule they have
sat and piped upon the stile and considered the
good cow grazing, confident that in the end she
must " bite off more than she can chew."

Still, the aristocracy of letters exists : and in *The " Out-*
it, if nowhere else, titles, social advantages, and *siders."*
commercial success alike count for nothing ;
while Royalty itself sits in the Court of the
Gentiles. And I am afraid we must include
in the crowd not only those affable politicians
who from time to time open a Public Library
and oblige us with their views upon literature,
little realizing what Hecuba is to them, and
still less what they are to Hecuba, but also
those affable teachers of religion, philosophy,

and science, who condescend occasionally to
amble through the garden of the Muses, and
rearrange its labels for us while drawing our attention to the rapid deterioration of the flower-
beds. The author of *The Citizen of the World*
once compared the profession of letters in England to a Persian army, "where there are many
pioneers, several suttlers, numberless servants,
women and children in abundance, and but
few soldiers." Were he alive to-day he would
be forced to include the Volunteers.

A CASE OF BOOKSTALL CENSORSHIP

March 16, 1895.

The "Woman Who Did," and Mr. Eason who wouldn't.

" In the romantic little town of 'Ighbury,
My father kept a Succulating Libary . . . "

—and, I regret to say, gave himself airs on the strength of it.

The persons in my instructive little story are—

H.H. Prince Francis of Teck.

Mr. Grant Allen, author of *The Woman Who Did.*

Mr. W. T. Stead, Editor of *The Review of Reviews.*

Messrs. Eason & Son, booksellers and newsvendors, possessing on the railways of Ireland a monopoly similar to that enjoyed by Messrs. W. H. Smith & Son on the railways of Great Britain.

Mr. James O'Hara, of 18, Cope Street, Dublin.

A Clerk.

Now, on the appearance of Mr. Grant Allen's *The Woman Who Did*, Mr. Stead conceived the desire of criticising it as the "Book of the Month" in *The Review of Reviews* for February, 1895. He strongly dissents from the doctrine of *The Woman Who Did*, and he also believes that the book indicts, and goes far to destroy, its own doctrine. This opinion, I may say, is shared by many critics. He says "Wedlock is to Mr. Grant Allen *Nehushtan*. And the odd thing about it is that the net effect of the book which he has written with his heart's blood to destroy this said *Nehushtan* can hardly fail to strengthen the foundation of reasoned conviction upon which marriage rests." And again—"Those who do not know the author, but who take what I must regard as the saner view of the relations of the sexes, will rejoice at what might have been a potent force for evil has been so strangely overruled as to become a reinforcement of the garrison defending the citadel its author desires so ardently to overthrow. From the point of view of the fervent apostle of Free Love, this is a Boomerang of a Book."

Believing this—that the book would be its

own best antidote—Mr. Stead epitomized it in
his *Review*, printed copious extracts, and wound
up by indicating his own views and what he
deemed the true moral of the discussion. The
Review was published and, so far as Messrs.
W. H. Smith & Son were concerned, passed
without comment. But to the Editor's surprise (he tells the story in the *Westminster
Gazette* of the 2nd inst.), no sooner was it
placed on the market in Ireland than he received word that every copy had been recalled
from the bookstalls, and that Messrs. Eason
had refused to sell a single copy. On tele-
graphing for more information, Mr. Stead was
sent the following letter :—

" DEAR SIR,—Allen's book is an avowed defence of
Free Love, and a direct attack upon the Christian view
of marriage. Mr. Stead criticises Allen's views ad-
versely, but we do not think the antidote can destroy
the ill-effects of the poison, and we decline to be made
the vehicle for the distribution of attacks upon the most
fundamental institution of the Christian state.—Yours
faithfully,   ——."

Mr. Stead thereupon wrote to the managing
Director of Messrs. Eason & Son, and received
this reply :—

" DEAR SIR,—We have considered afresh the character of the February number of your *Review* so far as

it relates to the notice of Grant Allen's book, and we are more and more confirmed in the belief that its influence has been, and is, most pernicious.

"Grant Allen is not much heard of in Ireland, and the laudations you pronounce on him as a writer, so far as we know him, appear wholly unmerited.

"At any rate, he appears in your *Review* as the advocate for Free Love, and it seems to us strange that you should place his work in the exaggerated importance of 'The Book of the Month,' accompanied by eighteen pages of comment and quotation, in which there is a publicity given to the work out of all proportion to its merits.

"I do not doubt that the topic of Free Love engages the attention of the corrupt Londoner. There are plenty of such persons who are only too glad to get the sanction of writers for the maintenance and practice of their evil thoughts, but the purest and best lives in all parts of the field of Christian philanthropy will mourn the publicity you have given to this evil book. It is not even improbable that the perusal of Grant Allen's book, which you have lifted into importance as 'The Book of the Month,' may determine the action of souls to their spiritual ruin.

"The problem of indirect influence is full of mystery, but, as the hour of our departure comes near, the possible consequences to other minds of the example and teaching of our lives may quicken our perceptions, and we may see and deeply regret our actions when not directed by the highest authority, the will of God.—We are, dear Sir, yours very truly (for Eason & Son, Limited),

"CHARLES EASON, Managing Director."

Exception may be taken to this letter on many points, some trivial and some important. Of the trivial points we may note with interest Mr. Eason's assumption that his opinion is wanted on the literary merits of the ware he vends ; and, with concern, the rather slipshod manner in which he allows himself and his assistants to speak of a gentleman as "Allen," or "Grant Allen," without the usual prefix. But no one can fail to see that this is an honest letter—the production of a man conscious of responsibility and struggling to do his best in circumstances he imperfectly understands. Nor do I think this view of Mr. Eason need be seriously modified upon perusal of a letter received by Mr. Stead from a Mr. James O'Hara, of 18, Cope Street, Dublin, and printed in the *Westminster Gazette* of March 11th. Mr. O'Hara writes :—

"DEAR SIR,—The following may interest you and your readers. I was a subscriber to the library owned by C. Eason & Co., Limited, and in December asked them for *Napoleon and the Fair Sex*, by Masson. The librarian informed me Mr. Eason had decided not to circulate it, as it contained improper details, which Mr. Eason considered immoral. A copy was also refused to one of the best-known pressmen in Dublin, a man of mature years and experience.

Mr. Eason in Two Attitudes.

"Three days afterwards I saw a young man ask the librarian for the same book, and Eason's manager presented it to him with a low bow. I remarked on this circumstance to Mr. Charles Eason, who told me that he had issued it to this one subscriber only, because he was Prince Francis of Teck.

"I told him it was likely, from the description he had given me of it, to be more injurious to a young man such as Prince Francis of Teck than to me; but he replied: 'Oh, these high-up people *are different*. Besides, they are so influential we cannot refuse them. However, if you wish, you can now have the book.'

"I told Mr. Eason that I did not wish to read it ever since he had told me when I first applied for it that it was quite improper."

The two excuses produced by Mr. Eason do not agree very well together. The first gives us to understand that, in Mr. Eason's opinion, ordinary moral principles cannot be applied to persons of royal blood. The second gives us to understand that though, in Mr. Eason's opinion, ordinary moral principles *can* be applied to princes, the application would involve more risk than Mr. Eason cares to undertake. Each of his excuses, taken apart, is intelligible enough. Taken together they can hardly be called consistent. But the effects of royal and semi-royal splendor upon the moral eyesight are well known, and need not be dwelt on here. After all, what concerns us is not Mr. Eason's attitude towards Prince Francis of Teck, but Mr. Eason's attitude towards the reading public. And in this respect, from one point of view—which happens to be his own—Mr. Eason's attitude seems to me irreproachable. He is clearly alive to his responsibility, and is honestly concerned that the goods he purveys to the public shall be goods of which his conscience approves. Here is no grocer who sands his sugar before hurrying to family prayer. Here is a man who carries his religion into his business, and stakes his honor on the purity of his wares. I think it would be wrong in the extreme to deride Mr. Eason's action in the matter of *The Woman Who Did* and Mr. Stead's review. He is doing his best, as Mr. Stead cheerfully allows.

But, as I said above, he is doing his best under circumstances he imperfectly understands —and, let me add here, in a position which is unfair to him. That Mr. Eason imperfectly understands his position will be plain (I think) to anyone who studies his reply to Mr. Stead. But let me make the point clear; for it is the crucial point in the discussion of the modern

273

Bookstall Censorship. A great deal may be said against setting up a censorship of literature. A great deal may be said in favor of a censorship. But if a censorship there must be, the censor should be deliberately chosen for his office, and, in exercising his power, should be directly responsible to the public conscience. If a censorship there must be, let the community choose a man whose qualifications have been weighed, a man in whose judgment it decides that it can rely. But that Tom or Dick or Harry, or Tom Dick Harry & Co. (Limited), by the process of collaring a commercial monopoly from the railway companies, should be exalted into the supreme arbiters of what men or women may or may not be allowed to read—this surely is unjustifiable by any argument? Mr. Eason may on the whole be doing more good than harm. He is plainly a very well-meaning man of business. If he knows a good book from a bad—and the public has no reason to suppose that he does—I can very well believe that when his moral and literary judgment came into conflict with his business interests, he would sacrifice his business interests. But the interests of good literature and profitable business cannot always be identi-

cal; and whenever they conflict they put Mr.
Eason into a false position. As managing
director of Messrs. Eason & Son, he must consider his shareholders; as supreme arbiter of
letters, he stands directly answerable to the
public conscience. I protest, therefore, that
these functions should never be combined in
one man. As readers of THE SPEAKER know,
I range myself on the side of those who would
have literature free. But even our opponents,
who desire control, must desire a form of control such as reason approves.

THE POOR LITTLE PENNY DREADFUL

Oct. 5, 1895. Our "Crusaders."

THE poor little Penny Dreadful has been catching it once more. Once more the British Press has stripped to its massive waist and solemnly squared up to this hardened young offender. It calls this remarkable performance a "Crusade."

I like these Crusades. They remind one of that merry passage in *Pickwick* (p. 254 in the first edition) :—

"Whether Mr. Winkle was seized with a temporary attack of that species of insanity which originates in a sense of injury, or animated by this display of Mr. Weller's valour, is uncertain ; but certain it is, that he no sooner saw Mr. Grummer fall, than *he made a terrific onslaught on a small boy who stood next to him;* whereupon Mr. Snodgrass——"

[Pay attention to Mr. Snodgrass, if you please, and cast your memories back a year or two, to the utterances of a famous Church Congress on the National Vice of Gambling.]

" —whereupon Mr. Snodgrass, in a truly Christian spirit, and in order that he might take no one unawares, announced in a very loud tone that he was going to begin, and proceeded to take off his coat with the utmost deliberation. He was immediately surrounded and secured ; and it is but common justice both to him and to Mr. Winkle to say that they did not make the slightest attempt to rescue either themselves or Mr. Weller, who, after a most vigorous resistance, was overpowered by numbers and taken prisoner. The procession then reformed, the chairmen resumed their stations, and the march was re-commenced."

" The chairmen resumed their stations, and the march was re-commenced."   Is it any wonder that Dickens and Labiche have found no fit successors ?   One can imagine the latter laying down his pen and confessing himself beaten at his own game ; for really this periodical " crusade " upon the Penny Dreadful has all the qualities of the very best vaudeville—the same bland exhibition of *bourgeois* logic, the same wanton appreciation of evidence, the same sententious alacrity in seizing the immediate explanation—the more trivial the better—the same inability to reach the remote cause, the same profound unconsciousness of absurdity.

You remember *La Grammaire* ? Caboussat's cow has eaten a piece of broken glass, with fatal results. Machut, the veterinary, comes :—

> *Caboussat.* " Un morceau de verre . . . est-ce drole ? Une vache de quatre ans."
>
> *Machut.* " Ah ! monsieur, les vaches . . . ça avale du verre à tout âge. J'en ai connu une qui a mangé une éponge à laver les cabriolets . . . à sept ans ! Elle en est morte."
>
> *Caboussat.* " Ce que c'est que notre pauvre humanité ! "

Penny Dreadfuls and Matricide.

Our friends have been occupied with the case of a half-witted boy who consumed Penny Dreadfuls and afterwards went and killed his mother. They infer that he killed his mother because he had read Penny Dreadfuls (*post hoc ergo propter hoc*) and they conclude very naturally that Penny Dreadfuls should be suppressed. But before roundly pronouncing the doom of this—to me unattractive—branch of fiction, would it not be well to inquire a trifle more deeply into cause and effect ? In the first place matricide is so utterly unnatural a crime that there must be something abominably peculiar in a form of literature that persuades to it. But a year or two back, on the occasion of a former crusade, I took the pains to study a con-

278

siderable number of Penny Dreadfuls. My reading embraced all those — I believe I am right in saying all — which were reviewed, a few days back, in the *Daily Chronicle;* and some others. I give you my word I could find nothing peculiar about them. They were even rather ostentatiously on the side of virtue. As for the bloodshed in them, it would not compare with that in many of the five-shilling adventure stories at that time read so eagerly by boys of the middle and upper classes. The style was ridiculous, of course: but a bad style excites nobody but a reviewer, and does not even excite him to deeds of the kind we are now trying to account for. The reviewer in the *Daily Chronicle* thinks worse of these books than I do. But he certainly failed to quote anything from them that by the wildest fancy could be interpreted as sanctioning such a crime as matricide.

Let us for a moment turn our attention from the Penny Dreadful to the boy — from the *éponge á laver les cabriolets* to *notre pauvre humanité.* Now — to speak quite seriously — it is well known to every doctor and every schoolmaster (and should be known, if it is

The Cause to be sought in the Boy rather than in the Book.

279

not, to every parent), that all boys sooner or later pass through a crisis in growth during which absolutely nothing can be predicted of their behavior. At such times honest boys have given way to lying and theft, gentle boys have developed an unexpected savagery, ordinary boys — " the small apple-eating urchins whom we know " — have fallen into morbid brooding upon unhealthy subjects. In the immense majority of cases the crisis is soon over and the boy is himself again; but while it lasts, the disease will draw its sustenance from all manner of things—things, it may be, in themselves quite innocent. I avoid particularizing for many reasons; but any observant doctor will confirm what I have said. Now the moderately affluent boy who reads five-shilling stories of adventure has many advantages at this period over the poor boy who reads Penny Dreadfuls. To begin with, the crisis has a tendency to attack him later. Secondly, he meets it fortified by a better training and more definite ideas of the difference between right and wrong, virtue and vice. Thirdly (and this is very important), he is probably under school discipline at the time—which means, that he is to some extent watched and shielded. When I think of these advantages, I frankly confess that the difference in the literature these two boys read seems to me to count for very little. I myself have written " adventure-stories " before now : stories which, I suppose—or, at any rate, hope—would come into the class of " Pure Literature," as the term is understood by those who have been writing on this subject in the newspapers. They were, I hope, better written than the run of Penny Dreadfuls, and perhaps with more discrimination of taste in the choice of adventures. But I certainly do not feel able to claim that their effect upon a perverted mind would be innocuous.

For indeed it is not possible to name any book out of which a perverted mind will not draw food for its disease. The whole fallacy lies in supposing literature the cause of the disease. Evil men are not evil because they read bad books : they read bad books because they are evil : and being evil, or diseased, they are quickly able to extract evil or disease even from very good books. There is talk of disseminating the works of our best authors, at a cheap rate, in the hope that they will drive the Penny

Fallacy of the " Crusade."

281

Dreadful out of the market. But has good literature at the cheapest driven the middle classes from their false gods? And let it be remembered, to the credit of these poor boys, that they do buy their books. The middle classes take *their* poison on hire or exchange.

But perhaps the full enormity of the cant about Penny Dreadfuls can best be perceived by travelling to and fro for a week between London and Paris and observing the books read by those who travel with first-class tickets. I think a fond belief in Ivanhoe-within-the-reach-of-all would not long survive that experiment.

IBSEN'S "PEER GYNT"

Oct. 7, 1892.
A Master-
piece.

" *Peer Gynt* takes its place, as we hold, on the sum-
mits of literature precisely because it means so much
more than the poet consciously intended. Is not this
one of the characteristics of the masterpiece, that everyone can read in it his own secret? In the material world
(though Nature is very innocent of symbolic intention)
each of us finds for himself the symbols that have relevance and value for him ; and so it is with the poems
that are instinct with true vitality."

I WAS glad to come across the above passage
in Messrs. William and Charles Archer's introduction to their new translation of Ibsen's
Peer Gynt (London : Walter Scott), because I
can now, with a clear conscience, thank the
writers for their book, even though I fail to find
some of the things they find in it. The play's
the thing after all. *Peer Gynt* is a great poem:
let us shake hands over that. It will remain a
great poem when we have ceased pulling it
about to find what is inside or search out texts

for homilies in defence of our own particular
views of life. The world's literature stands un-
affected, though Archdeacon Farrar use it for
chapter-headings and Sir John Lubbock wield it
as a mallet to drive home self-evident truths.

Peer Gynt is an extremely modern story
founded on old Norwegian folk-lore—the folk-
lore which Asbjörnsen and Moe collected, and
Dasent translated for our delight in childhood.
Old and new are curiously mixed; but the
result is piquant and not in the least absurd, because the story rests on problems which are
neither old nor new, but eternal, and on emotions which are neither older nor newer than the
breast of man. To be sure, the true devotee of
Ibsen will not be content with this. You will
be told by Herr Jaeger, Ibsen's biographer, that
Peer Gynt is an attack on Norwegian romanticism. The poem, by the way, is romantic to the
core—so romantic, indeed, that the culminating
situation, and the page for which everything
has been a preparation, have to be deplored
by Messrs. Archer as "a mere commonplace
of romanticism, which Ibsen had not outgrown
when he wrote *Peer Gynt*." But your true
votary is for ever taking his god off the ped-

*Not a
Pamphlet.*

284

estal of the true artist to set him on the tub of the hot-gospeller ; even so genuine a specimen of impressionist work as *Hedda Gabler* being claimed by him for a sermon.   And if ever you have been moved by *Ghosts*, or *Brand*, or *Peer Gynt* to exclaim " This is poetry ! " you have only to turn to Herr Jaeger—whose criticism, like his namesake's underclothing, should be labelled " All Pure Natural Wool "—to find that you were mistaken and that it is really pamphleteering.

To be sure, in one sense *Peer Gynt* is a sermon upon a text.   That is to say, it is written *Yet En-forcing a Moral.* primarily to expound one view of man's duty, not to give a mere representation of life.   The problem, not the picture, is the main thing. But then the problem, not the picture, is the main thing in *Alcestis, Hamlet, Faust.* In *Peer Gynt* the poet's own solution of the problem is presented with more insistence than in *Alcestis, Hamlet,* or *Faust :* but the problem is wider, too.

The problem is, What is self ? and how shall a man be himself ?   And the poet's answer is, " Self is only found by being lost, gained by being given away'': an answer at least as old as the gospels. The eponymous hero of the story is a man essentially half-hearted, "the incarnation of a compromising dread of self-committal to any one course," a fellow who says,

" Ay, think of it—wish it done—*will* it to boot,
    But *do* it——. No, that's past my understanding !"

—who is only stung to action by pique, or by what is called the " instinct of self-preservation," an instinct which, as Ibsen shows, is the very last that will preserve self.

The Story.   This fellow, Peer Gynt, wins the love of Solveig, a woman essentially whole-hearted, who has no dread of self-committal, who surrenders self. Solveig, in short, stands in perfect antithesis to Peer. When Peer is an outlaw she deserts her father's house and follows him to his hut in the forest. The scene in which she presents herself before Peer and claims to share his lot is worthy to stand beside the ballad of the Nut-browne Mayde: indeed, as a confessed romantic I must own to thinking Solveig one of the most beautiful figures in poetry. Peer deserts her, and she lives in the hut alone and

286

grows an old woman while her lover roams the
world, seeking everywhere and through the wildest adventures the satisfaction of his Self, acting
everywhere on the Troll's motto, " To thyself
be enough," and finding everywhere his major
premiss turned against him, to his own discom-
fiture, by an ironical fate. We have one
glimpse of Solveig, meanwhile, in a little scene
of eight lines. She is now a middle-aged
woman, up in her forest hut in the far north.
She sits spinning in the sunshine outside her
door and sings :—

" *Maybe both the winter and spring will pass by,*
And the next summer too, and the whole of the year;
But thou wilt come one day . . . .

. . . . .

God strengthen thee, whereso thou goest in the world!
God gladden thee, if at His footstool thou stand!
Here will I await thee till thou comest again;
And if thou wait up yonder, then there we'll meet,
my friend!"

At last Peer, an old man, comes home. On
the heath around his old hut he finds (in a
passage which the translators call " fantastic,"
intending, I hope, approval by this word) the
thoughts he has missed thinking, the watchword
he has failed to utter, the tears he has missed

shedding, the deed he has missed doing. The thoughts are thread-balls, the watchword withered leaves, the tears dewdrops, etc. Also he finds on that heath a Button-Moulder with an immense ladle. The Button-Moulder explains to Peer that he must go into this ladle, for his time has come. He has neither been a good man nor a sturdy sinner, but a half-and-half fellow without any real self in him. Such men are dross, badly cast buttons with no loops to them, and must go, by the Master's orders, into the melting-pot again. Is there no escape? None, unless Peer can find the loop of the button, his real Self, the Peer Gynt that God made. After vain and frantic searching across the heath, Peer reaches the door of his own old hut. Solveig stands on the threshold.

As Peer flings himself to earth before her, calling out upon her to denounce him, she sits down by his side and says—

" *Thou hast made all my life as a beautiful song.*
Blessed be thou that at last thou hast come!
Blessed, thrice-blessed our Whitsun-morn meeting!"

"But," says Peer, "I am lost, unless thou canst answer riddles." "Tell me them," tran-

quilly answers Solveig.   And Peer asks, while
the Button-Moulder listens behind the hut—

*" Canst thou tell me where Peer Gynt has been since we
     parted?"*
Solveig.—*Been?*
Peer.—   *With his destiny's seal on his brow ;*
     Been, as in God's thought he first sprang forth?
     *Canst thou tell me?   If not, I must get me
        home,—*
     Go down to the mist-shrouded regions.
Solveig (smiling).—*Oh, that riddle is easy.*
Peer.—   *Then tell what thou knowest !*
     *Where was I, as myself, as the whole man, the
        true man?*
     Where was I, with God's sigil upon my brow?
Solveig.—*In my faith, in my hope, in my love.*

"This," says the Messrs. Archer, in effect,
"may be—indeed is—magnificent : but it is
not Ibsen."   To quote their very words—

*A Shirking
of the
Ethical
Problem?*

" The redemption of the hero through a woman's
love . . .   we take to be a mere commonplace of
romanticism, which Ibsen, though he satirised it, had
by no means fully outgrown when he wrote *Peer Gynt*.
Peer's return to Solveig is (in the original) a passage of
the most poignant lyric beauty, but it is surely a shirking, not a solution, of the ethical problem.   It would be
impossible to the Ibsen of to-day, who knows (none
better) that *No man can save his brother's soul, or pay
his brother's debt.*"

In a footnote to the italicized words Messrs. Archer add the quotation—

" No, nor woman, neither."

" Peer's return to Solveig is surely a shirking, not a solution of the ethical problem." Of what ethical problem? The main ethical problem of the poem is, What is self? And how shall a man be himself? As Mr. Wicksteed puts it in his " Four Lectures on Henrik Ibsen," " What is it to be one's self? God *meant something* when He made each one of us. For a man to embody that meaning of God in his words and deeds, and so become, in a degree, ' a word of God made flesh ' is to be himself. But thus to be himself he must slay himself. That is to say, he must slay the craving to make himself the centre round which others revolve, and must strive to find his true orbit, and swing, self poised, round the great central light. But what if a poor devil can never puzzle out what God *did* mean when He made him? Why, then he must *feel* it. But how often your ' feeling ' misses fire! Ay, there you have it. The devil has no stancher ally than *want of perception*."

290

This is a fair statement of Ibsen's problem and his solution of it. In the poem he solves it by the aid of two characters, two diagrams we may say. Diagram I. is Peer Gynt, a man who is always striving to make himself the centre round which others revolve, who never sacrifices his Self generously for another's good, nor surrenders it to a decided course of action. Diagram II. is Solveig, a woman who has no dread of self-committal, who surrenders Self and is, in short, Peer's perfect antithesis. When Peer is an outlaw she forsakes all and follows him to his hut in the forest. Peer deserts her and roams the world, where he finds his theory of Self upset by one adventure after another and at last reduced to absurdity in the mad-house at Cairo. But though his own theory is discredited, he has not yet found the true one. To find this he must be brought face to face *And its Solution.* in the last scene with his deserted wife. There, for the first time, he asks the question and receives the answer. "Where," he asks, " has Peer Gynt's true self been since we parted : —

" Where was I, as myself, as the whole man, the true man ?
  Where was I with God's sigil upon my brow ? "

And Solveig answers :—

"In my faith, in my hope, in my love."

In these words we have the main ethical problem solved; and Peer's *perception* of the truth (*vide* Mr. Wicksteed's remarks quoted above) is the one necessary climax of the poem. We do not care a farthing—at least, I do not care a farthing—whether Peer escape the Button-Moulder or not. It may be too late for him, or there may be yet time to live another life; but whatever the case may be, it doesn't alter what Ibsen set out to prove. The problem which Ibsen shirks (if indeed he does shirk it) is a subsidiary problem—a rider, so to speak. Can Solveig by her love redeem Peer Gynt? Can the woman save the man's soul? Will she, after all, cheat the Button-Moulder of his victim?

The poet, by giving Solveig the last word, seems to think it possible. According to Mr. Archer, the Ibsen of to-day would know it to be impossible. He knows (none better) that "No man can save his brother's soul or pay his brother's debt." "No, nor women neither," adds Mr. Archer.

But is this so ?   *Peer Gynt* was published in *Is Peer's Redemption a romantic Fallacy ?* 1867.   I turn to *A Doll's House*, written twelve years later, and I find there a woman preparing to redeem a man just as Solveig prepares to redeem Peer.   I find in Mr. Archer's translation of that play the following page of dialogue :—

Mrs. Linden : There's no happiness in working for oneself, Nils ; give me somebody and something to work for.

Krogstad : No, no ; that can never be.   It's simply a woman's romantic notion of self-sacrifice.

Mrs. Linden : Have you ever found me romantic ?

Krogstad : Would you really——?   Tell me, do you know my past ?

Mrs. Linden : Yes.

Krogstad : And do you know what people say of me ?

Mrs. Linden : Didn't you say just now that with me you could have been another man ?

Krogstad : I am sure of it.

Mrs. Linden : Is it too late ?

Krogstad : Christina, do you know what you are doing ?   Yes, you do ; I see it in your face.   Have you the courage—— ?

Mrs. Linden : I need someone to tend, and your children need a mother.   You need me, and I——I need you.   Nils, I believe in your better self.   With you I fear nothing.

Again, we are not told if Mrs. Linden's experiment is successful ; but Ibsen certainly gives no hint that she is likely to fail.   This was in 1879.   In 1885 Ibsen paid a visit to Norway and made a speech to some workingmen at Drontheim, in which this passage occurred :—

"Democracy by itself cannot solve the social question.   We must introduce an aristocratic element into our life. I am not referring, of course, to an aristocracy of birth, or of purse, or even of intellect.   I mean an aristocracy of character, of will, of mind.   That alone can make us free. From two classes will this aristocracy I desire come to us—*from our women and our workmen.*   The social revolution, now preparing in Europe, is chiefly concerned with the future of the workers and the women.   On this I set all my hopes and expectations. . . ."

I think it would be easy to multiply instances showing that, though Ibsen may hold that no man can save his brother's soul, he does not extend this disability to women, but hopes and believes, on the contrary, that women will redeem mankind.   On men he builds little hope.   To speak roughly, men are all in Peer Gynt's case, or Torvald Helmer's.   They are swathed in timid conventions, blindfolded with selfishness, so that they cannot perceive, and unable with their own hands to tear off these bandages.   They are incapable of the highest

renunciation. "No man," says Torvald Helmer, "sacrifices his honor, even for one he
loves." Those who heard Miss Achurch deliver Nora's reply will not easily forget it.
"Millions of women have done so." The
effect in the theatre was tremendous. This
sentence clinched the whole play.

Millions of women are, like Solveig, capable
of renouncing all for love, of surrendering self
altogether ; and, as I read Ibsen, it is precisely
on this power of renunciation that he builds
his hope of man's redemption. So that, unless
I err greatly, the scene in *Peer Gynt* which
Mr. Archer calls a shirking of the ethical problem, is just the solution which Ibsen has been
persistent in presenting to the world.

Let it be understood, of course, that it is
only your Solveigs and Mrs. Lindens who
can thus save a brother's soul : women who
have made their own way in the world, thinking for themselves, working for themselves,
freed from the conventions which man would
impose on them. I know Mr. Archer will not
retort on me with Nora, who leaves her husband and children, and claims that her first

duty is to herself. Nora is just the woman who cannot redeem a man. Her Doll's House training is the very opposite of Solveig's and Mrs. Linden's. She is a silly girl brought up amid conventions, and awakened, by one blow, to the responsibilities of life. That she should at once know the right course to take would be incredible in real life, and impossible in a play the action of which has been evolved as inevitably as real life. Many critics have supposed Ibsen to commend Nora's conduct in the last act of the play. He neither sanctions nor condemns. But he does contrast her in the play with Mrs. Linden, and I do not think that contrast can be too carefully studied.

MR. SWINBURNE'S LATER MANNER

May 5, 1894.
Aloofness of Mr. Swinburne's Muse.

THERE was a time—let us say, in the early seventies—when many young men tried to write like Mr. Swinburne. Remarkably small success waited on their efforts. Still their numbers and their youth and (for a while also) their persistency seemed to promise a new school of poesy, with Mr. Swinburne for its head and great exemplar : exemplar rather than head, for Mr. Swinburne's attitude amid all this devotion was rather that of the god than of the priest. He sang, and left the worshippers to work up their own enthusiasm. And to this attitude he has been constant. Unstinting, and occasionally unmeasured, in praise and dispraise of other men, he has allowed his own reputation the noble liberty to look after itself. Nothing, for instance, could have been finer than the careless, almost disdainful, dignity of his bearing in the months that followed

Tennyson's death. The cats were out upon the tiles, then, and his was the luminous, expressive silence of a sphere. One felt, "whether he received it or no, here is the man who can wear the crown."

And Her Tendency towards Abstractions.

It was not, however, the aloofness of Mr. Swinburne's bearing that checked the formation of a Swinburnian school of poetry. The cause lay deeper, and has come more and more into the light in the course of Mr. Swinburne's poetic development—let me say, his thoroughly normal development. We can see now that from the first such a school, such a successful following, was an impossibility. The fact is that Mr. Swinburne has not only genius, but an extremely rare and individual genius. The germ of this individuality may be found, easily enough, in "Atalanta" and the Ballads; but it luxuriates in his later poems and throughout them—flower and leaf and stem. It was hardly more natural in 1870 to confess the magic of the great chorus, "Before the beginning of years," or of "Dolores," than to embark upon the vain adventure of imitating them. I cannot imagine a youth in all Great Britain so green or unknowing as to attempt an imitation

298

of "A Nympholept," perhaps the finest poem in the volume before me.

I say "in Great Britain;" because peculiar as Mr. Swinburne's genius would be in any country, it is doubly peculiar as the endowment of an English poet. If there be one quality beloved above others by the inhabitants of this island, it is concreteness; and I suppose there never was a poet in the world who used less concreteness of speech than Mr. Swinburne. Mr. Palgrave once noted that the landscape of Keats falls short of the landscape of Shelley in its comparative lack of the larger features of sky and earth; Keats's was "foreground work" for the most part. But what shall be said of Shelley's universe after the immense vague regions inhabited by Mr. Swinburne's muse? She sings of the sea; but we never behold a sail, never a harbor: she sings of passion—among the stars. We seem never to touch earth; page after page is full of thought—for, vast as the strain may be, it is never empty—but we cannot apply it. And all this is extremely distressing to the Briton, who loves practice as his birthright. He comes on a Jacobite song. "Now, at any rate," he tells himself, "we arrive at something definite: some allusion, however small, to Bonny Prince Charlie." He reads—

> " Faith speaks when hope dissembles ;
> Faith lives when hope lies dead :
> If death as life dissembles,
> And all that night assembles
> Of stars at dawn lie dead,
> Faint hope that smiles and trembles
> May tell not well for dread :
> But faith has heard it said."

" Very beautiful," says the Briton ; "but why call this a ' Jacobite Song ' ? " Some thorough-going admirer of Mr. Swinburne will ask, no doubt, if I prefer gush about Bonny Prince Charlie. Most decidedly I do not. I am merely pointing out that the poet cares so little for the common human prejudice in favor of concreteness of speech as to give us a Jacobite song which, for all its indebtedness to the historical facts of the Jacobite Risings, might just as well have been put in the mouth of Judas Maccabæus.

Somebody—I forget for the moment who it was—compared Poetry with Antæus, who was strong when his feet touched Earth, his mother ;

weaker when held aloft in air. The justice of this criticism I have no space here to discuss ; but the difference is patent enough between poetry such as this of Herrick—

> " When as in silks my Julia goes,
>   Then, then, methinks, how sweetly flows
>   The liquefaction of her clothes."

Or this, of Burns—

> " The boat rocks at the pier o' Leith,
>   Fu' loud the wind blaws frae the ferry,
>   The boat rides by the Berwick-law,
>   And I maun leave my bonny Mary."

Or this, of Shakespeare—

> " When daisies pied, and violets blue,
>   And lady smocks all silver-white,
>   And cuckoo-buds of yellow hue
>   Do paint the meadows with delight."

Or this, of Milton—

> " the broad circumference
> Hung on his shoulders like the moon, whose orb,
> Through optic glass the Tuscan artist views
> At evening from the top of Fesolé,
> Or in Valdarno . . ."

And such lines as these by Mr. Swinburne—

" The dark dumb godhead innate in the fair world's life
    Imbues the rapture of dawn and of noon with dread,

Infects the peace of the star-shod night with strife,
  Informs with terror the sorrow that guards the dead.
  No service of bended knee or of humbled head
May soothe or subdue the God who has change to
    wife :
    And life with death is as morning with evening
    wed."

Take Burns's song, " It was a' for our right-
fu' King," and set it beside the Jacobite song
quoted above, and it is clear at once that with
Mr. Swinburne we pass from the particular and
concrete to the general and abstract. And
in this direction Mr. Swinburne's muse has
steadily marched. In his "Erechtheus" he
tells how the gods gave Pallas the lordship of
Athens—

" The lordship and love of the lovely land,
  The grace of the town that hath on it for crown
      But a headband to wear
      Of violets one-hued with her hair."

Here at least we were allowed a picture of
Athens : the violet crown was something definite. But now, when Mr. Swinburne sings of
England, we have to precipitate our impressions from lines fluid as these :—

" Things of night at her glance took flight : the
    strengths of darkness recoiled and sank :

Sank the fires of the murderous pyres whereon wild
    agony writhed and shrank :
Rose the light of the reign of right from gulfs of
    years that the darkness drank."

Or—

" Change darkens and lightens around her, alternate
    in hope and in fear to be :
Hope knows not if fear speak truth, nor fear whether
    hope be not blind as she :
But the sun is in heaven that beholds her immortal,
    and girdled with life by the sea."

I suspect, then, that a hundred years hence,
when criticism speaks calm judgment upon all
Mr. Swinburne's writings, she will find that his
earlier and more definite poems are the edge of
his blade, and such volumes as " Astrophel "
the heavy metal behind it. The former pene-
trated the affections of his countrymen with
ease : the latter followed more difficultly through
the outer tissues of a people notoriously pachy-
dermatous to abstract speech. And criticism
will then know if Mr. Swinburne brought sufficient impact to drive the whole mass of metal
deep.

At present in these later volumes his must *A Voice chanting in the Void.*
seem to us a godlike voice chanting in the void.

For, fit or unfit as we may be to grasp the elu-
sive substance of his strains, all must confess
the voice of the singer to be divine. At once
in the range and suppleness of his music he
is not merely the first of our living poets, but
incomparable. In learning he has Robert
Bridges for a rival, and no other. But no
amount of learning could give us 228 pages of
music that from first to last has not a flaw.
Rather, his marvellous ear has taken him safely
through metres set by his learning as so many
traps. There is one metre, for instance, that
recurs again and again in this volume. Here
is a specimen of it :—

" Music bright as the soul of light, for wings an eagle,
        for notes a dove,
    Leaps and shines from the lustrous lines wherethrough
        thy soul from afar above
    Shone and sang till the darkness rang with light whose
        fire is the fount of love."

These lines are written of Sir Philip Sidney.
Could another man have written them they
had stood even better for Mr. Swinburne. But
we are considering the metre, not the meaning.
Now the metre may have great merits. I am
disposed to say that, having fascinated Mr.
Swinburne, it must have great merits. That I

dislike it is, no doubt, my fault, or rather my misfortune.   But undoubtedly it is a metre that no man but Mr. Swinburne could handle without producing a monotony varied only by discords.

A MORNING WITH A BOOK

April 29,
1893.
Hazlitt's
Stipula-
tion.
" Food, warmth, sleep, and a book ; these are all I
at present ask—the *Ultima Thule* of my wandering
desires.   Do you not then wish for—

> *a friend in your retreat*
> *Whom you may whisper, ' Solitude is sweet' ?*

Expected, well enough : gone, still better.   Such attrac-
tions are strengthened by distance."

S O Hazlitt wrote in his *Farewell to Essay
Writing.*   There never was such an epi-
cure of his moods as Hazlitt.   Others might
add Omar's stipulation—

> "—and Thou
> Beside me singing in the wilderness."

But this addition would have spoiled Hazlitt's
enjoyment.   Let us remember that his love
affairs had been unprosperous.   " Such attrac-
tions," he would object, " are strengthened by
distance."   In any case, the book and singer
go ill together, and most of us will declare for
a spell of each in turn.

Suppose we choose the book. What kind of book shall it be? Shall it be an old book which we have forgotten just sufficiently to taste surprise as its felicities come back to us, and remember just sufficiently to escape the attentive strain of a first reading? Or shall it be a new book by an author we love, to be glanced through with no critical purpose (this may be deferred to the second reading), but merely for the lazy pleasure of recognizing the familiar brain at work, and feeling happy, perhaps, at the success of a friend? There is no doubt which Hazlitt would have chosen; he has told us in his essay *On Reading Old Books*. But after a recent experience I am not sure that I agree with him.

What are " The Bes. Books " ?

That your taste should approve only the best thoughts of the best minds is a pretty counsel, but one of perfection, and is found in practice to breed prigs. It sets a man sailing round in a vicious circle. What is the best thought of the best minds? That approved by the man of highest culture. Who is the man of highest culture? He whose taste approves the best thoughts of the best minds. To escape from this foolish whirlpool, some of our stoutest bot-

toms run for that discredited harbor of refuge
—Popular Acceptance : a harbor full of shoals,
of which nobody has provided even the sketch
of a chart.

Some years ago, when the *Pall Mall Gazette*
sent round to all sorts and conditions of eminent men, inviting lists of "The Hundred
Best Books "—the first serious attempt to introduce a decimal system into Great Britain—I
remember that these eminent men's replies
disclosed nothing so wonderful as their unanimity. We were prepared for Sir John Lubbock, but not, I think, for the host of celebrities who followed his hygienic example, and
made a habit of taking the Rig Vedas to bed
with them. Altogether their replies afforded
plenty of material for a theory that to have
every other body's taste in literature is the
first condition of eminence in every branch of
the public service. But in one of the lists—I
think it was Sir Monier Williams's—the unexpected really happened. Sir Monier thought
that Mr. T. E. Brown's *The Doctor* was one
of the best books in the world.

Now, the poems of Mr. T. E. Brown are not

known to the million. But, like Mr. Robert Bridges, Mr. Brown has always had a band of readers to whom his name is more than that of many an acknowledged classic. I fancy it is a case of liking deeply or scarce at all. Those of us who are not celebrities may be allowed to have favorites who are not the favorites of others, writers who (fortuitously, perhaps) have helped us at some crisis of our life, have spoken to us the appropriate word at the moment of need, and for that reason sit cathedrally enthroned in our affections. To explain why the author of *Betsy Lee*, *Tommy Big-Eyes* and *The Doctor* is more to me than most poets—why to open a new book of his is one of the most exciting literary events that can befall me in now my twenty-ninth year—would take some time, and the explanation might poorly satisfy the reader after all.

But I set out to describe a morning with a book. The book was Mr. Brown's *Old John, and other Poems*, published but a few days back by Messrs. Macmillan & Co. The morning was spent in a very small garden overlooking a harbor. Hazlitt's conditions were fulfilled. I had enjoyed enough food and sleep

My Morning with a Book.

to last me for some little time : few people, I imagine, have complained of the cold, these last few weeks : and the book was not only new to me for the most part, but certain to please. Moreover, a small incident had already put me in the best of humors. Just as I was settling down to read, a small tug came down the harbor with a barque in tow whose nationality I recognized before she cleared a corner and showed the Norwegian colors drooping from her peak. I reached for the field-glass and read her name—*Henrik Ibsen !* I imagined Mr. William Archer applauding as I ran to my own flag-staff and dipped the British ensign to that name. The Norwegians on deck stood puzzled for a moment, but, taking the compliment to themselves, gave me a cheerful hail, while one or two ran aft and dipped the Norwegian flag in response. It was still running frantically up and down the halliards when I returned to my seat, and the lines of the bark were softening to beauty in the distance—for, to tell the truth, she had looked a crazy and not altogether seaworthy craft—as I opened my book, and, by a stroke of luck, at that fine poem, *The Schooner*.

" Just mark that schooner westward far at sea—
    'Tis but an hour ago

When she was lying hoggish at the quay,
   And men ran to and fro
And tugged, and stamped, and shoved, and pushed,
   and swore,
And ever an anon, with crapulous glee,
   Grinned homage to viragoes on the shore.

" So to the jetty gradual she was hauled :
   Then one the tiller took,
And chewed, and spat upon his hand, and bawled ;
   And one the canvas shook
Forth like a mouldy bat ; and one, with nods
And smiles, lay on the bowsprit end, and called
And cursed the Harbour-master by his gods.

" And, rotten from the gunwale to the keel,
   Rat riddled, bilge bestank,
Slime-slobbered, horrible, I saw her reel
   And drag her oozy flank,
And sprawl among the deft young waves, that
   laughed
And leapt, and turned in many a sportive wheel
As she thumped onward with her lumbering
   draught.

" And now, behold ! a shadow of repose
   Upon a line of gray
She sleeps, that transverse cuts the evening rose,
   She sleeps and dreams away,
Soft blended in a unity of rest
All jars, and strifes obscene, and turbulent throes
'Neath the broad benediction of the West—

" Sleeps ; and methinks she changes as she sleeps,
    And dies, and is a spirit pure ;
Lo ! on her deck, an angel pilot keeps
    His lonely watch secure ;
And at the entrance of Heaven's dockyard waits
    Till from night's leash the fine-breathed morning
      leaps,
And that strong hand within unbars the gates."

It is very far from being the finest poem in the volume. It has not the noble humanity of *Catherine Kinrade*—and if this be not a great poem I know nothing about poetry—nor the rapture of *Jessie,* nor the awful pathos of *Mater Dolorosa,* nor the gentle pathos of *Aber Stations,* nor the fine religious feeling of *Planting* and *Disguises.* But it came so pat to the occasion, and used the occasion so deftly to take hold of one's sympathy, that these other poems were read in the very mood that, I am sure, their author would have asked for them. One has not often such luck in reading—" Never the time and the place and the author all together," if I may do this violence to Browning's line. Yet I trust that in any mood I should have had the sense to pay its meed of admiration to this volume.

Now, having carefully read the opinions of

some half-a-dozen reviewers upon it, I can only wonder and leave the question to my reader, warning him by no means to miss *Mater Dolorosa* and *Catherine Kinrade.* If he remain cold to these two poems, then I shall still preserve my own opinion.

MR. JOHN DAVIDSON

April 7,
1894.
His Plays.

FOR some weeks now I have been meaning to write about Mr. John Davidson's "Plays" (Elkin Mathews and John Lane), and always shirking the task at the last moment. The book is an exceedingly difficult one to write about, and I am not at all sure that after a few sentences I shall not stick my hands in my pockets and walk off to something easier. The recent fine weather has, however, made me desperate. The windows of the room in which I sit face S. and S.-E.; consequently a deal of sunshine comes in upon my writing-table. In ninety-nine cases out of the hundred this makes for idleness; in this, the hundredth case, it constrains to energy, because it is rapidly bleaching the puce-colored boards in which Mr. Davidson's plays are bound—and (which is worse) bleaching them unevenly. I have tried (let the miserable truth be confessed) turning the book daily, as one turns a piece of

toast—But this is not criticism of Mr. Davidson's "Plays."

Now it would be easy and pleasant to ex- *His Style*
press my great admiration of Mr. Davidson's *full of Im-*
agination
Muse, and justify it by a score of extracts and *and Wit.*
so make an end : and nobody (except perhaps
Mr. Davidson himself) would know my dishon-
esty.   For indeed and out of doubt he is in
some respects the most richly-endowed of all
our younger poets.   Of wit and of imagination
he has almost a plethora : they crowd this book,
and all his books, from end to end.   And his
frequent felicity of phrase is hardly less remarkable. You may turn page after page, and with
each page the truth of this will become more
obvious.   Let me add his quick eye for natural
beauty, his penetrating instinct for the principles that lie beneath its phenomena, his sympathy with all men's more generous emotions—
and still I have a store of satisfactory illustrations at hand for the mere trouble of turning
the leaves.   Consider, for instance, the imagery
in his description of the fight by Bannockburn—

Now are they hand to hand !
How short a front !   How close !   *They're sewn together*
With steel cross-stitches, halbert over sword,

Spear across lance, and death the purfled seam !
I never saw so fierce, so lock'd a fight.
That tireless brand that like a pliant flail
Threshes the lives from sheaves of Englishmen—
Know you who wields it?   Douglas, who but he !
A noble meets him now.   Clifford it is !
No bitterer foes seek out each other there.
Parried ! That told ! And that ! Clifford, good night !
And Douglas shouts to Randolf ; Edward Bruce
Cheers on the Steward ; while the King's voice rings
In every Scotch ear : such a narrow strait
Confines this firth of war !
Young Friar: " God gives me strength
Again to gaze with eyes unseared. *Jewels !*
These must be jewels peering in the grass,
Cloven from helms, or on them: dead men's eyes
Scarce shine so bright. The banners dip and mount
Like masts at sea . . . ."

Or consider the fanciful melody of the Fairies'
song in *An Unhistorical Pastoral*—

" Weave the dance and sing the song ;
    Subterranean depths prolong
    The rainy patter of our feet ;
  Heights of air are rendered sweet
  By our singing.   Let us sing,
      Breathing softly, fairily,
      Swelling sweetly, airily,
    Till earth and sky our echo ring.
      Rustling leaves chime with our song :
      Fairy bells its close prolong
              Ding-dong, ding-dong."

—Or the closely-packed wit in such passages
as these—

Brown: " This world,
        This oyster with its valves of toil and play,
        Would round his corners for its own good ease,
        And make a pearl of him if he'd plunge in.

            *   *   *   *   *

Jones: And in this matter we may all be pearls.
Smith: Be worldlings, truly.   I would rather be
        A shred of glass that sparkles in the sun,
        And keeps a lowly rainbow of its own,
        Than one of these so trim and patent pearls
        With hearts of sand veneered, sewed up and
            down
        The stiff brocade society affects."

I have opened the book at random for these
quotations.   Its pages are stuffed with scores
as good.   Nor will any but the least intelligent
reviewer upbraid Mr. Davidson for deriving so
much of his inspiration directly from Shakespeare.   Mr. Davidson is still a young man ;
but the first of these plays, *An Unhistorical
Pastoral*, was first printed so long ago as 1877;
and the last, *Scaramouch in Naxos: a Panto-
mime*, in 1888.   They are the work therefore
of a very young man, who must use models
while feeling his way to a style and method of
his own.

Lack of "Architec- tonic" Quality.

But—there is a " but " ; and I am coming at length to my difficulty with Mr. David- son's work. Oddly enough, this difficulty may be referred to the circumstance that Mr. Davidson's poetry touches Shakespeare's great circle at a second point. Wordsworth, it will be remembered, once said that Shakespeare *could* not have written an Epic (Wordsworth, by the way, was rather fond of pointing out the things that Shakespeare could not have done). " Shakespeare *could* not have written an Epic ; he would have died of plethora of thought." Substitute " wit " for " thought," and you have my difficulty with Mr. Davidson. It is given to few men to have great wit : it is given to fewer to carry a great wit lightly. In Mr. Davidson's case it luxuriates over the page and seems persistently to choke his sense of form. One image suggests another, one phrase springs under the very shadow of another until the fabric of his poem is completely hidden beneath luxuriant flowers of speech. Either they hide it from the author himself; or, conscious of his lack of architectonic skill, he deliberately trails these creepers over his ill-constructed walls. I think the former is the true explanation, but am not sure.

Let me be cautious here, or some remarks I made the other day upon another poet—Mr. Hosken, author of *Phaon and Sappho*, and *Verses by the Way*—will be brought up against me. Defending Mr. Hosken against certain critics who had complained of the lack of dramatic power in his tragedies, I said, "Be it allowed that he has little dramatic power, and that (since the poem professed to be a tragedy) dramatic power was what you reasonably looked for. But an alert critic, considering the work of a beginner, will have an eye for the bye-strokes as well as the main ones: and if the author, while missing the main, prove effective with the bye—if Mr. Hosken, while failing to construct a satisfactory drama, gave evidence of strength in many fine meditative passages—then at the worst he stands convicted of a youthful error in choosing a literary form unsuited to convey his thought."

These observations I believe to be just, and having entered the *caveat* in Mr. Hosken's case, I should observe it in Mr. Davidson's also, did these five youthful plays stand alone. But Mr. Davidson has published much since these plays first appeared—works both in prose

Not in the "Plays" only.

319

and verse — *Fleet Street Eclogues, Ninian Jamieson, A Practical Novelist, A Random Itinerary, Baptist Lake :* and because I have followed his writings (I think from his first coming to London) with the greatest interest, I may possibly be excused for speaking a word of warning. I am quite certain that Mr. Davidson will never bore me : but I wish I could be half so certain that he will in time produce something in true perspective ; a fabric duly proportioned, each line of which from the beginning shall guide the reader to an end which the author has in view ; something which

> " *Servetur ad imum*
> *Qualis ab incepto processerit, et sibi constet.*"

Sibi constet, be it remarked. A work of art may stand very far from Nature, provided its own parts are consistent. Heaven forbid that a critic should decry an author for being fantastic, so long as he is true to his fantasy.

But Mr. Davidson's wit is so brilliant within the circles of its temporary coruscation as to leave the outline of his work in a constant penumbra. Indeed, when he wishes to unburden his mind of an idea, he seems to have less capacity than many men of half his ability to determine the form best suited for conveying it. If anything can be certain which has not been tried, it is that his story *A Practical Novelist* should have been cast in dramatic form. His vastly clever *Perfervid: or the Career of Ninian Jamieson* is cast in two parts which neither unite to make a whole, nor are sufficiently independent to stand complete in themselves. I find it characteristic that his *Random Itinerary*—that fresh and agreeable narrative of suburban travel—should conclude with a crashing poem, magnificent in itself, but utterly out of key with the rest of the book. Turn to the *Compleat Angler*, and note the exquisite congruity of the songs quoted by Walton with the prose in which they are set, and the difference will be apparent at once. Fate seems to dog Mr. Davidson even into his illustrations. *A Random Itinerary* and this book of *Plays* (both published by Messrs. Mathews and Lane) have each a conspicuously clever frontispiece. But the illustrator of *A Random Itinerary* has chosen as his subject the very poem which I have mentioned as out of harmony with the book; and I must protest that the vilely sensual faces in Mr. Beardsley's frontispiece to these *Plays* are hopelessly out of keeping with the sunny paganism of *Scaramouch in Naxos.* There is nothing Greek about Mr. Beardsley's figures : their only relationship with the Olympians is derived through the goddess Aselgeia.

With all this I have to repeat that Mr. Davidson is in some respects the most richly endowed of all the younger poets. The grand manner comes more easily to him than to any other : and if he can cultivate a sense of form and use this sense as a curb upon his wit, he has all the qualities that take a poet far.

Nov. 24, 1894. " Ballads and Songs."

At last there is no mistake about it : Mr. John Davidson has come by his own. And by " his own " I do not mean popularity—though I hope that in time he will have enough of this and to spare—but mastery of his poetic method. This new volume of " Ballads and Songs " (London : John Lane) justifies our hopes and removes our chief fear. You remember Mr. T. E. Brown's fine verses on " Poets and Poets " ?—

He fishes in the night of deep sea pools :
    For him the nets hang long and low,
Cork-buoyed and strong ; the silver-gleaming schools
    Come with the ebb and flow
Of universal tides, and all the channels glow.

Or holding with his hand the weighted line
    He sounds the languor of the neaps,
Or feels what current of the springing brine
    The cord divergent sweeps,
The throb of what great heart bestirs the middle deeps.

Thou also weavest meshes, fine and thin,
    And leaguer'st all the forest ways ;
But of that sea and the great heart therein
    Thou knowest nought ; whole days
Thou toil'st, and hast thy end—good store of pies and
    jays.

Mr. Davidson has never allowed us to doubt
to which of these two classes he belongs. "For
him the nets hang long and low." But though
it may satisfy the Pumblechook within us to
recall our pleasant prophesyings, we shall find
it more salutary to remember our fears. We
watched Mr. Davidson struggling in the thicket
of his own fancies, and saw him too often break
his shins over his own wit. We asked : Will
he in the end overcome the defect of his qualities? Will he remain unable to see the wood
for the trees ? Or will he some day be giving

us poems of which the whole conception and structure shall be as beautiful as the casual fragment or the single line? For this architectonic quality is just that "invidious distinction" which the fabled undergraduate declined to draw between the major and minor prophets.

The "Ballad of a Nun." Since its appearance, a few weeks back, all the critics have spoken of "A Ballad of a Nun," and admitted its surprising strength and beauty. They have left me in the plight of that belated fiddle in "Rejected Addresses," or of the gentleman who had to be content with saying "ditto" to Mr. Burke. For once they seem unanimous, and for once they are right. The poem is beautiful indeed in detail:

> " The adventurous sun took Heaven by storm;
>   Clouds scattered largesses of rain;
> The sounding cities, rich and warm,
>   Smouldered and glittered in the plain."

Dickens, reading for the first time Tennyson's "Dream of Fair Women," laid down the book, saying, "What a treat it is to come across a fellow who can *write!*" The verse that moved him to exclaim it was this—

" Squadrons and squares of men in brazen plates,
    Scaffolds, still sheets of water, divers woes,
  Ranges of glimmering vaults with iron grates ;
    And hushed seraglios."

It is not necessary to compare these two stanzas. Tennyson's depicts a confused and moving dream ; Mr. Davidson's a wide earthly
prospect. The point to notice in each is the superlative skill with which the poet chooses the
essential points of the picture and presents them
so as to convey their full meaning, appealing
at once to the senses and the intelligence. Tennyson, who is handling a mental condition in
which the sensations are less sharply and logically separated than in a waking vision, can
enforce this second appeal—this appeal to the
intelligence — by introducing the indefinite
" divers woes " between the definite "sheets of
water " and the definite " ranges of glimmering
vaults with iron grates " : just as Wordsworth, to
convey the vague unanalyzed charm of singing,
combines the indefinite " old unhappy far-off
things" with the definite " battles long ago."
Mr. Davidson, on the other hand, is describing
what the eye sees, and conveying what the mind
suspects, in their waking hours, and is therefore
restricted in his use of the abstract and indefi-

nite. Notice, therefore, how he qualifies that
which can be seen—the sun, the clouds, the
plain, the cities that "smoulder" and "glitter"
—with the epithets "sounding," "rich," and
" warm," each an inference rather than a direct
sensation : for nobody imagines that the sound
of the cities actually rang in the ear of the
Nun who watched them from the mountain-
side. The whole picture has the effect of one
of those wide conventional landscapes which
old painters delighted to spread beyond the
court-yard of Nazareth, or behind the pillars of
the temple at Jerusalem. My attempt to ana-
lyze it is something of a folly ; to understand
it is impossible :

> " but *if* I could understand
> What you are, root and all, and all in all,"—

I should at length comprehend the divine and
inexplicable gift of song.

The " Bal-
lad of the
Making of
a Poet."
But beautiful as it is in detail, this poem,
and at least one other in the little volume,
have the great merit which has hitherto been
lacking in the best of Mr. Davidson's work.
They are thoroughly considered ; seen as solid
wholes ; seen not only in front but round at

the back. In fact, they are natural growths
of Mr. Davidson's philosophy of life. In his
" Ballad of the Making of a Poet " Mr. Davidson lets us know his conception of the poet's
proper function.

> " I am a man apart :
> A mouthpiece for the creeds of all the world ;
> A soulless life that angels may possess
> Or demons haunt, wherein the foulest things
> May loll at ease beside the loveliest ;
> A martyr for all mundane moods to tear ;
> The slave of every passion ; and the slave
> Of heat and cold, of darkness and of light ;
> A trembling lyre for every wind to sound.

> *   *   *   *   *   *

> Within my heart
> I'll gather all the universe, and sing
> As sweetly as the spheres ; and I shall be
> The first of men to understand himself.   .   .   ."

Making, of course, full concessions to the demands of poetical treatment, we may assume
pretty confidently that Mr. Davidson intended
this " Ballad in Blank Verse of the Making of
a Poet " for a soul's autobiography, of a kind.
If so, I trust he will forgive me for doubting
if he is at all likely to fulfil the poet's office

as he conceives it here, or even to approach
within measurable distance of his ideal—

" A trembling lyre for every wind to sound."

That it is one way in which a poet may attain, I am not just now denying. But luck-
ily men attain in many ways: and the man
who sits himself down of fixed purpose to be
an Æolian harp for the winds of the world, is
of all men the least likely to be merely Æolian.
For the first demand of Æolian sound is that
the instrument should have no theories of its
own ; and explicitly to proclaim yourself Æolian is implicitly to proclaim yourself didactic.
As a matter of fact, both the " Ballad of the
Making of a Poet " and the " Ballad of a Nun "
contain sharply pointed morals very stoutly
driven home. In each the poet has made up
his mind ; he has a theory of life, and presents
that theory to us under cover of a parable.
The beauty of the " Ballad of a Nun "—or so
much of it as stands beyond and above mere
beauty of language—consists in this, that it is
informed, and consciously informed, by a
spirit of tolerance so exceedingly wide that
to match it I can find one poem and one
only among those of recent years : I mean

" Catherine Kinrade.''   In Mr. Brown's poem
the Bishop is welcomed into Heaven by the
half - witted harlot he had once condemned
to painful and public punishment.   In Mr.
Davidson's poem, Mary, the Mother of Heav-
en, herself takes the form and place of the
wandering nun and fills it until the peni-
tent returns.   Take either poem : take Mr.
Brown's—

" Awe-stricken, he was 'ware
  How on the Emerald stair
    A woman sat divinely clothed in white,
    And at her knees four cherubs bright,
      That laid
    Their heads within their lap.   Then, trembling, he
      essayed
      To speak—' Christ's mother, pity me ! '
      Then answered she—
  ' Sir, I am Catherine Kinrade.' ''

Or take Mr. Davidson's—in a way, its converse—

  " The wandress raised her tenderly ;
      She touched her wet and fast-shut eyes ;
  ' Look, sister ; sister, look at me ;
      Look ; can you see through my disguise ? '

    She looked and saw her own sad face,
        And trembled, wondering, ' Who art thou ? '
  ' God sent me down to fill your place ;
      I am the Virgin Mary now.'

And with the word, God's mother shone ;
　The wanderer whispered ' Mary, hail ! '
The vision helped her to put on
　Bracelet and fillet, ring and veil.

' You are sister to the mountains now,
　And sister to the day and night ;
Sister to God.'　And on her brow
　She kissed her thrice and left her sight."

The voice in each case is that of a prophet rather than that of a reed shaken by the wind, or an Æolian harp played upon by the same.

*March,
1895.
Second
Thoughts.*

I have to add that, apart from the beautiful language in which they are presented, Mr. Davidson's doctrines do not appeal to me.　I cannot accept his picture of the poet's as " a soulless life　.　.　.　wherein the foulest things may loll at ease beside the loveliest." It seems to me at least as obligatory on a poet as on other men to keep his garden weeded and his conscience active.　Indeed, I believe some asceticism of soul to be a condition of all really great poetry.　Also Mr. Davidson appears to be confusing charity with an approbation of things in the strict sense damnable when he makes the Mother of Christ abet a Nun whose wanderings have no nobler excuse than a carnal desire—*savoir enfin ce que c'est un homme.* Between forgiving a lapsed man or woman and abetting the lapse I now, in a cooler hour, see an immense, an essential, moral difference. But I confess that the foregoing paper was written while my sense of this difference was temporarily blinded under the spell of Mr. Davidson's beautiful verse.

It may still be that his Nun had some nobler motive than I am able, after two or three readings of the ballad, to discover. In that case I can only ask pardon for my obtuseness.

BJÖRNSTERNE BJÖRNSON

June 1, 1895. Björnson's First Manner.

I SEE that the stories promised in Mr. Heinemann's new series of translations of Björnson are *Synnövé Solbakken, Arne, A Happy
Boy, The Fisher Maiden, The Bridal March,
Magnhild,* and *Captain Mansana.* The first,
Synnövé Solbakken, appeared in 1857. The
others are dated thus:— *Arne* in 1858, *A
Happy Boy* in 1860, *The Fisher Maiden* in
1868, *The Bridal March* in 1873, *Magnhild*
in 1877, and *Captain Mansana* in 1879.
There are some very significant gaps here, the
most important being the eight years' gap between *A Happy Boy* and *The Fisher Maiden.*
Again, after 1879 Björnson ceased to write
novels for a while, returning to the charge in
1884 with *Flags are Flying in Town and
Haven,* and following up with *In God's Way,*
1889. Translations of these two novels have
also been published by Mr. Heinemann (the
former under an altered title, *The Heritage of*

the Kurts) and, to use Mr. Gosse's words, are the works by which Björnson is best known to the present generation of Englishmen. "They possess elements which have proved excessively attractive to certain sections of our public ; indeed, in the case of *In God's Way*, a novel which was by no means successful in its own country at its original publication, has enjoyed an aftermath of popularity in Scandinavia, founded on reflected warmth from its English admirers."

Taking, then, Björnson's fiction apart from his other writings (with which I confess myself unacquainted), we find that it falls into three periods, pretty sharply divided. The earliest is the idyllic period, pure and simple, and includes *Synnöve, Arne,* and *A Happy Boy*. Then with *The Fisher Maiden* we enter on a stage of transition. It is still the idyll ; but it grows self-conscious, elaborate, confused by the realism that was coming into fashion all over Europe ; and the trouble and confusion grow until we reach *Magnhild*. With *Flags are Flying* and *In God's Way* we reach a third stage—the stage of realism, some readers would say. I should not agree. But these tales certainly differ remarkably from their predecessors. They are much longer, to begin with ; in them, too, realism at length preponderates ; and they are probably as near to pure realism as Björnson will ever get.

If asked to label these three periods, I should call them the periods of (1) Simplicity, (2) Confusion, (3) Dire Confusion.

I speak, of course, as a foreigner, obliged to read Björnson in translations. But perhaps the disability is not so important as it seems at first sight. Translations cannot hide Björnson's genius ; nor obscure the truth that his genius is essentially idyllic. Now if one form of literary expression suffers more than another by translation it is the idyll. Its bloom is peculiarly delicate ; its freshness peculiarly quick to disappear under much handling of any kind. But all the translations leave *Arne* a masterpiece, and *Synnöve* and *The Happy Boy*.

How many artists have been twisted from their natural bent by the long vogue of " naturalism " we shall never know. We must make the best of the great works which have been produced under its influence, and be content with that. But we may say with some confidence that Björnson's genius was unfortunate in the date of its maturity. He was born on the 8th of December, 1832, in a lonely farmhouse among the mountains, at the head of the long valley called Osterdalen; his father being priest of Kvikne parish, one of the most savage in all Norway. After six years the family removed to Naesset, in the Romsdal, "a spot as enchanting and as genial as Kvikne is the reverse." Mr. Gosse, who prefaces Mr. Heinemann's new series with a study of Björnson's writings, quotes a curious passage in which Björnson records the impression of physical beauty made upon his childish mind by the physical beauty of Naesset :—

" Here in the parsonage of Naesset—one of the loveliest places in Norway, where the land lies broadly spreading where two fjords meet, with the green braeside above it, with waterfalls and farmhouses on the opposite shore, with billowy meadows and cattle away towards the foot of the valley, and, far overhead, along the line of the fjord, mountains shooting promontory after promontory out into the lake, a big farmhouse at the extremity of each—here in the parsonage of Naesset, where I would stand at the close of the day and gaze at the sunlight playing over mountain and fjord, until I wept, as though I had done something wrong ; and where I, descending on my snow-shoes into some valley, would pause as though bewitched by a loveliness, by a longing, which I had not the power to explain, but which was so great that above the highest ecstasy of joy I would feel the deepest apprehension and distress— here in the parsonage of Naesset were awakened my earliest sensations."

The passage is obviously important. And Björnson shows how much importance he attaches to the experience by introducing it, or something like it, time after time into his stories. Readers of *In God's Way*—the latest of the novels under discussion — will remember its opening chapter well.

It was good fortune indeed that a boy of such gifts should pass his early boyhood in such surroundings. Nor did the luck end here. While the young Björnson accumulated these impressions, the peasant-romance, or idyll of country life, was taking its place and growing into favor as one of the most beautiful forms of modern prose-fiction. Immermann wrote *Der Oberhof* in 1839. Weill and Auerbach took up the running in 1841 and 1843. George Sand followed, and Fritz Reuter. Björn-

son began to write in 1856. *Synnövé Solbakken* and *Arne* came in on the high flood of this
movement. "These two stories," writes Mr.
Gosse, "seem to me to be almost perfect;
they have an enchanting lyrical quality, without bitterness or passion, which I look for elsewhere in vain in the prose literature of the second half of the century." To my mind, without any doubt, they and *A Happy Boy* are the
best work Björnson has ever done in fiction, or
is ever likely to do. For they are simple, direct,
congruous; all of one piece as a flower is of a
piece with its root. And never since has Björnson written a tale altogether of one piece.

For here the luck ended. All over Europe
there began to spread influences that may
have been good for some artists, but were
(we may say) peculiarly injurious to so *naïf*
and, at the same time, so personal a writer as
Björnson. I think another age will find much
the same cause to mourn over Daudet when
it compares his later novels with the promise
of *Lettres de Mon Moulin* and *Le Petit Chose*.
Naturalism demands nothing more severely
than an impersonal treatment of its themes.
Of three very personal and romantic writers,

*His later
Manner.*

our own Stevenson escaped the pit into which both Björnson and Daudet stumbled. You may say the temptation came later to him. But the temptation to follow an European fashion does, as a rule, befall a Briton last of all men, for reasons of which we need not feel proud : and the date of Mr. Hardy's stumbling is fairly recent, after all. Björnson, at any rate, began very soon to be troubled. Between 1864 and 1874, from his thirty-second to his forty-second year, his invention seemed, to some extent, paralyzed. *The Fisher Maiden*, the one story written during that time, starts as beautifully as *Arne ;* but it grows complicated and introspective : the psychological experiences of the stage - struck heroine are not in the same key as the opening chapters. Passing over nine years, we find *Magnhild* much more vague and involved—

" Here he is visibly affected by French models, and by the methods of the naturalists, but he is trying to combine them with his own simpler traditions of rustic realism. . . . The author felt himself greatly moved by fermenting ideas and ambitions which he had not completely mastered. . . . There is a kind of uncomfortable discrepancy between the scene and the style, a breath of Paris and the boulevards blowing through the pine-trees of a puritanical Nor-

wegian village. . . . But the book is a most
interesting link between the early peasant-stories and
the great novels of his latest period."

Well, of these same " great novels "—of
Flags are Flying and *In God's Way*—people
must speak as they think. They seem to me
the laborious productions of a man forcing
himself still further and further from his right
and natural bent. In them, says Mr. Gosse,
" Björnson returns, in measure, to the poetical
elements of his youth. He is now capable
again, as for instance in the episode of Ragni's
symbolical walk in the woodlands, *In God's
Way*, of passages of pure idealism." Yes, he
returns—" in measure." He is " capable of
idyllic passages." In other words, his nature
reasserts itself, and he remains an imperfect con-
vert. " He has striven hard to be a realist, and
at times he has seemed to acquiesce altogether
in the naturalistic formula, but in truth he has
never had anything essential in common with
M. Zola." In other words, he has fallen between two stools. He has tried to expel nature
with a pitchfork and still she runs back upon
him. He has put his hand to the plough and
has looked back : or (if you take my view of
" the naturalistic formula ") he has sinned, but

has not sinned with his whole heart. For to produce a homogeneous story, either the acquired Zola or the native Björnson must have been cast out utterly.

Value of Early Impressions to a Novelist. I have quoted an example of the impressions of Björnson's childhood. I do not think critics have ever quite realized the extent to which writers of fiction—especially those who use a personal style—depend upon the remembered impressions of childhood. Such impressions—no matter how fantastic—are an author's first-hand stock : and in using them he comes much closer to nature than when he collects any number of scientifically approved data to maintain some view of life which he has derived from books. Compare *Flags are Flying* with *Arne*, and you will see my point. The longer book is ten times as realistic in treatment, and about one-tenth as true to life.

MR. GEORGE MOORE

March 31, 1894.
"Esther Waters."

IT is good, after all, to come across a novel written by a man who can write a novel. We have been much in the company of the Amateur of late, and I for one am very weary of him—weary of his preposterous goings-out and comings-in, of his smart ineptitudes, of his solemn zeal in reforming the decayed art of fiction, of his repeated failures to discover beneficence in all those institutions, from the Common Law of England to the Scheme of the Universe, which have managed to leave him and his aspirations out of count. I am weary of him and of his deceased wife's sister, and of their fell determination to discover each other's soul in a bottle of hay. Above all, I am weary of his writings, because he cannot write, neither has he the humility to sit down and learn.

Mr. George Moore, on the other hand, has steadily labored to make himself a fine artist, and his training has led him through many

341

strange places. I should guess that among living novelists few have started with so scant an equipment. As far as one can tell he had, to begin with, neither a fertile invention nor a subtle dramatic instinct, nor an accurate ear for language. A week ago I should have said this very confidently : after reading *Esther Waters* I say it less confidently, but believe it to be true, nevertheless. Mr. Moore has written novels that are full of faults. These faults have been exposed mercilessly, for Mr. Moore has made many enemies. But he has always possessed an artistic conscience and an immense courage. He answered his critics briskly enough at the time, but an onlooker of common sagacity could perceive that the really convincing answer was held in reserve—that, as they say in America, Mr. Moore "allowed" he was going to write a big novel one of these days, and meanwhile we had better hold our judgment upon Mr. Moore's capacity open to revision.

What, then, is to be said of *Esther Waters*, this volume of a modest 377 pages, upon which Mr. Moore has been at work for at least two years ?

Mr. George Moore

"Esther" and Mr. Hardy's "Tess."

Well, in the first place, I say, without hesitation, that *Esther Waters* is the most important novel published in England during these two years. We have been suffering from the Amateur during that period, and no doubt (though it seems hard) every nation has the Amateur it deserves. To find a book to compare with *Esther Waters* we must go back to December, 1891, and to Mr. Hardy's *Tess of the D'Urbervilles*. It happens that a certain similarity in the motives of these two stories makes comparison easy. Each starts with the seduction of a young girl ; and each is mainly concerned with her subsequent adventures. From the beginning the advantage of probability is with the younger novelist. Mr. Moore's "William Latch" is a thoroughly natural figure, and remains a natural figure to the end of the book : an uneducated man and full of failings, but a man always, and therefore to be forgiven by the reader only a little less readily than Esther herself forgives him. Mr. Hardy's "Alec D'Urberville" is a grotesque and violent lay figure, a wholly incredible cad. Mr. Hardy, by killing Tess's child, takes away the one means by which his heroine could have been led to return to D'Urberville

343

without any loss of the reader's sympathy. Mr. Moore allows Esther's child to live, and thus has at hand the material for one of the most beautiful stories of maternal love ever imagined by a writer. I dislike extravagance of speech, and would run my pen through these words could I remember, in any novel I have read, a more heroic story than this of Esther Waters, a poor maid-of-all-work, without money, friends, or character, fighting for her child against the world, and in the end dragging victory out of the struggle. In spite of the Æschylean gloom in which Mr. Hardy wraps the story of Tess, I contend that Esther's fight is, from end to end, the more heroic.

Also Esther's story seems to me informed with a saner philosophy of life. There is gloom in her story ; and many of the circumstances are sordid enough ; but throughout I see the recognition that man and woman can at least improve and dignify their lot in this world. Many people believe *Tess* to be the finest of its author's achievements. A devoted admirer of Mr. Hardy's genius, I decline altogether to consent. To my mind, among recent developments of the English novel nothing is more lamentable than the manner in which this distinguished writer has allowed himself of late to fancy that the riddles of life are solved by pulling mouths at Providence (or whatever men choose to call the Supreme Power) and depicting it as a savage and omnipotent bully, directing human affairs after the fashion of a practical joker fresh from a village ale-house. For to this teaching his more recent writings plainly tend ; and alike in *Tess* and *Life's Little Ironies* the part played by the " President of the Immortals " is no sublimer—save in the amount of force exerted—than that of a lout who pulls a chair suddenly from under an old woman. Now, by wedding Necessity with uncouth Jocularity, Mr. Hardy may have found an hypothesis that solves for him all the difficulties of life. I am not concerned in this place to deny that it may be the true explanation. I have merely to point out that art and criticism must take some time in getting accustomed to it, and that meanwhile the traditions of both are so far agreed in allowing a certain amount of free will to direct the actions of men and women that a tale which should be all necessity and no free will would, in effect, be necessity's own contrary—a merely wanton freak.

345

For, in effect, it comes to this :—The story of Tess, in which attention is so urgently directed to the hand of Destiny, is not felt to be inevitable, but freakish. The story of Esther Waters, in which a poor servant-girl is allowed to grapple with her destiny and, after a fashion, to defeat it, is felt (or has been felt by one reader, at any rate) to be absolutely inevitable. To reconcile us to the black flag above Wintoncester prison as to the appointed end of Tess's career, a curse at least as deep as that of Pelops should have been laid on the D'Urberville family. Tess's curse does not lie by nature on all women ; nor on all Dorset women ; nor on all Dorset women who have illegitimate children ; for a very few even of these are hanged. We feel that we are not concerned with a type, but with an individual case deliberately chosen by the author ; and no amount of talk about the "President of the Immortals" and his "Sport" can persuade us to the contrary. With Esther Waters, on the other hand, we feel we are assisting in the combat of a human life against its natural destiny ; we perceive that the woman has a chance of winning ; we are happy when she wins ; and we are the better for helping her with our sym-

pathy in the struggle. That is why, using the
word in the Aristotelian sense, I maintain that
Esther Waters is a more "philosophical"
work than *Tess*.

The atmosphere of the low-class gambling in
which Mr. Moore's characters breathe and live
is no doubt a result of his careful study of Zola.
It is, as everyone knows, M. Zola's habit to
take one of the many pursuits of men—from
War and Religion down to Haberdashery and
Veterinary Surgery—and expand it into an
atmosphere for a novel. But in Mr. Moore's
case it may safely be urged that gambling on
racehorses actually is the atmosphere in which
a million or two of Londoners pass their lives.
Their hopes, their very chances of a satisfying
meal, hang from day to day on the performances of horses they have never seen. I cannot
profess to judge with what accuracy Mr. Moore
has reproduced the niceties of handicapping,
bookmaking, place-betting, and the rest, the
fluctuations of the gambling market, and their
causes. I gather that extraordinary care has
been bestowed upon these details; but criticism here must be left to experts. I only know
that, not once or twice only in the course of

his narrative, Mr. Moore makes us study the
odds against a horse almost as eagerly as if it
carried our own money : because it does indeed carry for a while the destiny of Esther
Waters — and yet for a while only.   We feel
that, whichever horse wins the ultimate issues
are inevitable.

It will be gathered from what I have said
that Mr. Moore has vastly outstripped his own
public form, even as shown in *A Mummer's
Wife*.   But it may be as well to set down, beyond possibility of misapprehension, my belief
that in *Esther Waters* we have the most artistic, the most complete, and the most inevitable
work of fiction that has been written in England for at least two years.   Its plainness of
speech may offend many.   It may not be a
favorite in the circulating libraries or on the
bookstalls.   But I shall be surprised if it fails
of the place I predict for it in the esteem of
those who know the true aims of fiction and
respect the conscientious practice of that great
art.

MRS. MARGARET L. WOODS

Nov. 28, 1891. "*Esther Vanhom-righ.*"

AMONG considerable novelists who have handled historical subjects—that is to say, who have brought into their story men and women who really lived and events which have really taken place—you will find one rule strictly observed, and no single infringement of it that has been followed by success. This rule is that the historical characters and events should be mingled with poetical characters and events, and *made subservient to them.* And it holds of books as widely dissimilar as *La Vicomte de Bragelonne* and *La Guerre et la Paix ; The Abbot* and *John Inglesant.* In history Louis XIV. and Napoleon are the most salient men of their time : in fiction they fall back and give prominence to D'Artagnan and the Prince André. They may be admirably painted, but unless they take a subordinate place in the composition, the artist scores a failure.

The reason of this is, of course, very

349

simple. If an artist is to have full power
over his characters, to know their hearts, to
govern their emotions and sway them at his
will, they must be his own creatures and the
life in them derived from him. He must
have an entirely free hand with them. But
the personages of history have an independent life of their own, and with them his
hand is tied. Thackeray has a freehold on
the soul of Beatrix Esmond, but he takes the
soul of Marlborough furnished, on a short
lease, and has to render an account to the
Muse of History. He is lord of one and
mere occupier of the other. Nor will it do
to say that an artist by sympathetic and intelligent study can master the motives of any
group of historical characters sufficiently for
his purpose. For, since they have anticipated
him and lived their lives without his help,
they leave him but a choice between two
poor courses. If he narrate their lives and
adventures as they really befel, he is writing
history. If, on the other hand, he disregard
historical accuracy, he might just as well have
used another set of characters or have given
his characters other names. Indeed, it would
be much better. For if Alcibiades went as a

matter of fact to Sparta and as a matter of fiction you make him stay at home, you merely advertise to the world that there was something in Alcibiades you don't understand. And if you are writing about an Alcibiades whom you don't quite understand, you will save your readers some risk of confusion by calling him Charicles.

Now Jonathan Swift and Esther Johnson and Esther Vanhomrigh really lived; and by living, became historical. But Mrs. Woods sets forth to translate them back into fiction, not as subordinate characters, but as protagonists. She has chosen to work within the difficult limits I have indicated. But there are others which might easily have cramped her hand even more closely.

The story of Swift and Esther Vanhomrigh is a story of passion, and runs on the confines of madness. But it happened in the Age of Reason. Doubtless men and women felt madness and passion in that age: doubtless, too, they spoke of madness and passion, but not in their literature. And now that the lips are dust and the fiery conversations lost, Mrs.

A Tale of Passion to be told in Terms of Reason.

Woods has only their written prose to turn to
for help. To satisfy the pedant she must tell
her story of passion in terms of reason. In one
respect Thackeray had a more difficult task in
Esmond; for he aimed to make his book a
reflection, in every page and line, of the days
of Queen Anne. Not only had he, like Mrs.
Woods, to make his characters and their talk
consistent with that age; but every word of
the story is supposed to be told by a gentleman
of that age, whereas Mrs. Woods in her narrative prose may use the language of her own
century. On the other hand, the story of
Esmond deals with comparatively temperate
emotions. There is nothing in Thackeray's
masterpiece to strain the prose of the Age of
Reason. It is pitched in the key of those
times, and the prose of those times is sufficient
and exactly sufficient for it. That it should be
so is all the more to Thackeray's honor, for
the artist is to be praised in the conception as
duly as in the execution of his work. But, the
conception being granted, I think *Esther Vanhomrigh* must have been a harder book than
Esmond to write.

For even the prose of Swift himself is in-

adequate to Swift. He was a great and glaring
anomaly who never fell into perspective with
his age while he lived, and can hardly be
pulled into perspective now with the drawing
materials which are left to us. Men of like
abundant genius are rarely measurable in language used by their contemporaries; and this
is perhaps the reason why they disquiet their
contemporaries so confoundedly. Where in the
books written by tye-bewigged gentlemen, or
in the letters written by Swift himself, can you
find words to explain that turbulent and potent
man? He bursts the capacity of Addison's
phrase and Pope's couplet. He was too big
for a bishop's chair, and now, if a novelist
attempt to clothe him in the garments of his
time, he splits them down the back.

It is in meeting this difficulty that Mrs.
Woods seems to me to display the courage and
intelligence of a true artist. She is bound to
be praised by many for her erudition; but
perhaps she will let me thank her for having
trodden upon her erudition. In the first
volume it threatened to overload and sink her.
But no sooner does she begin to catch the
wind of her subject than she tosses all this

superfluous cargo overboard. From the point
where passion creeps into the story this learning
is carried lightly and seems to be worn unconsciously. Instead of cataloguing the age, she
comprehends it.

To me the warmth and pathos she packs into
her eighteenth‑century conversation, without
modernizing it thereby, is something amazing.
For this alone the book would be notable ; and
it can be proved to come of divination, simply
because nothing exists from which she could
have copied it. More obvious, though not
more wonderful, is her feminine gift of rendering a scene vivid for us by describing it, not as
it is, but as it excites her own intelligence or
feelings. Let me explain myself : for it is the
sorry fate of a book so interesting and suggestive as *Esther Vanhomrigh* to divert the critic
from praise of the writer to consider a dozen
problems which the writer raises.

*Women and
" le don pit-
toresque."* Well, then, M. Jules Lemaître has said somewhere — and with considerable truth — that
women when they write have not *le don pittor-
esque*. By this he means that they do not
strive to depict a scene exactly as it strikes upon

354

their senses, but as they perceive it after testing its effect upon their emotions and experience. Suppose now we have to describe a moonlit night in May. Mrs. Woods begins as a man might begin, thus—

" The few and twinkling lights disappeared from the roadside cottages. The full white moon was high in the cloudless deep of heaven, and the sounds of the warm summer night were all about their path ; the splash of leaping fish, the sleepy chirrup of birds disturbed by some night-wandering creature ; the song of the reed-warbler, the persistent churring of the night jar, and the occasional hoot of the owl, far off on some ancestral tree."

Now all this, except, perhaps, the " ancestral " tree, is a direct picture, and with it some men might stop. But no woman could stop here, and Mrs. Woods does not. She goes on—

" It was such an exquisite May night, full of the mystery and beauty of moonlight and the scent of haw-thorn, as makes the earth an Eden in which none but lovers should walk—happy lovers or young poets, whose large eyes, so blind in the daylight world of men, can see God walking in the Garden." . . .

You see it is sensation no longer, but reflection and emotion.

Now I am only saying that women cannot

avoid this.   I am not condemning it.   On the contrary, it is beautiful in Mrs. Woods's hand, and sometimes luminously true.   Take this, for instance, of the interior of a city church : —

" It had none of the dim impressiveness of a mediæval church, that seems reared with a view to Heaven rather than Earth, and whose arches, massive or soaring, neither gain nor lose by the accidental presence of ephemeral human creatures below them.   No, the building seemed to cry out for a congregation, and the mind's eye involuntarily peopled it with its Sunday complement of substantial citizens and their families."

This is not a picturesque but a reflective description.   Yet how it illuminates !   If we had never thought of it before we know now, once and for all, the essential difference between a Gothic church and one of Wren's building. And further, since Mrs. Woods is writing of an age that slighted Gothic for the architecture of Wren and his followers, we get a brilliant side-flash to help our comprehension.   It is a hint only, but it assures us as we read that we are in the eighteenth century, when men and women were of more account than soaring aspirations.

And the conclusion is that if Mrs. Woods could not conquer the difficulties which beset any attempt to make protagonists of two historical characters, if she was obliged to follow the facts to the detriment of composition, she has vitalized and recreated a dead age in a fashion to make us all wonder. *Esther Vanhomrigh* is a great feat, and its authoress is one of the few of whom almost anything may be expected.

In her latest book,* Mrs. Woods returns to that class of life—so far as life may be classified—which she handled so memorably in *A Village Tragedy*. There are differences, though. As the titles indicate, the life in the earlier story was stationary : in the latter it is nomadic—the characters are artistes in a travelling show. This at once suggests comparison with M. Edmond de Goncourt's *Les Frères Zemganno ;* or rather a contrast : for the two stories, conceived in very similar surroundings, differ in at least two vital respects.

Jan. 26, 1895.
" The Vagabonds."

For what, in short, is the story of *Les Frères Zemganno ?* Two brothers, Gianni and Nello,

* *The Vagabonds.* By Margaret L. Woods. London : Smith, Elder & Co.

tumblers in a show that travels round the village fairs and small country towns of France, are seized with an ambition to excel in their calling. They make their way to England, where they spend some years clowning in various circuses. Then they return to make their *debut* in Paris. Gianni has invented at length a trick act, a feat that will make the brothers famous. They are performing it for the first time in public, when a circus girl, who has a spite against Nello, causes him to fall and break both his legs. He can perform no more : and henceforward, as he watches his brother performing, a strange jealousy awakes and grows in him, causing him agony whenever Gianni touches a trapèze. Gianni discovers this and renounces his art.

Now here in the first place it is to be noted that the whole story depends upon the circus profession, and the brothers' love for it and desire to excel in it. The catastrophe ; Nello's jealousy ; Gianni's self-sacrifice ; are inseparable from the atmosphere of the book. The catastrophe is a professional catastrophe ; the jealousy a professional jealousy ; the sacrifice a sacrifice of a profession. And in the second place we

know, even if we had not his own word for it,
that M. de Goncourt—contrary to his habit—
deliberately etherealized the atmosphere of the
circus-ring and idealized the surroundings. He
calls his tale an essay in poetic realism. " Je
me suis trouvé dans une de ces heures de la vie,
vieillissantes, maladives, lâches devant le travail
poignant et angoisseux de mes autres livres, en
un état de l'âme où la vérité trop vraie m'était
antipathique à moi aussi!—et j'ai fait cette
fois de l'imagination dans du rêve mêlé à du
souvenir." We know from the Goncourt Jour-
nals exactly what is meant by "du souvenir."
We know that M. Edmond de Goncourt is
but translating into the language of the circus-
ring and symbolizing in the story of Gianni
and Nello the story of his own literary col-
laboration with his brother Jules—a collab-
oration of quite singular intimacy, that ceased
only with Jules's death in 1870. Possibly,
as M. Zola once suggested, M. Edmond de
Goncourt did at first intend to depict the
circus-life, after his wont, in true "naturalistic" manner, softening and extenuating
nothing: but "par une délicatesse qui s'ex-
plique, il a reculé devant le milieu brutal de
cirques, devant certaines laideurs et certaines

monstruosités des personnages qu'il choisis-
sait.'' The two facts remain that in *Les
Frères Zemganno* M. de Goncourt (1) made
professional life in a circus the very blood and
tissue of his story; and (2) that he softened
the details of that life, and to a certain degree
idealized it.

Turning to Mrs. Woods's book and taking
these two points in reverse order, we find to
begin with that she idealizes nothing and
softens next to nothing. Where she does
soften, she softens only for literary effect—
to give a word its due force, or a picture its
proper values. She does not, for instance,
accurately report the oaths and blasphemies:—

" The tents and booths of the show were disappearing
rapidly like stage scenery. The red-faced Manager,
Joe, and several others in authority, ran hither and
thither shouting their orders to a crowd of workmen in
jackets and fustian trousers, who were piling rolls of
canvas, and heavy chests, and mountains of planks and
long vibrating poles, on the great waggons. Others were
harnessing the big powerful horses to the carts, horses
that were mostly white, and wore large red collars. The
scene was so busy, so full of movement, that it would
have been exhilarating had not the fresh morning air
been full of senseless blasphemies and other deformities

of speech, uttered casually and constantly, without any apparent consciousness on the part of the speakers that they were using strong language. Probably the lady who dropped toads and vipers from her lips whenever she opened them came in process of time to consider them the usual accompaniments of conversation."

There are a great many reasons against copious profanity of speech. Here you have the artistic reason, and, by implication, that which forbids its use in literature — namely, its ineffectiveness. But though she selects, Mrs. Woods does not refine. She exhibits the life of the travelling show in its habitual squalor as well as in its occasional brightness. How she has managed it passes my understanding : but her book leaves the impression of confident familiarity with this kind of life, of knowledge not merely accumulated, but assimilated. Knowing as we do that Mrs. Woods was not brought up in a circus, we infer that she must have spent much labor in research : but, taken by itself, her book permits no such inference. The truth is that in the case of a genuine artist no line can be drawn between knowledge and imagination. Probably—almost certainly —Mrs. Woods has to a remarkable degree that gift which Mr. Henry James describes as " the

faculty which when you give it an inch takes an
ell, and which for an artist is a much greater
source of strength than any accident of residence or of place in the social scale . . .
the power to guess the unseen from the seen, to
trace the implication of things, to judge the
whole piece by the pattern ; the condition
of feeling life in general so completely that you
are well on your way to knowing a particular
corner of it." Be this as it may, Mrs. Woods
has written a novel which, for mastery of
an unfamiliar *milieu*, is almost fit to stand
beside *Esther Waters*. I say "almost" : for,
although Mrs. Woods's mastery is easier and less
conscious than Mr. Moore's, it neither goes so
deep to the springs of action nor bears so
intimately on the conduct of the story. But of
this later.

If one thing more than another convinces
me that Mrs. Woods has thoroughly realized
these queer characters of hers, it is that she
makes them so much like other people. Whatever our profession may be, we are generally
silent upon the instincts that led us to adopt it
—unless, indeed, we happen to be writers and
make a living out of self-analysis. So these

strollers are silent upon the attractiveness of
their calling.   But they crave as openly as any
of us for distinction, and they worship " respectability " as heartily and outspokenly as
any of the country-folk for whose amusement
they tumble and pull faces. It is no small
merit in this book that it reveals how much
and yet how very little divides the performers
in the ring from the audience in the sixpenny
seats.   I wish I had space to quote a particularly fine passage—you will find it on pp. 72–74
—in which Mrs. Woods describes the progress
of these motley characters through Midland
lanes on a fresh spring morning ; the shambling
white horses with their red collars, the painted
vans, the cages " where bears paced uneasily
and strange birds thrust uncouth heads out
into the sunshine," the two elephants and the
camel padding through the dust and brushing
the dew off English hedges, the hermetically
sealed omnibus in which the artistes bumped
and dozed, while the wardrobe-woman, Mrs.
Thompson, held forth undeterred on " those
advantages of birth, house-rent, and furniture,
which made her discomforts of real importance,
whatever those of the other ladies in the show
might be."

But in bringing her Vagabonds into relation with ordinary English life, Mrs. Woods loses all, or nearly all, of that esoteric professional interest which, at first sight, would seem the chief reason for choosing circus people to write about. The story of *Les Frères Zemganno* has, as I have said, this esoteric professional interest. The story of *The Vagabonds* is the story of a husband and of a young wife who does not love him, but discovers that she loves another man—a story as old as the hills and common to every rank and every calling. Mrs. Woods has made the husband a middle-aged clown, the wife a girl with strict notions about respectability, and the lover, Fritz, a handsome young German gymnast. But there was no fundamental reason for this choice of professions. The tale might be every bit as true of a grocer, and a grocer's wife, and a grocer's assistant. Once or twice, indeed, in the earlier chapters we have promise of a more peculiar story when we read of Mrs. Morris's objection to seeing her husband play the clown. "No woman," she says, "that hadn't been brought up to the business would like to see her husband look like that." And of Joe Morris we read that he took an artistic pride in his clowning. But there follows no serious struggle between love and art — no such struggle, for instance, as Zola has worked out to tragic issues in his *L'Œuvre*. Mrs. Morris's shame at her husband's ridiculous appearance merely heightens the contrast in her eyes between him and the handsome young gymnast.

But though the circus-business is not essential, Mrs. Woods makes most effective use of it. I will select one notable illustration of this. When Mrs. Morris at length makes her confession—it is in the wagon, and at night—the unhappy husband wraps her up carefully in her bed and creeps away with his grief to the barn where Chang, a ferocious elephant amenable only to him, has been stabled :—

" He opened the door ; the barn was pitch dark, but as he entered he could hear the noise of the chain which had been fastened to the elephant's legs being suddenly dragged. He spoke to Chang, and the noise ceased. Then running up a short ladder which was close to the door, he threw himself down on the straw and stared up into the darkness, which to his aching eyes seemed spangled with many colours. Presently he was startled by something warm touching him on the face.

" ' Who's there ? ' he called out.

" There was no answer, but the soft thing, something like a hand, felt him cautiously and caressingly all over.

" ' Oh, it's you, Chang, my boy, is it?' said Joe.
' What! are you glad to have me, old chappie? No
humbug about yer, are yer sure? No lies?' ' "

The circus-business is employed again in the
catastrophe : but, to my mind, far less happily.
In spite of very admirable writing, there remains something ridiculous in the spectacle of
an injured husband, armed with a Winchester
rifle and mounted on a frantic elephant, pursuing his wife's lover by moonlight across an
English common and finally " treeing " him
up a sign-post. Mrs. Woods, indeed, means it
to be grotesque : but I think it is something
more.

The problem of the story is the commonest
in fiction. And when I add that the injured
husband has been married before and that his
first wife, honestly supposed to be dead, returns
to threaten his happiness, you will see that Mrs.
Woods sets forth upon a path trodden by many
hundreds of thousands of incompetent feet.
To start with such a situation almost suggests
bravado. If it be bravado, it is entirely justified as the tale proceeds : for amid the crowd
of failures Mrs. Woods's solution wears the
singular distinction of truth. That the book

is written in restrained and beautiful English goes without saying : but the best tribute one can pay to the writing of it is to say that its style and its truthfulness are at one. If complaint must be made, it is the vulgar complaint against truth—that it leaves one a trifle cold. A less perfect story might have aroused more emotion. Yet I for one would not barter the pages that tell of Joe Morris's final surrender of his wife—with their justness of imagination and sobriety of speech—for any amount of pity and terror.

A word on the few merely descriptive passages in the book. Mrs. Woods's scene-painting has all a Frenchman's accomplishment with the addition of that open-air feeling and intimate knowledge of the phenomena of " out-of-doors " which a Frenchman seldom or never attains to. Though not, perhaps, her strongest gift, it is the one by which she stands most conspicuously above her contemporaries. The more credit, then, that she uses it so temperately.

367

MR. HALL CAINE

*August 11,
1894.*
" *The
Manx-
man.*"

MR. HALL CAINE'S new novel *The
Manxman* (London: William Heine-
mann) is a big piece of work altogether. But,
on finishing the tale, I turned back to the beginning and read the first 125 pages over again,
and then came to a stop. I wish that portion
of the book could be dealt with separately. It
cannot: for it but sets the problem in human
passion and conduct which the remaining 300
pages have to solve. Nevertheless the temptation is too much for me.

As one who thought he knew how good Mr.
Hall Caine can be at his best, I must confess to
a shock of delight, or rather a growing sense
of delighted amazement, while reading those
125 pages. Yet the story is a very simple one
—a story of two friends and a woman. The
two friends are Philip Christian and Pete Quil-
liam: Philip talented, accomplished, ambitious,

of good family, and eager to win back the social position which his father had lost by an
imprudent marriage; Pete a nameless boy—
the bastard son of Philip's uncle and a gawky
country-girl—ignorant, brave, simple-minded,
and incurably generous.   The boys have grown
up together, and in love are almost more than
brothers when the time comes for them to part
for a while—Philip leaving home for school,
while Pete goes as mill-boy to one Cæsar Cregeen, who combined the occupations of miller
and landlord of "The Manx Fairy" public-
house.   And now enters the woman—a happy
child when first we make her acquaintance—in
the shape of Katherine Cregeen, the daughter of Pete's employer.   With her poor simple
Pete falls over head and ears in love.   Philip,
too, when home for his holidays, is drawn by
the same dark eyes; but stands aside for his
friend.   Naturally, the miller will not hear of
Pete, a landless, moneyless, nameless, lad, as a
suitor for his daughter; and so Pete sails for
Kimberley to make his fortune, confiding Kitty
to Philip's care.

It seems that the task undertaken by Philip
—that of watching over his friend's sweetheart

—is a familiar one in the Isle of Man, and he who discharges it is known by a familiar name.

> " They call him the *Dooiney Molla*—literally, the ' man-praiser ' ; and his primary function is that of an informal, unmercenary, purely friendly and philanthropic match-maker, introduced by the young man to persuade the parents of the young woman that he is a splendid fellow, with substantial possessions or magnificent prospects, and entirely fit to marry her. But he has a secondary function, less frequent, though scarcely less familiar ; and it is that of a lover by proxy, or intended husband by deputy, with duties of moral guardianship over the girl while the man himself is off ' at the herrings,' or away ' at the mackerel,' or abroad on wider voyages."

And now, of course, begins Philip Christian's ordeal : for Kitty discovers that she loves him and not Pete, and he that he loves Kitty madly. On the other hand there is the imperative duty to keep faith with his absent friend ; and more than this. His future is full of high hope ; the eyes of his countrymen and of the Governor himself are beginning to fasten on him as the most promising youth in the island ; it is even likely that he will be made Deemster, and so win back all the position that his father threw away. But to marry Kitty—even if he can bring himself to break faith with Pete—will

be to marry beneath him, to repeat his father's
disaster, and estrange the favor of all the high
"society" of the island. Therefore, even
when the first line of resistance is broken down
by a report that Pete is dead, Philip determines to cut himself free from the temptation.
But the girl, who feels that he is slipping away
from her, now takes fate into her own hands.
It is the day of harvest-home—the "Melliah"
—on her father's farm. Philip has come to
put an end to her hopes, and she knows it.
The "Melliah" is cut and the usual frolic
begins:

> "Then the young fellows went racing over the field,
> vaulting the stooks, stretching a straw rope for the girls
> to jump over, heightening and tightening it to trip them
> up, and slackening it and twirling it to make them skip.
> And the girls were falling with a laugh, and, leaping up
> again and flying off like the dust, tearing their frocks
> and dropping their sun-bonnets as if the barley-grains
> they had been reaping had got into their blood.
> "In the midst of this maddening frolic, while Cæsar
> and the others were kneeling by the barley-stack, Kate
> snatched Philip's hat from his head and shot like a gleam
> into the depths of the glen.
> "Philip dragged up his coat by one of its arms and
> fled after her."

Here, then, in Sulby Glen, the girl stakes her

last throw—the last throw of every woman—
and wins. It is the woman—a truly Celtic
touch—who wooes the man, and secures her
love and, in the end, her shame.

> "When a good woman falls from honour, is it merely
> that she is the victim of a momentary intoxication, of
> stress of passion, of the fever of instinct? No. It is
> mainly that she is the slave of the sweetest, tenderest,
> most spiritual, and pathetic of all human fallacies—the
> fallacy that by giving herself to the man she loves she
> attaches him to herself for ever. This is the real be-
> trayer of nearly all good women that are betrayed. It
> lies at the root of tens of thousands of the cases that
> make up the merciless story of man's sin and woman's
> weakness. Alas! it is only the woman who clings the
> closer. The impulse of the man is to draw apart. He
> must conquer it, or she is lost. Such is the old cruel
> difference and inequality of man and woman as Nature
> made them—the old trick, the old tragedy."

And meanwhile Pete is not dead; but re-
covered, and coming home.

Here, on p. 125, ends the second act of the
drama: and the telling has been quite masterly.
The passage quoted above has hitherto been
the author's solitary comment. Everything
has been presented in that fine objective manner which is the triumph of story-telling. As

I read, I began to say to myself, "This is good"; and in a little while, "Ah, but this is very good"; and at length, "But this is amazing. If he can only keep this up, he will have written one of the finest novels of his time." The whole story was laid out so easily; with such humor, such apparent carelessness, such an instinct for the right stroke in the right place, and no more than the right stroke; the big scenes—Pete's love-making in the dawn and Kate's victory in Sulby Glen—were so poetically conceived (I use the adverb in its strictest sense) and so beautifully written; above all, the story remained so true to the soil on which it was constructed. A sworn admirer of Mr. Brown's *Betsy Lee* and *The Doctor* has no doubt great advantage over other people in approaching *The Manxman*. Who, that has read his *Fo'c's'le Yarns* worthily, can fail to feel kindly towards the little island and its shy, home-loving folk? And—by what means I do not know—Mr. Hall Caine has managed from time to time to catch Mr. Brown's very humor and set it to shine on his page. The secret, I suppose, is their common possession as Manxmen: and, like all the best art, theirs is true to its country and its material.

373

Pete comes home, suspecting no harm; still childish of heart and loud of voice—a trifle too loud, by the way; his shouts begin to irritate the reader, and the reader begins to feel how sorely they must have irritated his wife: for the unhappy Kate is forced, after all, into marrying Pete. And so the tragedy begins.

I wish, with my heart, I could congratulate Mr. Hall Caine as warmly upon the remainder of the book as upon its first two parts. He is too sure an artist to miss the solution—the only adequate solution—of the problem. The purification of Philip Christian and Kitty must come, if at all, "as by fire"; and Mr. Hall Caine is not afraid to take us through the deepest fire. No suffering daunts him—neither the anguish of Kitty, writhing against her marriage with Pete, nor the desperate pathos of Pete after his wife has run away, pretending to the neighbors that she has only gone to Liverpool for her health, and actually writing letters and addressing parcels to himself and posting them from out-of-the-way towns to deceive the local postman; nor the moral ruination of Philip, with whom Kitty is living in hiding; nor his final redemption by the ordeal of a public confession before

374

the great company assembled to see him reach
the height of worldly ambition and be appointed governor of his native island.

And yet—I have a suspicion that Mr. Hall
Caine, who deals by preference with the elemental emotions, would rejoice in the epithet
" Æschylean " applied to his work.   The epithet would not be unwarranted : but it is precisely when most consciously Æschylean that
Mr. Hall Caine, in my poor judgment, comes
to grief.   This is but to say that he possesses
the defects of his qualities.   There is altogether
too much of the " Go to : let me be Titanic "
about the book.   Æschylus has grown a trifle
too well aware of his reputation, has taken to
underscoring his points, and tends to prolixity
in consequence.   Mr. Hall Caine has not a
little of Hugo's audacity, but, with it, not a
little of Hugo's diffuseness.   Standing, like
Destiny, with scourge lifted over the naked
backs of his two poor sinners, he spares them
no single stroke—not so much as a little one.
Every detail that can possibly heighten their
suffering is brought out in its place, until we
feel that Life, after all, is more careless, and tell
ourselves that Fate does not measure out her

revenge with an inch rule. We see the machinery of pathos at work: and we are rather made incredulous than moved when the machinery works so accurately that Philip is made to betray Pete on the very night when Pete goes out to beat a big drum in Philip's honor. Nor is this by any means the only harrowing coincidence of the kind. Worse than this—for its effect upon us as a work of art—our emotions are so flogged and out-tired by detail after detail that they cannot rise at the last big fence, and so the scene of Philip's confession in the Courthouse misses half its effect. It is a fine scene. I am no bigoted admirer of Hawthorne—a very cold one, indeed—and should be the last to say that the famous scene in *The Scarlet Letter* cannot be improved upon. Nor do I make any doubt that, as originally conceived by Mr. Hall Caine, the story had its duly effective climax here. But still less do I doubt that the climax, and therefore the whole story, would have been twice as impressive had the book, from p. 125 onwards, contained just half its present number of words. But whether this opinion be right or wrong, the book remains a big book, and its story a beautiful story.

MR. ANTHONY HOPE

A S I set down the titles of these two new stories by Mr. Anthony Hope, it occurs to me that combined they would make an excellent title for a third story yet to be written. For Mr. Hope's duchess, if by any chance she found herself travelling with a god in a car, would infallibly seize the occasion for a *tour de force* in charming indiscretion. That the car would travel for some part of the distance in that position of unstable equilibrium known to skaters as the "outside edge" may, I think, be taken for granted. But far be it from me to imagine bungling developments of the situation I here suggest to Mr. Hope's singular and agreeable talents. Like Mr. Stevenson's smatterer, who was asked, "What would be the result of putting a pound of potassium in a pot of porter?" I content myself with anticipating "that there would probably be a number of interesting bye-products."

Oct. 27, 1894. "*The God in the Car*" *and* "*The Indiscretion of the Duchess.*"

Be it understood that I suggest only a combination of the titles—not of the two stories as Mr. Hope has written them : for these move on levels altogether different. The constant reader of *The Speaker's* " Causeries " will be familiar with the two propositions—not in the least contradictory—that a novel should be true to life, and that it is quite impossible for a novel to be true to life. He will also know how they are reconciled. A story, of whatever kind, must follow life at a certain remove. It is a good and consistent story if it keep at that remove from first till last. Let us have the old tag once more :

" Servetur ad imum
Qualis ab incepto processerit, et sibi constet."

A good story and real life are such that, being produced in either direction and to any extent, they never meet. The distance between the parallels does not count : or rather, it is just a matter for the author to choose. It is here that Mr. Howells makes his mistake, who speaks contemptuously of Romance as *Puss in Boots*. *Puss in Boots* is a masterpiece in its way, and in its way just as true to life—*i.e.*, to its distance from life—as that very

378

different masterpiece *Silas Lapham.* When Mr. Howells objects to the figure of Vautrin in *Le Père Goriot,* he criticizes well: Vautrin in that tale is out of drawing and therefore monstrous. But to bring a similar objection against Porthos in *Le Vicomte de Bragelonne* would be very bad criticism; for it would ignore all the postulates of the story. In real life Vautrin and Porthos would be equally monstrous: in the stories Vautrin is monstrous and Porthos is not.

But though the distance from real life at which an author conducts his tale is just a matter for his own choice, it usually happens to him after a while, either from taste or habit, to choose a particular distance and stick to it, or near it, henceforth in all his writings. Thus Scott has his own distance, and Jane Austen hers. Balzac, Hugo, Charlotte Brontë, Dickens, Tolstoi, Mr. Howells himself—all these have their favorite distances, and all are different and cannot be confused. But a young writer usually starts in some uncertainty on this point. He has to find his range, and will quite likely lead off with a miss or a ricochet, as Mr. Hardy led off with *Desperate Remedies* before finding the target with *Under the Greenwood Tree*. Now Mr. Hope—the application of these profound remarks is coming at last—being a young writer, hovers in choice between two ranges. He has found the target with both, and cannot make up his mind between them: and I for one hope he will keep up his practice at both: for his experiments are most interesting, and in the course of them he is giving us capital books. Of the two before me, *The God in the Car* belongs to the same class as his earliest work—his *Father Stafford*, for instance, a novel that did not win one-tenth of the notice it deserved. It is practice at short range. It moves very close to real life. Real people, of course, do not converse as briskly and wittily as do Mr. Hope's characters: but these have nothing of the impossible in them, and even in the whole business of Omofaga there is nothing more fantastic than its delightful name. The book is genuinely tragic; but the tragedy lies rather in what the reader is left to imagine than in what actually occurs upon the stage. That it never comes to a more explicit and vulgar issue stands not so much to the credit of the heroine (as I suppose we must call Mrs. Dennison) as to the force of circumstances as

manipulated in the tactful grasp of Mr. Hope.
Nor is it to be imputed to him for a fault that
the critical chapter xvii. reminds us in half a
dozen oddly indirect ways of a certain chapter
in *Richard Feverel*. The place, the situation,
the reader's suspense, are similar ; but the actors, their emotions, their purposes are vastly
different. It is a fine chapter, and the page
with which it opens is the worst in the book—
a solitary purple patch of " fine writing." I
observe without surprise that the reviewers—
whose admiring attention is seldom caught but
by something out of proportion—have been
fastening upon it and quoting it ecstatically.

The Indiscretion of the Duchess is the tale in
Mr. Hope's second manner — the manner of
The Prisoner of Zenda. Story for story, it
falls a trifle sort of *The Prisoner of Zenda*. As
a set-off, the telling is firmer, surer, more accomplished. In each an aimless, superficially
cynical, but naturally amiable English gentleman finds himself casually involved in circumstances which appeal first to his sportsmanlike
love of adventure, and so by degrees to his
chivalry, his sense of honor, and his passions.
At first amused, then perplexed, then nettled,

then involved heart and soul, he is left to fight
his way through with the native weapons of his
order—courage, tact, honesty, wit, strength of
self-sacrifice, aptitude for affairs. The *donnée*
of these tales, their spirit, their postulates, are
nakedly romantic. In them the author deliberately lends enchantment to his view by
withdrawing to a convenient distance from real
life. But, once more, the enchantment is everything and the distance nothing. If I must find
fault with the later of the stories, it will not be
with its general extravagance—for extravagance
is part of the secret of Romance—but with the
sordid and very nasty Madame Delhasse. She
would be repulsive enough in any case : but as
Marie's mother she is peculiarly repulsive and,
let me add, improbable. Nobody looks for
heredity in a tale of this sort : but even in the
fairy tales it is always the heroine's *step*-mother
who ends very fitly with a roll downhill in a
barrel full of spikes.

But great as are the differences between *The
God in the Car* and *The Indiscretion of the
Duchess*—and I ought to say that the former
carries (as it ought) more weight of metal—
they have their points of similarity. Both

illustrate conspicuously Mr. Hope's gift of advancing the action of his story by the sprightly conversation of his characters. There is a touch of Dumas in their talk, and more than a touch of Sterne — the Sterne of the *Sentimental Journey*.

" I beg your pardon, madame," said I, with a whirl of my hat.

" I beg your pardon, sir," said the lady, with an inclination of her head.

" One is so careless in entering rooms hurriedly," I observed.

" Oh, but it is stupid to stand just by the door ! " insisted the lady.

To sum up, these are two most entertaining books by one of the writers for whose next book one searches eagerly in the publishers' lists. If, however, he will not resent one small word of caution, it is that he should not let us find his name there too often. As far as we can see, he cannot write too much for us. But he may very easily write too much for his own health.

"TRILBY"

Sept. 14, 1895.
Hypnotic Fiction.

A NUMBER of people—and I am one—cannot "abide" hypnotism in fiction. In my own case the dislike has been merely instinctive, and I have never yet found time to examine the instinct and discover whether or not it is just and reasonable. The appearance of a one-volume edition of *Trilby*—undoubtedly the most successful tale that has ever dealt with hypnotism—and the success of the dramatic version of *Trilby* presented a few days ago by Mr. Tree, invite one to apply the test. Clearly there are large numbers of people who enjoy hypnotic fiction, or whose prejudices have been effectively subdued by Mr. du Maurier's tact and talent. Must we then confess that our instinct has been unjust and unreasonable, and give it up? Or—since we *must* like *Trilby*, and there is no help for it—shall we enjoy the tale under protest and in spite of its hypnotism?

384

I think my first objection to these hypnotic Analysis of an Aversion.
tales is the terror they inspire. I am not talk-
ing of ordinary human terror, which, of course,
is the basis of much of the best tragedy. We
are terrified by the story of Macbeth; but it is
with a rational and a salutary terror. We are
aware all the while that the moral laws are at
work. We see a hideous calamity looming,
approaching, imminent : but we can see that
it is the effect of causes which have been duly
exhibited to us. We can reason it out : we
know where we stand : our conscience approves
the punishment even while our pity calls out
against it. And when the blow falls, it shakes
away none of our belief in the advantages of
virtuous conduct. It leaves the good old impregnable position, "Be virtuous and you
will be happy," stronger than ever. But the
terror of these hypnotic stories resembles that
of a child in a dark room. For artistic reasons
too obvious to need pointing out, the hypno-
tizer in these stories is always the villain of the
piece. For the same or similar reasons, the
"subject" is always a person worthy of our
sympathy, and is usually a woman. Let us
suppose it to be a good and beautiful woman—
for that is the commonest case. The author

gives us to understand that by hypnotism this good and beautiful woman is for a while completely in the power of a man who is *ex hypothesi* a beast, and who *ex hypothesi* can make her commit any excesses that his beastliness may suggest. Obviously we are removed outside the moral order altogether; and in its place we are presented with a state of things in which innocence, honesty, love, and the rest are entirely at the disposal and under the rule of malevolent brutality; the result, as presented to us, being qualified only by such tact as the author may choose to display. That Mr. du Maurier has displayed great tact is extremely creditable to Mr. du Maurier, and might have been predicted of him. But it does not alter the fact that a form of fiction which leaves us at the mercy of an author's tact is a very dangerous form in a world which contains so few Du Mauriers. It is lamentable enough to have to exclaim—as we must over so much of human history—

> " Ah ! what avails the sceptred race
> And what the form divine ? . . ."

But it must be quite intolerable when a story leaves us demanding, " What avail native inno-

cence, truthfulness, chastity, when all these
can be changed into guile and uncleanliness at
the mere suggestion of a dirty mesmerist?"

The answer to this, I suppose, will be, "But
hypnotism is a scientific fact. People can be
hypnotized, and are hypnotized. Are you one
of those who would exclude the novelist from
this and that field of human experience?"
And then I am quite prepared to hear the old
tag, "*Homo sum,*" etc., once more misapplied.

Let us distinguish. Hypnotism is a proved *Limitation
of Hypnotic
Fiction.*
fact: people are hypnotized. Hypnotism is
not a delimited fact: nobody yet knows precisely its conditions or its effects; or, if the
discovery has been made, it has certainly not
yet found its way to the novelists. For them
it is as yet chiefly a field of fancy. They invent vagaries for it as they invent ghosts. And
as for the " *humanum nihil a me alienum* "
defence, my strongest objection to hypnotic
fiction is its inhumanity. An experience is
not human in the proper artistic sense (with
which alone we are concerned) merely because
it has befallen a man or a woman. There was
an Irishman, the other day, who through mere

inadvertence cut off his own head with a scythe. But the story is rather inhuman than not. Still less right have we to call everything human which can be supposed by the most liberal stretch of the imagination to have happened to a man or a woman. A story is only human in so far as it is governed by the laws which are recognized as determining human action. Now according as we regard human action, its two great determinants will be free will or necessity. But hypnotism entirely does away with free will: and for necessity, fatal or circumstantial, it substitutes the lawless and irresponsible imperative of a casual individual man, who (in fiction) usually happens to be a scoundrel.

A story may be human even though it discard one or more of the recognized conditions of human life. Thus in the confessedly supernatural story of Dr. Jekyll and Mr. Hyde, the conflict between the two Jekylls is human enough and morally significant, because it answers to a conflict which is waged day by day—though as a rule less tremendously—in the soul of every human being. But the double Trilby signifies nothing. She is naturally in love with Little Billee: she is also in love with Svengali, but quite unnaturally and irresponsibly. There is no real conflict. As Gecko says of Svengali—

"He had but to say '*Dors!*' and she suddenly became an unconscious Trilby of marble, who could produce wonderful sounds—just the sounds he wanted and nothing else—and think his thoughts and wish his wishes—and love him at his bidding with a strange, unreal, factitious love . . . just his own love for himself turned inside out—à l'envers—and reflected back on him as from a mirror . . . un écho, un simulacre, quoi? pas autre chose! . . . It was not worth having! I was not even jealous!"

This last passage, I think, suggests that Mr. du Maurier would have produced a much less charming story, indeed, but a vastly more artistic one, had he directed his readers' attention rather upon the tragedy of Svengali than upon the tragedy of Trilby. For Svengali's position as complete master of a woman's will and yet unable to call forth more than a factitious love—"just his own love for himself turned inside out and reflected back on him as from a mirror"—is a really tragic one, and a fine variation on the old Frankenstein *motif*. The tragedy of Frankenstein resides in Frankenstein himself, not in his creature.

389

In short, *Trilby* seems — as *Peter Ibbetson* seemed — to fall into two parts, the natural and supernatural, which will not join. They might possibly join if Mr. du Maurier had not made the natural so exceedingly domestic, had he been less successful with the Trilby, and Little Billee, and Taffy, and the Laird, for all of whom he has taught us so extravagant a liking. But his very success with these domestic (if oddly domestic) figures, and with the very domestic tale of Little Billee's affair of the heart, proves our greatest stumbling-block when we are invited to follow the machinations of the superlative Svengali. That the story of Svengali and of Trilby's voice is a good story only a duffer would deny. So is Gautier's *La Morte Amoureuse ;* perhaps the best story of its kind ever written. But suppose Thackeray had taken *La Morte Amoureuse* and tried to write it into *Pendennis !*

MR. STOCKTON

Sept. 21, 1895.
Stevenson's Testimony.

IN his chapter of "Personal Memories," printed in the *Century Magazine* of July last, Mr. Gosse speaks of the peculiar esteem in which Mr. Frank R. Stockton's stories were held by Robert Louis Stevenson. "When I was going to America to lecture, he was particularly anxious that I should lay at the feet of Mr. Frank R. Stockton his homage, couched in the following lines :—

> My Stockton if I failed to like,
>   It were a sheer depravity ;
> For I went down with the ' Thomas Hyke,'
>   And up with the ' Negative Gravity.'

He adored these tales of Mr. Stockton's, a taste which must be shared by all good men."

It is shared at any rate by some thousands of people on this side of the Atlantic. Only, one is not quite sure how far their admiration extends. As far as can be guessed—for I have never come across any British attempt at a

serious appreciation of Mr. Stockton — the
general disposition is to regard him as an
amusing kind of "cuss" with a queer kink in
his fancy, who writes puzzling little stories that
make you smile. As for taking him seriously,
"why he doesn't even profess to write seriously"—an absurd objection, of course; but
good enough for the present - day reviewer,
who sits up all night in order that the public may have his earliest possible opinion on
the Reminiscences of Bishop A, or the Personal Recollections of Field-Marshal B, or a
Tour taken in Ireland by the Honorable Mrs. C.
For criticism just now, as a mere matter of
business convenience, provides a relative importance for books before they appear; and
in this classification the space allotted to fiction and labelled "important" is crowded for
the moment with works dealing with religious
or sexual difficulties. Everyone has read *Rud-
der Grange, The Lady or the Tiger ?* and *A
Borrowed Month ;* but somehow few people
seem to think of them as subjects for serious
criticism.

And yet these stories are almost classics.
That is to say, they have the classical qualities,

and only need time to ripen them into class- *" Classi-*
ics : for nothing but age divides a story of the *cal" qual-*
ities.
quality of *The Lady or the Tiger ?* (for instance)
from a story of the quality of *Rip Van Winkle*.
They are full of wit ; but the wit never chokes
the style, which is simple and pellucid.   Their
fanciful postulates being granted, they are absolutely rational.   And they are in a high
degree original.   Originality, good temper,
good sense, moderation, wit—these are classical qualities : and he is a rare benefactor who
employs them all for the amusement of the
world.

At first sight it may seem absurd to compare *A Com-*
Mr. Stockton with Defoe.   You can scarcely *parison.*
imagine two men with more dissimilar notions
of the value of gracefulness and humor, or with
more divergent aims in writing.   Mr. Stockton
is nothing if not fanciful, and Defoe is hardly
fanciful at all.   Nevertheless in reading one I
am constantly reminded of the other.   You
must remember Mr. Stockton's habit is to con-
fine his eccentricities of fancy to the postulates
of a tale.   He starts with some wildly unusual
—but, as a rule, not impossible—conjuncture of
circumstances.   This being granted, however,

he deduces his story logically and precisely, appealing never to our passions and almost constantly to our common sense. His people are as full of common-sense as Defoe's. They may have more pluck than the average man or woman, and they usually have more adaptability; but they apply to extraordinary circumstances the good unsentimental reasoning of ordinary life, and usually with the happiest results. The shipwreck of Mrs. Lecks and Mrs. Aleshine was extraordinary enough, but their subsequent conduct was rational almost to precision : and in story-telling rationality does for fancy what economy of emotional utterances does for emotion. We may apply to Mr. Stockton's tales a remark which Mr. Saintsbury let fall some years ago upon dream-literature. He was speaking particularly of Flaubert's *Tentation de Saint Antoine* :—

" The capacities of dreams and hallucinations for literary treatment are undoubted. But most writers, including even De Quincey, who have tried this style, have erred, inasmuch as they have endeavoured to throw a portion of the mystery with which the waking mind invests dreams over the dream itself. Anyone's experience is sufficient to show that this is wrong. The events of dreams as they happen are quite plain and matter-of-fact, and it is only in the intervals, and, so to speak, the

scene-shifting of dreaming, that any suspicion of strange-
ness occurs to the dreamer."

A dream, however wild, is quite plain and
matter-of-fact to the dreamer ; therefore, for
verisimilitude, the narrative of a dream should
be quite plain and matter-of-fact. In the
same way the narrator of an extremely fanciful tale should — since verisimilitude is the
first aim of story-telling—attempt to exclude
all suspicion of the unnatural from his reader's
mind. And this is only done by persuading
him that no suspicion of the unnatural occurred
to the actors in the story. And this again is
best managed by making his characters persons
of sound every-day common sense. " If *these*
are not upset by what befalls them, why "—is
the unconscious inference—" why in the world
should *I* be upset ? "

So, in spite of the enormous difference between the two writers, there has been no one
since Defoe who so carefully as Mr. Stockton regulates the actions of his characters by
strict common sense. Nor do I at the moment remember any writer who comes closer
to Defoe in mathematical care for detail.
In the case of the True-born Englishman this

carefulness was sometimes overdone—as when he makes Colonel Jack remember with exactness the lists of articles he stole as a boy, and their value. In the *Adventures of Captain Horn* the machinery which conceals and guards the Peruvian treasure is so elaborately described that one is tempted to believe Mr. Stockton must have constructed a working model of it with his own hands before he sat down to write the book. In a way, this accuracy of detail is part of the common-sense character of the narrative, and undoubtedly helps the verisimilitude enormously.

A Genuine American. But to my mind Mr. Stockton's characters are even more original than the machinery of his stories. And in their originality they reflect not only Mr. Stockton himself, but the race from which they and their author spring. In fact, they seem to me about the most genuinely American things in American fiction. After all, when one comes to think of it, Mrs. Lecks and Captain Horn merely illustrate that ready adaptation of Anglo - Saxon pluck and businesslike common sense to savage and unusual circumstances which has been the real secret of the colonization of the North

American Continent. Captain Horn's discovery and winning of the treasure may differ accidentally, but do not differ in essence, from a thousand true tales of commercial triumph in the great Central Plain or on the Pacific Slope. And in the heroine of the book we recognize those very qualities and aptitudes for which we have all learnt to admire and esteem the American girl. They are hero and heroine, and so of course we are presented with the better side of a national character; but then it has been the better side which has done the business. The bitterest critic of things American will not deny that Mr. Stockton's characters are typical Americans, and could not belong to any other nation in the world. Nor can he deny that they combine sobriety with pluck, and businesslike behavior with good feeling; that they are as full of honor as of resource, and as sportsmanlike as sagacious. That people with such characteristics should be recognizable by us as typical Americans is a sufficient answer to half the nonsense which is being talked just now *à propos* of a recent silly contest for the America Cup.

Nationality apart, if anyone wants a good stirring story, *Captain Horn* is the story for his money. It has loose ends, and the concluding chapter ties up an end that might well have been left loose ; but if a better story of adventure has been written of late I wish somebody would tell me its name.

BOW-WOW

August 26, 1893. Dauntless Anthology.

IT is really very difficult to know what to say to Mr. Maynard Leonard, editor of *The Dog in British Poetry* (London : David Nutt). His case is something the same as Archdeacon Farrar's. The critic who desires amendment in the Archdeacon's prose, and suggests that something might be done by a study of Butler or Hume or Cobbett or Newman, is met with the cheerful retort, " But I have studied these writers, and admire them even more than you do." The position is impregnable ; and the Archdeacon is only asserting that two and two make four when he goes on to confess that, " with the best will in the world to profit by the criticisms of his books, he has never profited in the least by any of them."

Now, Mr. Leonard has at least this much in common with Archdeacon Farrar, that before him criticism must sit down with folded hands.

399

In the lightness of his heart he accepts every fresh argument against such and such a course as an added reason for following it :—

> " While this collection of poems was being made," he tells us, " a well-known author and critic took occasion to gently ridicule (*sic*) anthologies and anthologists. He suggested, as if the force of foolishness could no further go, that the next anthology would deal with dogs."

" Undismayed by this," to use his own words, Mr. Leonard proceeded to prove it. Now it is obvious that no man can set a term to literary activity if it depend on the Briton's notorious unwillingness to recognize that he is beaten. I might dare, for instance, a Scotsman to compile an anthology on " The Eel in British Poetry " ; but of what avail is it to challenge an indomitable race ?

I am sorry Mr. Leonard has not given the name of this critic ; but have a notion it must be Mr. Andrew Lang, though I am sure he is innocent of the split infinitive quoted above. It really ought to be Mr. Lang, if only for the humor of the means by which Mr. Leonard proposes to silence him. " I am confident," says he, " that the voice of the great dog-loving public in this country would drown that of the critic in question." Mr. Leonard's metaphors, you see, like the dyer's hand, are subdued to what they work in. But is not the picture delightful? Mr. Lang, the gentle of speech; who, with his master Walton, "studies to be quiet"; who tells us in his very latest verse

> " I've maistly had my fill
> O' this world's din "—

—Mr. Lang set down in the midst of a really representative dog show, say at Birmingham or the Crystal Palace, and there howled down! His *blandi susurri* drowned in the combined clamor of mongrel, puppy, whelp, and hound, and " the great dog-loving public in this country"!

" *Solvitur ululando*," hopes Mr. Leonard; and we will wait for the voice of the great dog-loving public to uplift itself and settle the question. Here, at any rate, is the book, beautiful in shape, and printed by the Constables upon sumptuous paper. And the title-page bears a rubric and a reference to Tobias' dog. " It is no need," says Wyclif in one of

his sermons, " to busy us what hight Tobies'
hound "; but Wyclif had never to reckon with
a great dog-loving public.   And Mr. Leonard,
having considered his work and dedicated it
" To the Cynics "—which, I suppose, is Greek
for " dog - loving public " — observes, " It is
rather remarkable that no one has yet published
such a book as this."   Perhaps it is.

But if we take it for granted (1) that it was
worth doing, and (2) that whatever be worth
doing is worth doing well, then Mr. Leonard
has reason for his complacency.   " It was never
my intention," he says, " to gather together a
complete collection of even British poems about
dogs."—When will *that* come, I wonder?—
" I have sought to secure a representative rather
than an exhaustive anthology."   His selections
from a mass of poetry ranging from Homer to
Mr. Mallock are judicious.   He is not concerned (he assures us) to defend the poetical
merits of all this verse:—

> "—O, the wise contentment
>   Th' anthologist doth find ! "

—but he has provided it with notes—and capital notes they are—with a magnificent Table of

Contents, an Index of Authors, an Index of
First Lines, an Index of Dogs Mentioned by
Name in the Poems, and an Index of the
Species of Dogs Mentioned. So that, even if
he miss transportation to an equal sky, the dog
has better treatment on earth than most authors.
And Mr. Nutt and the Messrs. Constable have
done their best; and everyone knows how good
is that best. And the wonder is, as Dr. Johnson remarked (concerning a dog, by the way),
not that the thing is done so well, but that it
should be done at all.

OF SEASONABLE NUMBERS:

A Baconian Essay

Dec. 26,
1891.

T HAT was a Wittie Invective made by *Mon-*
taigny upon the *Antipodeans*, Who said they
must be Thieves that pulled on their breeches
when Honest Folk were scarce abed. So is
it Obnoxious to them that purvey *Christmas*
Numbers, *Annuals*, and the like, that they
commonly write under *Sirius* his star as it were
Capricornus, feigning to Scate and Carol and
blow warm upon their Fingers, while yet they
might be culling of Strawberries. And all to
this end, that Editors may take the cake. I
know One, the Father of a long Family, that
will sit a whole June night without queeching
in a Vessell of Refrigerated Water till he be In-
gaged with hard Ice, that the *Publick* may be
docked no pennyweight of the Sentiments incident to the *Nativity*. For we be like Grapes,
and goe to Press in August. But methinks
these rigours do postulate a *Robur Corporis*

404

more than ordinary (whereas 'tis but one in ten
if a Novelist overtop in Physique) ; and besides
will often fail of the effect.   As I *myself* have
asked—the Pseudonym being but gauze—

> "O !   Who can hold a fire in his hand
>   By thinking on the frosty Caucasus ? "

Yet sometimes, because some things are in kind
very Casuall, which if they escape prove Excellent (as the man who by Inadvertence inherited
the throne of the *Grand Turk* with all apper-
tayning) so that the kind is inferiour, being
subject to Perill, but that which is Excellent
being proved superiour, as the Blossom of
March and the Blossom of May, whereof the
French verse goeth :—

> " Bourgeon de Mars, enfant de Paris ;
>   Si un eschape, il en vaut dix."

—so, as I was saying (till the Mischief in-
fected my Protasis), albeit the gross of writings
will moulder between *St. John's* feast and *St.
Stephen's*, yet, if one survive, 'tis odds he will
prove Money in your Pocket.   Therefore I
counsel that you preoccupate and tie him, by
Easter at the latest, to *Forty thousand words*,
naming a Figure in excess : for Operation

shrinketh all things, as was observed by Gal-
enus, who said to his Friend, "I will cut off
your Leg, and then you will be lesse by a
Foot." Also you will do well to provide a
Pictura in Chromo-Lithography. For the
Glaziers like it, and no harm done if they blush
not : which is easily avoided by making it out
of a little Child and a Puppy-dog, or else a
Mother, or some such trivial Accompaniment.
But Phryne marrs all. It was even rashly done
of that Editor who issued a Coloured Plate,
calling it "*Phryne Behind the Areopagus*":
for though nothing was Seen, the pillars and
Grecian elders intervening, yet 'twas Felt a
great pity. And the Fellow ran for it, saying
flimsily :—

"Populus me sibilat. At mihi plaudo."

Whereas I rather praise the dictum of that
other writer, who said, "In this house I had
sooner be turned over on the Drawing-room
Table than roll under that in the Dining-room,"
meaning to reflect on the wine, but the Hostess
took it for a compliment.

But to speak of the Letter Press. For the
Sea you will use Clark Russell ; for the East,

Rudyard Kipling; for *Blood*, Haggard; for neat pastorall Subjects, Thomas Hardy, so he be within Bounds. I mislike his " Noble Dames." Barrie has a prettier witt; but Besant will keep in all weathers, and serve as right *Pemmican*. As for conundrums and poetry, they are but Toys: I have seen as good in crackers; which we pull, not as meaning to read or guess, but read and guess to cover the Shame of our Employment. Yet for Conundrums, if you hold the Answers till your next issue they Raise the Wind among Fools.

He that hath *Wife and Children* hath given Hostages to *Little Folks :* he will hardly redeem but by sacrifice of a Christmas Tree. The learned Poggins, that had twelve Sons and Daughters, used to note ruefully that he might never escape but by purchase of a *dozen Annuals*, citing this to prove how greatly Tastes will diverge among the Extreamely Young, even though they come of the same geniture. So will Printed Matter multiply faster than our Parents. Yet 'tis discutable that this phrensy of *Annuals* groweth staler by Recurrence. As that Helvetian lamented, whose Cuckoo-clock failed of a ready Purchaser, and he had to live with it. "*What Again?*" said he, and "*Surely Spring is not come yet, dash it?*" Also I cannot stomach that our Authors portend a Severity of Weather unseasonable in these Muggy Latitudes. I will eat my Hat if for these twenty Christmasses I have made six Slides worthy the Mention. Yet I know an Author that had his *Hero and Heroine* consent together very prettily; but 'twas in a *Thaw*, and the Editor being stout, the match was broken off unblessedly, till a Pact was made that it should indeed be a Thaw, but sufficient only to let the Heroine drop through the Ice and be Rescewed.

Without *Ghosts*, we twiddle thumbs . . .